WORKING FOR PEACE

WORKING FOR PEACE

A Handbook of
Practical Psychology
and Other Tools

Rachel M. MacNair, Ph.D., Editor
and
Psychologists for
Social Responsibility

Foreword by Arun Gandhi
Director, M. K. Gandhi Institute for Nonviolence

Impact *Publishers*®
ATASCADERO, CALIFORNIA

ATTENTION ORGANIZATIONS AND CORPORATIONS:
This book is available at quantity discounts on bulk purchases for educational, business, or sales promotional use. For further information, please contact Impact Publishers, P.O. Box 6016, Atascadero, California 93423-6016.
Phone: 805-466-5917, e-mail: info@impactpublishers.com

Library of Congress Cataloging-in-Publication Data

Working for peace : a handbook of practical psychology and other tools/ Rachel M. MacNair, Editor ; and Psychologists for Social Responsibility.
    p. cm.
  Includes bibliographical references and index.
  ISBN 1-886230-72-2 (alk. paper)
1. Peace. 2. Peace—Psychological aspects. 3. Social action—Psychological aspects. I. MacNair, Rachel. II. Psychologists for Social Responsibility.
  JZ5538.W69 2006
  303.6'6—dc22

2006007229

Publisher's Note: This publication is designed to provide accurate and authoritative information in regard to the subject matter covered. It is sold with the understanding that the publisher is not engaged in rendering psychological, medical, legal, or other professional services. If expert assistance or counseling is needed, the services of a competent professional should be sought.

Impact Publishers and colophon are registered trademarks of Impact Publishers, Inc.

Cover design by Gail Camposagrado, K.A. White Design, Templeton, California
Composition by UB Communications, Parsippany, New Jersey
Printed in the United States of America on acid-free, recycled paper
Published by **Impact 🖋 Publishers**®
        POST OFFICE BOX 6016
    ATASCADERO, CALIFORNIA 93423-6016
        www.impactpublishers.com

CONTENTS

FOREWORD

Arun Gandhi

What is Peace? Much more than the absence of war. Reconciliation, harmony, serenity, freedom of opportunity, all these things *and* the absence of both physical and passive violence are characteristics of genuine peace. To work for peace, then, is to work for a world of compassion, free of all forms of violence.

Mohandas Gandhi emphasized the need to understand the manifold ways in which humans practice violence. Superficial calm in a society does not indicate the lack of turmoil and conflict. Apart from physical violence — wars, killings, beatings, murders, rape, etc. — we commit an inordinately large amount of passive violence both consciously and unconsciously in the form of hate, prejudice, discrimination, oppression, name-calling, teasing, looking down on people, speaking to people impolitely, classifying people by their religion, their economic standing, their gender, their habits and the millions of other ways in which our actions or even inaction hurt people. In a selfish, self-centered world we ignore the plight of millions. We continue to over-consume the resources of the world, to create economic imbalance, and to generate anger. Passive violence is, therefore, the fuel that ignites physical violence so, logically, if we want to put an end to physical violence we have to cut-off the fuel supply.

We are building mega urban societies around the world that lack soul and substance. We ignore the basic question: Can a society be cohesive, compassionate and caring if every member is taught to be selfish and self-centered? In Gandhian terms a society is an enlarged family and should possess the same positive characteristics —

compassion and cohesiveness. However, we have created a materialistic society that not only fosters selfishness but encourages it in our children when we advise them to be successful at whatever cost.

Passive violence festers in every society until it becomes unbearable and eventually explodes into physical violence. It incidentally, brings into question our concept of justice. In a world steeped in the culture of violence, justice has come to mean revenge — an eye for an eye, Gandhiji said, only makes the whole world blind. In a culture of nonviolence, justice would mean reformation, recognizing that those who do wrong do it out of ignorance or extenuating circumstances. Punishing the person instead of resolving the problem only aggravates physical violence in the form of crime and violence.

The story of the starfish has an appropriate moral lesson for us. A man once went early in the morning to the beach for a walk. Dawn was still minutes away. He saw a figure near the water's edge picking something up and throwing it into the water. He went to enquire and was told that during the night the tide comes in and washes starfish ashore; when the sun comes out they all perish. The curious man saw thousands of starfish stranded on the shore. He said: "You aren't going to be able to save all these starfish, so what difference is it going to make?" The Good Samaritan had a starfish in his hand, about to it toss into the water. He turned and answered: "It will make a big difference to this guy."

Let us not be overwhelmed by the state of the world and do nothing to try to change the world. Gandhiji always believed that small acts of change can ultimately make a big difference. That is the essence of Gandhiji's message.

Working for Peace offers many helpful suggestions for becoming more effective in your own small acts of change. You can make a difference.

Arun Gandhi is the fifth grandson of Mohandas K. (Mahatma) Gandhi, and Director of the M.K. Gandhi Institute for Nonviolence. This statement was adapted from Arun Gandhi's paper, *Nonviolence — The Only Hope*. The full text of the paper appears on the web site of the Gandhi Institute, www.gandhiinstitute.org.

INTRODUCTION

THE CHOIR'S GOTTA KNOW HOW TO SING

Rachel M. MacNair, with Neil Wollman

The wise see knowledge and action as one. They see truly. Take either path and tread it to the end. The end is the same. There the followers of action meet the seekers after knowledge in equal freedom.

— *Bhagavad Gita*

Are you someone who wants to find better ways to work for peace or otherwise improve the world? If you've gotten tired of merely preaching to the choir and would like to get out and help make social change — well, remember that choir has to be well organized and know what it's talking about. You and any group you're in have to have your act together to have the impact you're hoping for. And if you've been in the work a long time, then all the more will you know how important it is to get practical ideas from those who study how to do it well.

Here's How *Working for Peace* Can Help You

If you are *wanting to improve your personal effectiveness* . . . take a look at chapters

If you are *feeling overwhelmed* . . . take a look at chapters
2 — Cultivating Inner Peace
4 — Overcoming Anger and Anxiety
5 — Overcoming Helplessness and Discouragement
6 — Overcoming Burnout
9 — Peace Within, Peace Between, Peace Among
10 — Working for Peace and Social Justice? Who's watching?
14 — How to Know When It's Not Time to Get Discouraged
22 — Moving from the Clenched Fist to Shaking Hands: Working
      with Negative Emotions Provoked by Conflict
34 — Humor for Peace: Finding Laughing Matters

If you are *wanting to help your local group work better* . . . take a
look at chapters
7 — Dealing with the Distressed
11 — Motivating Others to Work with You
12 — Effective Group Meetings and Decision Making
13 — Changing Within to Bring Change Outside: Promoting Healthy
      Group Dynamics
16 — Three Examples of Successful Social Action Groups
24 — Effective Media Communication
25 — Attracting an Audience: The Psychology of Layout and Design
28 — Regrets, Realizations, and Resolutions of an Online Activist
30 — Principles of Opinion Change
31 — Techniques of Behavior Change

If you are *looking for ideas on how to make a greater impact* . . .
take a look at chapters
1 — Building Confidence for Social Action
3 — Improving Your Personal Appeal
15 — Storytelling: A Workshop for Inspiring Group Action
20 — Resolving Conflict from the Third Side
21 — Conflict Transformation Skills for Left and Right
23 — Preparing for Nonviolent Confrontations
24 — Effective Media Communication
25 — Attracting an Audience: The Psychology of Layout and Design
28 — Regrets, Realizations, and Resolutions of an Online Activist
29 — Creating a Peaceful Climate for Peace Work
30 — Principles of Opinion Change
31 — Techniques of Behavior Change

And if you can't see what you need in the Table of Contents, try the Index.

How the Book Is Organized

Working for Peace builds on a classic book from 1985; some of the chapters are updated from that book. It follows a similar order:

Part I lets peace begin with you — it provides help in getting your personal act together, motivating yourself, overcoming obstacles like anger and anxiety and burnout, and making it easier for others to listen to you.

Part II expands to the group — with ideas on recruiting members, getting organized, holding better meetings, and dealing with difficult members.

Conflict is the central theme of **Part III** — it covers how to communicate and how to resolve and transform conflict to make it constructive.

In **Part IV**, you'll find lots of ideas about communicating your message to diverse audiences — the media, the classroom, and online.

Finally, **Part V** talks about persuasion — changing people's attitudes and behavior.

We thought this was a logical order, but it's not one you need to follow. This isn't a novel with a defined story line. All chapters were written independently of one another, and you can skip around and read what you need, when you need it. You can sit and read in whatever order makes sense to you, and you can leave it handy on the shelf and refer to the chapters as a reference when it would be helpful.

From the Editor's Introduction of the 1985 Book, Neil Wollman

As you pick up this book, you may ask yourself, Why another book about peace? Aren't there enough books about war and peace? Aren't there enough manuals about fundraising, writing letters, canvassing, and holding meetings and demonstrations?

I agree, if you're only interested in facts and theories about war and peace, or the nuts and bolts of political organizing, the existing books are sufficient. But, there is far more involved in being a successful peace worker than understanding the issues and knowing how to prepare a press release, run a meeting, or set up a speaker system. This book presents personal and interpersonal psychological principles that will help you effectively put your knowledge and organizing skills to work.

Psychologists certainly have no corner on the market on how to make peace workers more effective. But psychologists do have a valuable perspective to offer — one that has worked well in other situations but which has been only minimally applied in the peace movement. . . .

Though the examples here are geared to peace, I believe the book also will be useful to those working for other causes. The basic principles of good organization and effective communication remain essentially the same, regardless of the issue with which you are dealing.

You'll find that *Working for Peace* contains several different approaches to some topics. As with other complex life issues, there is usually no one, right way to do things. There are different approaches to making group decisions or changing attitudes about peace, just as there are different approaches to successfully raising children. You can't use all the techniques suggested here for any given topic. You don't need to in order to be successful. Choose and combine the techniques which best fit your needs, abilities, situation, group, and moral beliefs. Take from the book what best fits you and work with it.

Where We Are Currently

A lot can happen in 20 years! Along with the fact that further study means more knowledge and that we no longer feel the need to explain the uses of a computer word processor, there have been some stupendous historical developments. In 1985, the major focus was on the nuclear arms race, and many peace arguments were about the Soviet Union. Now terrorism is the first thing that pops into people's minds when it comes to the dangers of war. The nuclear danger is still there but different, more in loose nukes and bunker busters and less in an arms race. Additional concerns besides the international, such as family or structural or environmental violence, have become more prominent.

How did we get from then to now? Go back to 1985 and make the prediction that a surge of nonviolent rebellions in Eastern Europe would free one country after another, with the Berlin Wall being literally torn to pieces by jubilant crowds. Soon thereafter, a nonviolent uprising in the Soviet Union would make a coup fall in a matter of days. The entire Soviet empire would crumble due primarily to nonviolent action.

That prediction would have made you a hopeless, utterly laughable idealist. None of us ever dared to put forward that speedy scenario as a serious possibility. Yet it's exactly what happened.

Remember that, the next time you get discouraged. Those events didn't burst out spontaneously. They culminated from year after tedious year of long, hard work by peace workers — peace workers such as you.

PART I
PEACE WORKERS
GETTING YOURSELVES TOGETHER

Let there be peace on earth, and let it begin with me.

Building Confidence for
Social Action

Barry Childers

Like any other kind of learning, learning to be active and effective in response to peace issues takes time. You can learn by reading and by talking with others who are more experienced, but most of all, you learn by doing. Social action at its best represents an attempt by you (alone or with others) to bring your particular interests and talents to bear on a problem of your own choosing. Generally, social action can be classified as research, education, or direct action.

Following is a list of social actions in which people engage. You will need to duplicate the list in some form. There are several purposes for the list. It is intended to help you (a) assess your unique interests and skills in relation to social action, (b) evaluate the difficulties that particular kinds of activities present so that you can better understand them, and (c) choose the most appropriate tasks and build confidence in undertaking them.

The list can be used most effectively in a support group, with sharing of experiences and mutual exploration of problems and options, but it can also be used alone. In the former case, there should be no pressure to achieve or to conform. The best results will be obtained if you can make an honest assessment of what you wish to do, unpressured by others' expectations.

For each item on the list, mark down how difficult it would be for you to do that particular action (very hard — VH, moderately hard — MH, or fairly easy — FE). Why an action is difficult for you is not important at this point; just get a fairly quick, gut-level reaction about each item.

_____ 1. Join a national organization that is active on peace issues.

_____ 2. Write a letter to the editor of a local paper encouraging people to think about a peace issue.

_____ 3. Spend several hours a week doing volunteer office work for a peace organization.

_____ 4. Obtain a peace-related slide show to present to my church group.

_____ 5. Encourage my local political party to endorse peace policies.

_____ 6. Ask some friends to come to my home and discuss a peace issue.

_____ 7. Write a letter to my congressperson urging her or him to vote a certain way on an upcoming bill.

_____ 8. Spend time learning about organizations that work on a particular issue so that I can discuss the groups with others.

_____ 9. Circulate among my friends a petition supporting action on a peace-related problem.

_____10. Raise funds for a cause by organizing an event (a garage sale, a bake sale, a walk or run, a book sale, a craft fair, etc.).

_____11. Write a letter to a government official, criticizing her or his decision on an issue.

_____12. Set aside twenty minutes a day to think about and study an issue and consider what I can do about it.

_____13. Talk about a peace issue with someone I just met at a party.

_____14. Write a letter to the editor of a local paper criticizing actions of the city council or a local business firm.

_____15. Join a social action group that is not too popular in my community because of its outspokenness on a peace issue.

_____16. Make it a point to bring a peace issue into conversations whenever the opportunity presents itself.

_____17. Think about my own particular interests and skills, and figure out how I can contribute to solving a global conflict problem and enjoy myself at the same time.

_____18. Organize a speakers' bureau in my community.

_____19. Persuade several friends to join a group to which I belong.

_____20. Take an unpopular position on an issue that arose during a local civic group meeting I attended.

_____21. Send a gift subscription for a peace-oriented magazine to a friend who might be interested.

_____22. Explore how people in my profession can contribute to peace.

_____23. Withhold a percentage of my taxes to protest government spending that contributes to a military conflict.

_____24. Talk with my clergyperson about directing certain congregation funds toward peacemaking.

_____25. Write a letter to a magazine journalist criticizing her or his article.

_____26. Stop buying a product that I know is produced by exploiting poor people in another country.

_____27. Write a letter to my congressperson criticizing militaristic statements he or she made at a news conference.

_____28. Join a nonviolent demonstration obstructing the gates of a nearby defense plant.

_____29. Call in to radio talk shows to express a peace concern.

_____30. Set up a booth at a community or county fair to provide literature and talk with people about militarism.

_____31. Help a group to which I belong plan a public meeting on a peace issue.

_____32. Volunteer for a low-paying job with a peace group overseas.

_____33. Run a newspaper ad regularly about world conflict.

_____34. Prepare an annotated reading list on an issue to distribute among friends and groups to which I belong.

_____35. Join a peace demonstration marching through the middle of town, knowing the stance is not popular with local people.

_____36. Telephone my congressperson to convey my peace concerns.

_____37. Canvass local businesses, asking permission to place a peace sign (or a sign publicizing a local group) in their windows.

_____38. Actively help plan a demonstration at a local defense-related industry.

_____39. Feed and house people who come to my area to speak or do other peace work.

_____40. Write a letter to the president of a large corporation to complain about its ties to military defense.

_____41. Canvass the neighborhood door to door to raise funds or survey attitudes about peace.

_____42. Try to arrange a dialogue between opposing factions in a dispute about peace.

_____43. Appear on a TV talk show to discuss a peace issue.

_____44. Be a part of a phone tree to alert people to a peace issue needing urgent action.

_____45. Organize a rally in a local park to protest government action in a conflict somewhere in the world.

_____46. Write to national radio and TV networks urging them to carry a program on war and peace.

_____47. Contribute part of my monthly budget to a peace-related cause.

_____48. Explore ways to introduce war and peace issues into the curriculum of elementary schools.

_____49. Purchase and distribute materials on conflict where I think they might create some interest.

_____50. Write a grant proposal for money to develop a local peace program.

_____51. Take part in a march across the country to make people more aware of an issue.

_____52. Become known as a person willing to speak about peace.

_____53. Organize a benefit concert with area musicians to raise funds for a cause.

_____54. Volunteer my vacation time to work on a peace project.

_____55. Spend several months learning all I can about a peace issue.

_____56. Start refusing when people ask me to do things that I know contribute to world conflict.

_____57. Do library research on a peace issue for our local group.

_____58. Contact a local TV or radio station and try to persuade them to give some time to a peace issue in the public interest.

_____59. Chair a committee in my church/temple/mosque to decide what my congregation should do to promote peace.

_____60. Help write materials for a local organization (descriptive flyers, meeting announcements, calls to action, etc.).

_____61. Stand on a busy street corner to distribute leaflets and talk with passers-by about militarism.

_____62. Bring in a speaker or show a film on peace, arranging for publicity in the local media.

_____63. Talk with the local high school principal to find out how peace and conflict issues are covered in the curriculum, and encourage more attention to them.

_____64. Start a peace-oriented newsletter among people I know.

_____65. Attend a conference on a peace issue held in a nearby city.

_____66. Do in-depth research on a peace issue and write a report for a local or national organization.

_____67. Speak to a junior high or high school class about a peace issue.

_____68. Volunteer one day a week to work with a state peace group.

_____69. Organize a meeting to start a local chapter of a national peace organization.

_____70. Help organize a street theater group to dramatize issues at public events.

_____71. Wear a peace symbol button or lapel pin.

_____72. Engage in a house-to-house petition campaign for a peace issue.

_____73. Simplify my lifestyle as a contribution to solving global conflict problems.

_____74. Write an article about a peace issue for a national magazine.

_____75. Create a photo display about a peace issue and show it at a local shopping center once a week.

_____76. Try to persuade friends to join a social action group to which I belong.

_____77. Organize a letter-writing or email network to focus on peace action.

_____78. Join an organization that I know is considered radical by many community people, including my friends.

_____79. Write an article on peace for the local newspaper.

_____80. Attend a rally in the center of town protesting local government action.

_____81. Ask a local civic group to which I belong to have one of her or his meetings focus on a peace issue.

_____82. Talk with people at a local college or university and try to persuade them to offer a course on peace and conflict.

_____83. Write a will leaving some of my assets to a peace group.

_____84. Personally confront a board member of a corporation to explain my concern about the corporation's activities.

_____85. Organize a telephone or email lobbying network to influence my congressperson on peace-related legislation.

_____86. Stand up in a question-and-answer period following a speech and express criticism of something the speaker said.

_____87. Give a talk promoting peace to a local civic group.

_____88. Organize a vigil in front of the governor's mansion to call attention to an issue.

_____89. Serve as a contact person in my area for a peace group.

_____ 90. Give up a large portion of my leisure time to do peace-related activities.

_____ 91. Participate in a small nonviolent protest, knowing that I will probably be arrested and jailed.

_____ 92. Solicit funds from local businesses to support a peace group.

_____ 93. Boycott a company that contributes to a conflict somewhere.

_____ 94. Take a job with a social action organization, even if it would mean a drop in income.

_____ 95. Speak at a local rally that is protesting government action.

_____ 96. Attend a meeting of the city council and speak to them about declaring a day for peace.

_____ 97. Travel a long distance to attend the annual conference of a national or international peace organization.

_____ 98. Participate in a panel discussion on peace given by a local group.

_____ 99. Quit my job if it is contributing to world conflict.

_____100. Make a speech promoting peace to a large audience at a religious conference.

_____101. Prepare and teach a class on peace and conflict at a community college.

When you have completed marking the list, go back and find the items you marked very hard (VH). Try to get a sense of what makes them difficult for you. If you're in a group, do a sharing discussion with one or two other members of the group. Afterward, briefly write what you think makes them difficult for you — just a few words to identify the difficulty. Examples: "I find writing very difficult — I'm more of an action-oriented person." "I enjoy talking with individuals, but talking in front of a group really scares me." "I tend to shy away from situations where there might be conflict." "I prefer intellectual activities and tend to avoid action groups." "I've never had much experience at organizing and think I'd be very poor at it." "I'm a procrastinator." And so on. . .

Now that you have a better idea which things are difficult for you and why, begin to think about what you would like to do. Choose an item of moderate difficulty that appeals to you and that represents something you could, in fact, do now. Think through a plan for doing it, or discuss a plan with your small group. If it is something that cannot be done alone, include in your program a way of joining with others to do it.

After you have finished, write a brief description of your plan, including a time schedule for following through on it. If you are part of a group, you may want to get together with others after you complete your activity to share your experiences. You may want to talk about (a) how easy or difficult the activity was and why, (b) what problems arose that you hadn't foreseen, (c) what things you might want to do differently to be more effective if you repeat the activity later, and (d) your plans for the next step you want to take. Through this exercise you are engaging in a learning and confidence-building process that you can continue at your own pace. Choose activities that will keep you moving gradually in the direction you want to go, and stay with each level until you feel fairly satisfied with your performance. Comments from others can be helpful, but remember that you are the final and best judge of your own progress.

A Final Note

One thing that discourages many people unnecessarily is the feeling that they don't know enough to participate in social action. They feel that many of the actions require that one be an "expert." It is true, of course, that a few of the listed actions require some knowledge and experience, and the more you know about an issue, the more effective you can be. But one can learn in the process of doing, and most actions can be undertaken by anyone at any stage of understanding.

Cultivating Inner Peace

Christina Michaelson

Peace. It does not mean to be in a place where there is no noise, trouble, or hard work. It means to be in the midst of those things and still be calm in your heart.

— Unknown

Peace activists invest tremendous amounts of time, talent, energy, and resources into changing the world. You work for peace between individuals, among groups, and between nations, but are you at peace? Do you experience inner peace? Within each of us are the seeds of peace, love, and compassion and also the seeds of violence, anger, and hate. We can choose which seeds we will nurture and cultivate. When we choose to cultivate peace within ourselves, we can transform ourselves and the world.

While your focus on peace work is on change in the external world, you probably spend much less time on developing peace in your inner world — such as practicing methods to create peacefulness in your thoughts and emotions. Perhaps that's because you feel that inner peace isn't really important to your peace work or that you don't have time to devote to developing inner peace. Yet inner peace is a vitally important component in peacemaking because you cannot give what you do not have. If you're to bring peace to others, then you first must manifest peace in your own life.[1] Your peace work in the world should begin with cultivating an inner state of peacefulness, and then you truly can offer peace to others. Mahatma Gandhi said, "Be the change you want to see in the world." If you want to see peace in the world, then you must "be" peace in the world.

What Is Inner Peace?

Inner peace is a subjective experience for each person. The experiences of peace change over time and circumstances and therefore can be described in many different ways. In general, inner peace is a calm and tranquil state of mind. Author Don Miguel Ruiz offered the following description, "The voice in your head is like a wild horse taking you wherever it wants to go. . . . When the voice in your head finally stops talking, you experience inner peace."[2]

Inner peace is transformational. It can make deep changes in you and in how you relate to the world. The path to inner peace is to quiet and focus your thoughts and patterns of thinking. This, in turn, can have profound effects on other areas of your functioning. Your thoughts, emotions, physical functioning, and behavior are interrelated, and changes in one area affect the other areas in continuous feedback.[3] Therefore, as you induce inner peace and calm your thoughts, you also will feel more tranquil emotionally and physically, and your behavior can become more peaceful.

Why Should You Care about Inner Peace?

Inner peace can help you to be more effective in your work.

One day, when my son was 12 years old, he told me that he didn't want to go to another protest against the war in Iraq. When I asked him why, he responded, "Because the protesters are too angry about what they're fighting for. They're angry for peace — it's ironic."

It's very easy to get angry about the causes for peacemaking or to feel depressed, frustrated, or afraid. However, these feelings, if left unchecked, can interfere with accomplishing your goals. Your anger can distract others from hearing your message. Instead, they just remember the anger. For example, the public may remember the arrests for disorderly conduct at a human rights demonstration, while the real issues of concern get lost in the media coverage of the arrests.

Feeling depressed and hopeless about the hard work of peacemaking can make you less motivated to work for peace and can even leave you immobilized. Strong, unregulated emotions can impair your ability to express yourself clearly and appropriately and to think and respond "on your feet" in difficult circumstances. Yelling at legislators surely lets them know that you feel deeply about the issues, but it usually is not effective for engaging them in a dialog.

Inner peace can help. Practicing inner peace can help you manage strong emotions, and thus you can more effectively keep your message of peace clear and strong, without feeling overwhelmed by negative emotions.

I used to work as a psychotherapist with adults who were sexually abused as children, and I often became very angry listening to my clients' stories of victimization. However, my outrage was not helpful to them. Instead, it distracted me from my purpose of being truly present for my clients and focused on their recoveries from their pasts. I needed to find a way to manage my strong negative feelings, and practicing strategies to induce inner peace was a very effective way of accomplishing this. Outside of therapy sessions, as I focused on clearing and calming my thoughts, my emotions also quieted. No longer distracted by intense thoughts and emotions, I was able to develop new insights and understanding. Inner peace truly allowed me to become more useful to my clients.

Perhaps the most important reason to cultivate inner peace in your peace work is that you model peacemaking to others. By inducing inner peace, you can interact with others in a more peaceful manner. In turn, this can improve your relationships, enhance the outcome of your interactions, and model peacefulness to others. By your personal example, you demonstrate that while you remain strongly focused on the purpose of your peacemaking, you can effect change peacefully.

Inner peace can keep you healthier.

Peace work can be stressful, and stress can make you sick. There's a large body of research that shows a link between stress and many diseases, including everyday illnesses such as colds and headaches and more serious health problems such as heart disease and diabetes.[4] For health reasons, it's wise to engage in stress management techniques. Practicing inner peace can be an important method in your efforts to care for your health. Inner peace calms your mind, body, and emotions, and this can help you recover from the effects of stress.

With continued practice, as you change your patterns of thinking you may respond to stressors in a different way. Thus, inner peace even can help you prevent stress responses from occurring. In practicing inner peace, you are increasing your potential for good health.

How Do You Cultivate Inner Peace?

There are many paths to inner peace. You can try any or all of the methods I describe and add some of your own. I recommend practicing and developing a repertoire of inner peace practices so that you have a choice of coping strategies ready whenever needed.

Meditation.

Throughout history, people in cultures around the world have used meditation to experience inner peace. Meditation practices are numerous, but all have in common calming the mind while remaining alert and training the mind in focused attention. Most meditative techniques also include focusing mental attention on breathing, and this contributes to both training the mind and calming the body. In addition to being a method for inducing inner peace, meditation has positive effects on many areas of psychological and physical functioning, including memory, anxiety, stress management, happiness, and heart disease.[5] Meditation also was found to increase activity in parts of the brain that create positive emotions and to improve the functioning of the immune system.[6] This supports the use of meditation to help keep you happy and healthy and to manage the effects of stress.

If you're interested in meditating, I recommend taking a class in your community or self-study with books and Internet resources. Here, I briefly outline several types of meditation:

- *One-pointed awareness meditation.* This meditation trains your mind by having you focus on the inhalation and exhalation of each breath and away from all other distracting thoughts. As the mind wanders, you gently guide it back to the point of awareness, which is the focus on the breath. Alternatively, instead of focusing on the breath, you can focus your attention on a mantra, which is a word or sound repeated silently or aloud, or on your mind's image of a word or object.

- *Mindfulness meditation.* This type of meditation involves becoming an observer of your thoughts and emotions. In a nonjudgmental manner, you watch your thoughts and emotions as they rise and fall — like watching the water in a river flow by. This helps you develop an awareness of your experiences in the present moment. With practice, mindful awareness can be extended out of meditation time and into all experiences in your life. Mindfulness then becomes a way of being more present and aware in the world.

- *Guided meditation.* This meditation begins with inducing calmness through deep breathing and a focus on the breath. Then you are directed through relaxation exercises or to think about a beautiful place in nature, such as the woods or another relaxing location, to deepen your sense of tranquility. Guided meditations are available on tapes, on CDs, on the Internet, and written out in meditation books.

- *Reflective meditation.* After inducing calmness, reflective meditations allow you to focus on a question or concern. When distractions in thinking occur, you keep guiding your thoughts back to the question. When distracting thoughts and emotions are minimized, you can more easily develop insights and new ways of thinking about your areas of concern. With reflective meditation, you can directly address issues of peace by contemplating questions related to your peace work, such as, "How can I be more effective in expressing my views?" "How can I mobilize others to speak out for this cause?" or "How can I better understand the other person's perspective?"

- *Lovingkindness meditation.* This is a traditional Buddhist meditation for increasing peace. Lovingkindness is a state of mind of deep compassion for yourself and all others. This meditation begins with inducing mental and physical calming through focused attention on the breath. Next, you generate loving acceptance of yourself and wishes for your happiness and freedom from suffering. Then you systematically apply these principles to all others — beginning with those you love, then those you feel neutral about or have never met, on to those with whom you have conflicts or who are your enemies — and finish with sending lovingkindness to all types of beings in the world.

Nature.

Spending quiet time in nature helps many people experience inner peace. You can climb a mountain, walk the beach, or just sit in your own backyard. You can find peace by appreciating the glory of nature, from the delicate beauty of a flower to the magnificence of the ocean. What's important is that you allow your mind to become quiet and calm so that you can transcend the stressors of your life.

Prayer.

For centuries, religious traditions have emphasized the importance of inner peace. It's regarded as a highly valued spiritual goal and as a way to connect with God and bring peace to others. If it's consistent with your religious and spiritual beliefs, then engaging in prayer is a method that can help you develop inner peace. Also, becoming part of the community at your house of worship can connect you with like-minded others and support you in your spiritual peace practices.

Inner Peace in Action

There are many practices for inducing inner peace, and what's most important is that you discover the ones that are helpful to you. Inner peace is its own reward, because it relieves stress and brings calmness and tranquility to your psychological, emotional, and physical functioning. It also allows you to make your behavior more peaceful and to model peacemaking to others.

Even just a few deep breaths can help you decrease stress and become clearer in your thinking. A prayer or short focus on the breath can be done quickly and quietly anywhere, without others even knowing. This can allow you to induce a more tranquil inner state so that you can choose to interact with others in a more peaceful manner.

It's relatively easy to be peaceful in pleasant circumstances, but what about experiencing and expressing peacefulness in the midst of the difficult challenges of peace work? The seeds of inner peace are within everyone, but to access this, you often need to become quiet and removed from the noise of the world. With practice, you can carry your inner peace into the world and even remain peaceful in the midst of stress and chaos.

A survey of peace workers found that the most rewarding as well as the most stressful aspects of peace work were the interactions with the community of fellow activists.[7] Your relationships with the peace workers in your organization can be a good place to practice inner peace and observe its effects.

Let's use the example that you are angry with another peace activist because you feel she's not doing her fair share of the work. Holding a grudge against her, you find yourself disagreeing with her at meetings and arguing with her. You recognize that you don't have a peaceful relationship with her. Because of that awareness, you now can choose to change that relationship. The first step is to become peaceful, to induce a state of inner peace by quieting and focusing your thoughts. This can allow you to access your inner compassion and understanding while thinking of your colleague, and your view of her can change. Now you see her struggles and realize that her strengths are not being utilized by your organization. She has difficulties interfacing with other community groups, while her stronger skills lie in making plans for others behind the scenes. You have shifted your thinking about this person, and now you also can change your behavior toward her. You no longer see her as shirking her responsibilities, and you no longer find yourself arguing with her. You may even be able to help your group assign work to her that more effectively uses her strengths. You have worked on developing inner peace and changing your mind, and this is very important peace work. When peace starts with peace workers and peace organizations, you more effectively can bring peace to the world. With inner peace, you can give peace because you have peace.

Some may think that if you become too peaceful and calm, you cannot be effective for peace. Thich Nhat Hanh, a Zen Buddhist monk from Vietnam, teaches that practicing peace is not a sign of weakness but, rather, an act of courage.[8] Inner peace doesn't produce apathy or passivity in your desire to change the world. Instead, inner peace allows you to work from a position of strength to express peace to others. From this strength, you cultivate the seeds of inner peace and then you can grow peace in the world.

References

1. Leyden-Rubenstein, L. (2001). *Peace on earth begins with inner peace. Annals of the American Psychotherapy Association, November/December*, 24.
2. Ruiz, D. M. (2004). *The voice of knowledge: A practical guide to inner peace.* San Rafael, CA: Amber-Allen Publishing, Inc., p. 100.
3. Greenberger, D., & Padesky, C. A. (1995). *Mind over mood: Change how you feel by changing the way you think.* New York: The Guilford Press.
4. Sapolsky, R. M. (1994). *Why zebras don't get ulcers: A guide to stress, stress-related diseases, and coping.* New York: W. H. Freeman and Company.
5. Shapiro, S. L., & Walsh, R. (2003). An analysis of recent meditation research and suggestions for future directions. *The Humanistic Psychologist, 31,* 86–114.

6. Davidson, R. J., Kabat-Zinn, J., Schumacher, J., Rosenkranz, M., Muller, D., Santorelli, S. F., et al. (2003). Alterations in brain and immune function produced by mindfulness meditation. *Psychosomatic Medicine, 65,* 564–570.
7. Gomes, M. E. (1992). The rewards and stresses of social change: A qualitative study of peace activists. *Journal of Humanistic Psychology, 32,* 138–146.
8. Hanh, T. N. (2003). *Creating true peace.* New York: Free Press.

Suggested Readings

Borysenko, J. (2001). *Inner peace for busy people: 52 simple strategies for transforming your life.* Carlsbad, CA: Hay House, Inc.

    Includes strategies for taking care of yourself, changing your relationship to time, managing your mind, developing compassion, and creating a purpose in your life.

Chopra, D. (2005). *Peace is the way.* New York: Harmony Books.

    Insights into how violence has developed and been maintained in the world. Includes strategies for changing cultural belief systems and practices for being a peacemaker.

Kornfield, J. (2004). *Meditation for beginners.* Boulder, CO: Sounds True, Inc.

    Provides excellent descriptions of different types of meditation. Includes a CD of guided meditations.

Weiss, B. L. (2003). *Eliminating stress, finding inner peace.* Carlsbad, CA: Hay House, Inc.

    Good information about the relationship between stress and disease. Includes a CD of guided meditations.

IMPROVING YOUR PERSONAL APPEAL

Neil Wollman

Though you might hope that others' opinions will be affected only by the strengths of your position, this will not be the case. The greater people's liking for you, whatever the reason, the more likely they'll be open to your arguments. The importance of personal characteristics goes beyond just being friendly and sympathetic during conversations. Even seemingly trivial characteristics will have an effect — are you aware that every U.S. presidential election except for two since 1900 was won by the taller of the two candidates?

Though personal traits and other nonpolitical factors will not single handedly determine someone's views toward peace, they will have some effect on them. These secondary factors will most likely affect opinions for a short period of time, and primarily in people for whom the issue is of minor importance. On the surface it may seem that if this is the case, it's not worth worrying about, but such factors are worth considering for several reasons.

First, for some of your projects, a short-term attitude change (without deep commitment) is all that may be needed. A brief change of opinion on an issue not critical to someone may be enough to get them to sign a petition, give a financial contribution, or vote favorably in an immediately upcoming election.

Second, it will be easier to bring about a deeper commitment once you've changed an opinion temporarily.

Finally, secondary factors can be applied along with other attitude change techniques to make a more effective overall appeal.

Even if personal characteristics have their greatest effect in only certain situations, they will likely have some effect in all circumstances.

Why not use all the appeal available to you? The following are principles that are most likely to make others like you, and thus be more open to your message.

Personality Traits

The most powerful traits that cause liking seem vaguely similar to the Boy Scout pledge: loyalty, honesty, sincerity, competence, and physical attractiveness. The more you have (or appear to have) of these qualities, the greater the chance that people will like you. Presumably, it will not be difficult to be sincere and honest when talking to others about your concern for peace. If it is, it will probably become obvious to listeners in the long run, and perhaps even in more limited interactions. Likewise, if people think you're insincere, they'll have negative feelings about you and your message.

It may be more difficult to establish your competence with listeners if contacts are brief. Try to show it through the actions you take and the knowledge you express. If appropriate, mention your training, awards, work accomplished, degrees, etc.

Physical attractiveness, for better or worse, is a particularly important factor. Appearance may be improved by use of appropriate clothing and grooming. Whether you wish to be concerned with such matters is your own choice, but you should be aware that they'll have an effect on others' acceptance of you and your message. One needn't necessarily be "clean-cut" to be best received; listeners are usually most receptive to those who are dressed and groomed similar to themselves.

Rewards

People like others who provide them with pleasant things. Rewards can take many forms. For example, you could praise them for their openness and their giving of time, or you could compliment them on something not directly tied to the topic — clothing, a personality trait, some statement made during the course of conversation. People like to be liked, and you can certainly find something in your listeners to like. The more your liking can be genuinely conveyed, the more your audience will like you. Depending on the circumstances, other rewards might include (a) providing food or some other material goods, (b) doing or promising a favor, or (c) relieving some sort of stress or bad feelings that another is experiencing. Be aware of the needs of those you contact. By helping someone out, not only will she or he be better off, but you might be doing a little something indirectly for the cause of peace.

Interestingly, research also shows that when someone is rewarded, he or she will begin feeling good about other people who happen to be around at the time, even if they had nothing to do with the good feeling. Taking this a step further — if you happen to be around someone who is feeling good (regardless of what caused the good feeling), that person will like you more. Thus when you talk to others about peace, try to catch them when they're feeling good. Plan on approaching them at times and places when they're likely to be in a good mood. It turns out that this will cause them to better like not only you, but your ideas as well.

Another interesting finding is that we like not only those who give us rewards, but also those to whom we give rewards. If this is the case, it seems logical that those people working together cooperatively (and thus rewarding each other by helping) would like each other. This turns out to be true. Working cooperatively has such a strong effect on liking because not only are both parties giving rewards, but they are also receiving them.

Thus, the more you can cooperate with people or groups in any way, political or otherwise, the more they'll like you. Cooperation could involve anything from your peace group working with a local service club to register voters or raise money for charity to working cooperatively with someone while fixing a car or a meal. The type of cooperative ventures you undertake will depend upon whom you wish to approach about peace.

Finally, be aware that through cooperation you will also like the other person or group more, and some of their ideas may rub off on you as well.

Similarities

There's strong evidence that we like others who have opinions similar to our own. Surprisingly, the importance of the topic often doesn't matter. There's also a tendency for people with similar personalities to like each other; as the saying goes, "birds of a feather flock together." This is usually true unless the similar personalities tend to be conflicting; for instance, two very talkative people might not get along well if they had to compete for talking time.

Try applying these principles of similarity by having your peace message delivered by someone from your group who has similarities with the audience. Additionally, wherever possible, mention any similar interests or opinions you have with your listener(s), whether politically related or not. Sometimes something as simple as wearing a T-shirt with the name of a pro sports team can make others feel some identification with you and make you seem like a similar, average citizen.

Contact

The more time people spend together in neutral or pleasant circumstances, the more they will like each other. Only under unpleasant circumstances will greater contact lead to less liking. What this means is that the more times your listeners see you, the better, be it listening to a speech or just seeing you at a restaurant. There are many ways to be seen more often, some examples: scheduling many formal or informal political contacts, becoming involved in nonpolitical events and gatherings in the community, and being pictured on television or in newspaper photographs.

One final point: though you will be liked more the more often you are seen, be aware of the importance of making a good first impression. Research shows that first impressions are sometimes hard to shake — for better or worse.

Conclusion

Not all the factors that increase liking are presented here, but the most important ones have been described: those well-established by research and explained in greater depth in most textbooks of social psychology. By applying what's known about the effects of personality traits, rewards, similarities, and frequency of personal contact in your work for peace, you and your message can have more impact.

OVERCOMING ANGER AND ANXIETY

Helen Margulies Mehr

If I am not for myself, who will be for me? But if I am for myself alone, what am I? And if not now, when?

— Hillel

In our work for peace we often experience emotions affecting our health, such as the feeling that arises when we are the object of others' anger, or feeling hurt, anxious, or angry. This chapter will give some basic suggestions on how to overcome them.

Overcoming Feelings of Hurt

- Acknowledge and accept feelings of hurt, depression, or grief. Confronting a world filled with warring nations where people are tortured and where so much injustice prevails naturally results in reactions of overwhelming anger and grief. Accept these feelings as natural, normal, and healthy. Set aside a little time for reflecting or writing whenever these emotions develop, even just five to ten minutes.

- Release these feelings. Most of us are inclined to repress unpleasant feelings. When sledding on an icy road, your first reaction may be to slam on the brakes. But the way to handle a skid is to take your foot off the brake pedal and gently steer the car. This expresses the principle of "going along with a feeling." In a similar vein, one can be emotionally "safer" by expressing strong emotions. Many people in our society are ashamed of crying and showing emotions, considering it weakness. Yet if we think about our violence-ridden planet, crying is an appropriate reaction. Accept these feelings as natural, normal, and healthy.

- Express feelings to others. If you are depressed, words of cheer from others are usually not helpful. Rather, just having others listen and acknowledge your pain can many times bring relief.

I remember seeing a woman whose daughter was murdered. It was with apprehension that I approached her, asking myself what I could do to help her. She said her friends had told her to stop crying and go on with her life. I told her to tell her friends they were wrong. We both had tears in our eyes, and putting my arms around her, I supported her deep grief and her right to express it for as long as she needed to. This affirmed her need to express the hurt within her, and her pain was relieved. To think she had not allowed herself to grieve over the death of her own daughter!

- Seek out individuals or groups who have similar views. This will provide support and encouragement. I find the correspondence I engage in with other activists revitalizes my energies. The American colonists set up the "Committee of Correspondence" before the Revolutionary War so they could secretly keep in touch with each other while struggling to uphold their rights. This network played a big part in drawing the colonists together for their struggle with Great Britain. By staying in contact with other individuals and groups who are working for peace, we feel an interconnectedness that builds our personal strength.

- Stay physically fit. Taking care of yourself physically has a positive effect on mental health. Physical activity is a good way to deal with depression and stress. Staying healthy involves taking time for exercise, proper nutrition, relaxation and fun, and enough sleep; it also means avoiding or limiting smoking and alcohol. These behaviors will improve your mental attitude and give you the mental and physical energy to more effectively do your peace work.

- Develop and maintain hope. The best antidote to feelings of discouragement and pain is hope. But how can we stay hopeful? Where can we look for hope? In the story about the opening of Pandora's box and the releasing of evil, it is often forgotten that at the bottom of the box was hope. "Hoping is hard, active work. A person must use images and weave a pattern of ideas which presents the future in a potentially positive light."[1]

- Each day, at a regular time, take 10 or 15 minutes (or longer) for reflection and/or prayer.[2] During this time, close your eyes and allow an image to form, actually see the way you would want people to live if the world were at peace. Visualize symbols as well, like an image of the planet earth as seen in totality by the astronauts. A colleague of mine visualizes a long rainbow of circling colored scarves; for her it represents a personal commitment to the idea that we are all one. There was an organization in the early 1960s in Berkeley, California, called "Acts for Peace." Their idea was to do an act for peace each day: write a letter, talk to a person, read a book — do something.

During times of reflection, also think of the people who inspire you: friends and colleagues, people you know personally who have shown courage in overcoming obstacles, or public figures who helped advance peace and social justice through individual initiative, like Mohandas Gandhi, Martin Luther King, Jr., Thomas Merton, Cesar Chavez, and Bishop Desmond Tutu.

It's also inspiring to read about the accomplishments of individual (and often unknown) citizens who have brought about changes in their communities and beyond.[3,4] Helen Caldicott, as an Australian pediatrician, became concerned about radiation levels found in milk. She persuaded a majority of Australians to boycott French products, succeeded in stopping above-ground nuclear testing in the South Pacific, and went on to influence millions as president of Physicians for Social Responsibility in the United States.

Think of important victories in the past, victories that were won through the efforts of ordinary people and that helped what appeared to be insurmountable obstacles to be overcome: for example, the Quakers' 100-year struggle to abolish slavery, women's achievement of the right to vote in the U.S. after 70 years of effort, the ending of monarchies as the world's dominant political force, and the gradual deterioration of imperialism through the years. *[Editor's note: For events that have happened after this was written in 1985, wouldn't we hasten to add the fall of the Berlin Wall and the Soviet Empire, accomplished almost entirely through nonviolent rebellion? This would have been an entirely implausible fantasy at the time this was written. There have also been several successful "people power" revolutions that overturned rigged elections of dictators in the Philippines, Chile, Serbia, Ukraine, Georgia, and so on. This list just skims the surface.]*

History teaches us that many things that had once been unimaginable have come to pass. Such knowledge can inspire not just you, but perhaps also those you meet who say they might support your cause if it were not a "hopeless dream."

Dealing with Your Anger and Hostility

Perhaps some might assume that those who work for world peace are not the kind of people who get angry. But, of course, we know that this is not the case. As with the emotions of discouragement and grief, anger should be regarded as normal and natural. There will always be times when we feel annoyed, angry, or even enraged. Disagreements and arguments among peace workers and with others are inevitable. Unfortunately, peace workers (particularly pacifists) have a particularly hard time acknowledging and accepting anger in themselves.

When you start to get angry, sometimes it's beneficial to directly communicate that anger, in which case you can start by saying, "I feel angry because . . ." and end up with ". . . and I would *like* you to . . ." Don't blame the other person, but instead talk about *what needs to change* on the other person's part to improve the interaction. Better yet, if the circumstances allow it, say, "I feel angry because...and I would like us to . . ." Talk about what needs to change on both persons' parts to improve the interaction.

Whenever your anger has risen such that your body is becoming tense, perhaps feeling as if it will soon "explode," or whenever you begin feeling very frustrated or out of control, say to the other person, "I'm feeling angry and I need to take a break. I'll be back soon." Leave the other person and go for a brief walk or run, or do something else physical; doing so will help discharge the tension in your body.[5] *[Editor's note: This doesn't include the common idea of "letting off steam" or "catharsis" by punching a pillow or throwing darts at a picture. Around a thousand studies have shown this increases later aggression, rather than dissipating it. It puts your mind on violent activity and can be the first small step in a set of steps that gets worse and worse — a common pattern for getting*

*people into more violence. Furiously peddling a stationary bicycle,
however, is more likely to reduce tension. It's having a replacement
pretend target that gives more danger to a real target. Exercise is a
stress reducer.]*

Taking a "break" is hard to do initially but it becomes easier
with practice. And just acknowledging your anger to yourself, which
taking a break first requires, will in fact make you feel less angry.
The more you are aware of your anger and what effect it has on you,
the more control you will have in dealing with it.

While alone, take a number of deep breaths and relax your
muscles. Then, rather than blaming the other person (or yourself)
for the conflict, accept the anger that you feel ("I'm not happy about
the situation, but that's how I feel"). If you begin again to get angry
about the conflict, say to yourself, "I'm beginning to feel angry
again, and I need to take a break." Take a few more deep breaths.
Finally, come back and ask if the person is willing to first discuss
why the hostile situation developed before getting back to the
original topic of discussion.

There are some people who have difficulty recognizing they are
feeling angry. One reason is many people were taught as children
that anger is a "bad" emotion. As a result, they try to ignore or
suppress their anger. Anger that is not acknowledged often gets
expressed in unhealthy ways, such as in violence or in trying to make
other people feel inferior.

You will better understand and be able to deal with your anger
patterns if you look at messages you received in the past. How did
your parents or siblings behave during conflicts? Growing up, how
did you behave when you got angry? What signals did you get from
your parents or guardians regarding your expression of anger — was
it OK or not OK? Many people discover that their angry behavior as
adults is similar to that which they observed or were taught as
children. Having insight into your anger patterns makes it easier to
recognize, understand, and deal with your anger.

Dealing with Others' Anger, Ridicule, or Abuse

It is difficult to listen to others getting angry. When people express
anger toward you, you are apt to give another, and often inaccurate,
meaning to what they are conveying such as, "You're stupid." The
first step in dealing with others' anger is to avoid assuming that the

angered party is putting you down. If you view another's anger as a personal attack, you may become defensive and either retaliate automatically or think you have to respond in kind in order to "save face." In either case, a contest will likely develop in which you feel pressure to defeat, hurt, or prove wrong your "opponent."

Sometimes, of course, others will make personal attacks in the form of ridicule or criticism. But whether you incorrectly assume you are being personally attacked or are directly ridiculed does not matter. You will likely feel defensive to some extent. The trick then is to stop the cycle, which leads from feeling defensive to becoming angry to creating or intensifying a conflict.

Develop an "emergency kit" — through practice — that you can use in the midst of a barrage of another's anger: *take a deep breath*, and another. *Count to five* to yourself while inhaling; count to five to yourself while exhaling. This helps relieve the tension inside you that normally builds during another's attack.

Then, *consciously decide* not to give the other person the power to upset you. Eleanor Roosevelt once said that no one can make you feel inferior without your consent. Finally, *concentrate on your conviction* that if others are indeed attacking you personally, it is due either to their own insecurity or to the weakness of the position they are espousing.

Handling Anxiety

It is unrealistic to think you can eliminate anxiety. The types of activities that peace workers typically engage in do not allow that. For instance, you may plan a major event involving a great deal of time and energy. As the day approaches, it is likely you will experience a great deal of anxiety about the outcome. And there are times you will be anxious about talking to certain citizens or legislators who are important to some aspect of your work, such as the passage of a Congressional bill.

To deal with your worries, set aside a time each day for ten or fifteen minutes, or whatever time you need, to *actively worry*. Think of the worst thing that could happen for the events you'll be involved in, and what you would do about them. Then later, when you become aware of a worrisome thought, say to yourself, "I've already done my worrying." Then take several deep breaths and internally count each inhalation and each exhalation you take.

Switch your thoughts to pleasant experiences in which you have felt totally relaxed — lying at the beach, in the garden, whatever. Use all your senses, and if, for example, you imagine the beach, feel the warmth of the sun, hear the waves against the shore, and see the beauty of nature. Doing so will enable you to recapture a relaxed feeling. Learning to reduce worrying requires practice, as every skill does, but I have never found anyone who could not switch their unpleasant thoughts to more positive ones.

Practice the following relaxation technique so it will work for you when you need it — you can't just *tell* yourself to "relax" and expect it to happen. Sit in a comfortable chair or lie down, and take some deep breaths. Don't make a conscious effort to *try* to relax because that only increases the tension. Instead, just *let go;* imagine what a noodle looks like when you throw it in the water. It goes limp, and that is the message you want to give your muscles. After several deep breaths, start at the top of your head, loosening up the scalp muscles. Then proceed downward, systematically relaxing each set of muscles — face, chest, shoulders, arms, back, thighs, lower legs, and feet and toes. After this progressive relaxation you may wish to visualize a relaxing scene, as discussed in the section above.

Conclusion

Psychologists have worked with individuals who have had the most terrible childhoods and yet have become truly remarkable people. The research about these "super children" who have survived tragic childhoods shows that in some way they made a decision not to be engulfed in their pasts.[6] As did these children, we can see our circumstances as a challenge; we can *decide not to be victims* — to work for peace, regardless of failures in the past and many likely ones in the future. Thomas Merton said

> When you are doing the sort of work you have taken on . . . you may have to face the fact that your work will be apparently worthless and achieve no result at all, if not perhaps results opposite to what you expect. As you get used to this idea, you start more and more to concentrate not on the results but on the value, the rightness, the truth of the work itself.... Insisting on evidence of success might quickly lead to despair and paralysis. The big results are

not in your hands or mine, but they suddenly happen, and we can share in them.[7]

Sebastiane Olguin, a co-worker of Cesar Chavez, said at a conference on nonviolence that he didn't know whether the farm workers would ever get what they needed, but the process was in itself rewarding for him.

We can find rewards in the friendships we make with caring, fun, and interesting people who open up new vistas for us by telling about their lives.

Finally, Dr. Alan Nelson, a psychologist who closed his clinical practice in order to work full time for peace, told me after five years of full-time peace work, "I feel much greater hope, and my mental health and joy and peace of mind increase the more I do work on peace issues." Thus, although peace work has its times of despair, anger, and anxiety, it can also be filled with much joy and hope.

References

1. Breznitz, N. cited in Carol Turkington (1984). Israeli researcher finds hope eases stress, affects outcome. *APA Monitor* 18.
2. Nelson, A. (1984). Prayer for peace: Meditation, contemplation and nonviolence in our nuclear age. *Journal of Humanistic Psychology,* 24(3), 93.
3. Kresh, P. (1969). *The power of the unknown citizen.* New York: J.B. Lippincott.
4. Boulding, E. (1969). *The underside of history: A view of women through time.* Boulder, CO: Westview Press.
5. Sonkin, D. J., & Durphy, M. (1982). *Learning to live without violence.* San Francisco: Volcano Press.
6. Pines, M. (1979, January). Superkids. *Psychology Today,* 53-63.
7. Faust, J. (1980). *Thomas Merton: A pictorial biography.* New York: Paulist Press. p. 79.

Overcoming Helplessness and Discouragement

Gerald D. Oster

Mary worked actively for peace-related causes. She had been involved in peace organizations since her high school days, doing everything from writing articles and soliciting petition signatures to marching in demonstrations and speaking at rallies. Now, at 23, Mary found herself taking on so many responsibilities that she could no longer meet all her commitments. Rather than realizing that she was just taking on too big a load, she began criticizing herself for not being able to accomplish all she could. A pattern of self-criticism followed over the next several months. Before a demonstration that was projected to be exceedingly large, Mary suddenly became anxious for no apparent reason and expressed sadness and an uncharacteristic pessimism regarding the movement's success. Her once hectic life came to a standstill, and despite the support of her friends, Mary became increasingly depressed and inactive.

John yearned to be more of an activist but stayed in the background, yielding to his lack of confidence and shyness. He agreed with many of the peace-related issues but felt ineffective, helpless, and overwhelmed by the extent of the problems. After joining an organization that was attempting to stop the construction of a weapons-related facility, his feelings of self-worth dropped even further due to an unfortunate incident. Before the first major rally, there was a legal injunction against the event, which had the effect of halting any demonstration. John took this defeat very personally, thinking that if he could have worked harder or had known someone in the legislature, the rally would have taken place as planned. After this perceived failure, John felt that he was powerless to change the issues and he avoided all further involvement.

Learned Helplessness

Although these two fictitious individuals are of very different temperaments, both experienced similar feelings of helplessness and depression. Both felt that they had lost control of the outcomes in their lives, and this feeling began a cycle of self-degrading thoughts in each of them ("I am powerless to control any situation"). This culminated in a belief system of negative feelings about themselves and about the world in which they live. They became less active as they began to view themselves as powerless people who were unable to help themselves, let alone help change problems in society.

This perceived loss of control sometimes leads to a form of clinical depression called "learned helplessness."[1] Even though the above examples might be considered extreme, it's likely that everyone has at one time or another experienced a similar situation and has felt this negative thought process begin.

The Thought-Feeling Connection

Many theorists of modern psychology believe that how individuals view the world and themselves will ultimately determine how they will feel and act. Thoughts and disturbed feelings are interrelated. Rarely, they suggest, can one feel upset without also having associated disturbance-creating thoughts.[2,3,4] For instance, such unrealistic views as "I must be a success in everything I do" will ultimately stir up feelings of anxiety or sadness when faced with any failure. Conversely, sad feelings may produce irrational beliefs, such as, "I'll never experience success from now on." This type of thought-feeling connection can happen fairly regularly to peace workers, who often run into "brick walls" in their efforts for peace. Fortunately, much psychological research has shown that when people are able to alter their flow of disturbing thoughts, their feelings and subsequent behaviors become much more positive.[5]

Monitoring Your Activities and Associated Feelings and Thoughts

If you happen to find yourself in the early stages of this cycle, what can you do to avert these negative thoughts and resulting feelings? You might first attempt to create what is termed an "activity schedule."[6] This technique calls for you first to make an hour-by-hour list of your daily schedule, peace-related or otherwise, keeping a record of those activities that you find enjoyable and rating (on a scale of 1 to 5) how much pleasure you get from them. From this information you should soon realize that you're deriving more satisfaction from your daily activities than you had previously thought. This will disprove any notion you might have had that your situation was hopeless.

Next, you should rate the negative moods you experience during your day's activities — say, how much anxiety you felt during your telephone conversation with your boss. From these various ratings you'll discover that positive and negative feelings tend to be limited in time and are associated with specific activities.[6] You'll also discover that your mood improves when you've completed assignments or have engaged in particular activities. You can then begin to do more of those pleasurable activities and schedule more accomplishable tasks. Doing so will improve your mood and productive energy. (Hints for accomplishable tasks are covered later in the chapter.)

You can take these suggestions a step further by becoming more aware of those negative thoughts that lead to bad feelings. To begin, pay attention to your negative moods and replay in your mind exactly what went on before the bad mood began. Try to recall the thoughts that led to those feelings. For example, when you find yourself becoming nervous when planning a peace activity for your organization, examine the thoughts that preceded the anxiety. You might have been thinking about how you were criticized the last time you did the planning, and perhaps you had attributed that criticism to a lack of ability on your part. Ask yourself whether the criticism was valid — did the peace activity really turn out to be that bad? A past criticism can infringe on your present efficiency. You need to realize that things probably have changed since the original criticism.

Questioning Your Assumptions about Yourself

Are you:

1. assuming that your negative thoughts or self-criticisms are valid — confusing thoughts with facts?
2. holding beliefs without checking out your ideas with others?
3. overgeneralizing failures — thinking that you'll fail at everything?
4. not becoming aware of factors beyond your control that may have caused a failed project?
5. overlooking your obvious strengths or underestimating the impact you might have on others?
6. thinking that the present negative situation will never change?

Sue was beginning to believe that she had nothing valuable to contribute in group meetings as she always listened to someone else's view rather than expressing her own. Although she privately differed on many of the ideas being expressed, she had always taken criticisms of her opinion very personally. This led to increasing feelings of anxiety. When she attempted to understand why she always felt so nervous when wanting to say something, she discovered that she would say to herself things like, "What would the other group members think of my ideas?" "Will I be able to influence anyone with my ideas?" "Will the others just think I'm jealous of the person I oppose?" "Does what I have to say really have any relevance?" "Wouldn't it be awful if I made a mistake in public?" It's these self-imposed statements that many psychologists think cause feelings of anxiety. They believe that emotions nearly always are created by personal thoughts and beliefs.[7] Fortunately, after receiving advice from a friend, Sue began questioning the assumptions she was making and thoughts she was having about her problem with public speaking. This led her to make an agreement with herself to increase the proportion of time spent expressing personal views in meetings. It was only after she tried this and discovered that nothing terrible happened when she made a mistake (and that she was not a terrible communicator even if she failed to influence anybody) that she overcame her fear of public speaking and participated actively in group meetings.

You can use the same basic technique in other situations to monitor and question the thoughts that lead to negative moods. Try to think of some examples in your daily life where different moods may have been precipitated by your thoughts or beliefs.

Plan Accomplishable Activities

Another practical strategy you can use to improve your mood and increase your energy is to plan more accomplishable activities and then reward yourself for even minor successes.

Say, for instance, that you've been wanting to write a pamphlet concerning the atrocities of war but have never found the time to do it or don't know where to begin. If you *don't* break the task down into small steps, you may feel overwhelmed and give up before trying. By breaking the activity down into smaller parts, you're more likely to accomplish it. In writing the pamphlet, you could begin by going to the library for fifteen minutes to find what books are available on the topic. Then on the next visit, go inside and skim several relevant books and articles for thirty minutes, taking notes on which sources deserve further use. Return to the library for an hour to study and outline, and so on.

As you progress through the project, you should reward yourself for each success, perhaps stopping for ice cream or a beer after visiting the library, or going someplace special at the end of a productive week. The actual writing of the pamphlet may also be a stumbling block; again, break it down into small accomplishable steps — write for ten minutes and not more on the first night, fifteen minutes on the second, twenty on the third, etc. This time-management technique of breaking activities down into easily accomplished subgoals can be applied to almost any task you might want to attempt.

The following scenario demonstrates another method of establishing goals and subgoals and how they can enhance feelings of success:

Tom was in charge of a large political organization that seemed to be getting bogged down by its own weight. Because of constant phone calls, distractions from visitors, and meetings that seemed unfocused, very little work was getting done, and Tom began blaming himself for the group's inefficiency. In order to accomplish more objectives and thus feel better about the job he was supposed to be doing, he rearranged the group's structure in the following manner:

1. He identified as many goals as possible for the organization;
2. He listed the goals in order, from the most important to the least, and put his energy into them accordingly;
3. He broke down all complex tasks into simple steps (say, to prepare a report he went to the library for background information, then checked previous reports, next used someone as a "sounding board," and finally set a deadline and began writing);
4. He assigned as much work as possible to others;
5. He established a quiet time for two hours of the day when he would not be interrupted by phone calls or visitors.[8]

With the introduction of this program, the organization became much more effective and Tom overcame his disturbing thoughts, which were beginning to be self-defeating.

Conclusion

Psychologists have learned that it's a person's distortion of actual facts that begins a vicious cycle of thoughts and moods that lead to the expectation that nothing can change the situation, and any attempts to change will always fail. The result usually means less motivation and possible feelings of helplessness.

These techniques encourage positive beliefs and expectations with pleasurable activities and tasks that can be accomplished. Small task successes increase feelings of mastery and control and, in turn, the chances for further success. You must also question negative faulty beliefs and assumptions about yourself that lead to anxious and sad feelings. Using these techniques can help you keep positive attitudes about yourself and your work.

References

1. Peterson, C., Maier, S. F., & Seligman, M. E. P. (1995). *Learned helplessness: A theory for the age of personal control.* New York: Oxford University Press.
2. Ellis, A. (2001). *Overcoming destructive beliefs, feelings, and behaviors: New directions for rational emotive behavior therapy.* Amherst, NY: Prometheus Books.

3. Alford, B. A., & Beck, A. T. (1998). *The integrative power of cognitive therapy*. New York: The Guilford Press.
4. Burns, D. (1999). *Feeling good: The new mood therapy*. New York: Avon.
5. Meichenbaum, D. (2003). *Treatment of individuals with anger-control problems and aggressive behaviors*. Norwalk, CT: Crown House Publishing.
6. Emery, G. (2000). *Overcoming depression: Client manual*. Oakland, CA: New Harbinger Publications.
7. Ellis, A. (2000). *How to control your anxiety before it controls you*. New York: Citadel Press.
8. Morgenstern, J. (2004). *Time management from the inside out: The foolproof system for taking control of your schedule—and your life*. New York: Owl Books.

Suggested Readings

Burns, D. (1999). *Ten days to self-esteem*. New York: Quill.

Dr. Burns presents innovative, clear, and compassionate methods that will help you identify the causes of your mood slumps and develop a more positive outlook on life. You'll learn that negative feelings like guilt, anger, and depression don't result from the bad things that happen to you but from the way you think about these events. You'll also discover why you get depressed and learn how to brighten your outlook when you're in a slump, without drugs or lengthy therapy. The methods are based on common sense and are not difficult to apply. Research shows that they really work!

Seligman, M. E. P. (1998). *Learned optimism: How to change your mind and your life*. New York: Free Press.

Martin Seligman, a renowned psychologist and clinical researcher for over twenty-five years, provides this book as a psychological discussion of pessimism, optimism, learned helplessness (giving up because you feel unable to change things), explanatory style (how you habitually explain to yourself why events happen), and depression and how these affect success, health, and quality of life. Seligman supports his points with animal research and human cases and his chapters teach the skills of changing from pessimism to optimism.

OVERCOMING BURNOUT

Christina Maslach and Mary E. Gomes

Being an activist requires enormous energy and personal sacrifice. It's not always easy to sustain, and many activists report experiencing *burnout*. The initial "fire" of enthusiasm, dedication, and commitment to the cause has "burned out," leaving behind the smoldering embers of exhaustion, cynicism, and ineffectiveness.

In literature, this is portrayed in Graham Greene's novel, *A Burnt-out Case*.[1] A spiritually tormented and disillusioned architect quits his job and withdraws into the African jungle. But this isn't merely fictional — and isn't rare. Burnout is a fairly common and widespread experience.

Burnout has been a special concern among many caregiving occupations, where people often work very hard for few rewards but are strongly motivated by core values. Activism shares many of the characteristics of this kind of dedicated commitment and sacrifice, so it's not surprising that many activists, both paid and unpaid, report burnout at some time.

Activists also have other unique characteristics that can make them vulnerable to burnout. The very nature of activist work involves cultivating and maintaining awareness of large and overwhelming social problems, often carrying a burden of knowledge that society as a whole is unable or unwilling to face. This can lead to feelings of pressure and isolation that easily feed into burnout.

If severe enough, burnout can mark the turning point when people withdraw and leave their activist work behind. But people who are able to cope effectively can keep going over a long time. We have studied the factors that distinguish between these two paths, offering many insights.[2,3]

Understanding Burnout

Because it's catchy, "burnout" has been a popular way of referring to all kinds of problems. So let's begin with a clear definition. Burnout is not about feeling blue or bored or having an occasional bad day. It's a chronic state of being stressed and out of synch with work. The three key parts are:

• *Exhaustion* — the individual stress component

You feel drained and used up, without any source of replenishment. You lack energy to face another day or another challenge. As one activist put it, "I'm feeling totally overwhelmed by the immensity of the problem — feeling like I have to do everything, support every struggle, every issue...feeling small and helpless, getting lethargic, not knowing what to do, and ending up doing nothing."

• *Cynicism* — the interpersonal component

This is a negative, callous, or excessively detached response to various aspects of the work. It usually develops in response to the overload of exhaustion. At first, it's self-protective, an emotional buffer. If you're working too hard and doing too much, you might begin to back off and to cut down on your tasks. Excessive detachment can mean a loss of the idealism, passion, and enthusiasm that initially fueled your commitment to activism.

As cynicism develops, you shift from trying to do your very best to doing the bare minimum, and you begin to resent colleagues who seem to pose more obstacles than support. "I feel overwhelmed, and sometimes I look at the stuff I have to do and I get angry. Like, why doesn't somebody else do some of this stuff? Why is it just me? And I begin to think that other people don't have the same dedication." This anger can even evolve into self-righteous bitterness toward an unresponsive public. "I find myself thinking, Oh, a pox on them! They don't want to save themselves, so why should I go out of my way for these people?"

• *Inefficacy* — the self-evaluation component

This is a feeling of a lack of achievement and resulting doubts about self-worth. It's exacerbated by a lack of enough resources to do the job well and a lack of needed help and support. As one activist put it, "You have to deal with people who don't know what they're doing — that's the worst thing. And you can't count on them. I don't think I ask people for a whole heck of a lot, and then when they don't come through, it's very demoralizing." Activist work involves large, long-term goals that often seem unreachable. Progress in social change is often nonlinear,[4] leaving activists vulnerable to feeling discouraged. If you come to feel you have nothing to show for all your hard work or you've made a mistake in choosing your life path, then you're at risk for low self-esteem and depression, and you're more likely to leave activism.

Six Strategies for Dealing with Burnout

What leads people to feel burnout? An imbalance, or mismatch, between the person and the situation is a key underlying cause. There are six areas in which imbalances can occur:[5]

1. *Work Overload* — a mismatch between the demands of the work and your ability to meet those demands

There's too much to do, with not enough time or resources. There can also be an imbalance between workload and home life, when you may have to sacrifice family time or vacation time to do your work. Imbalances in workload are a major theme in comments from activists — indeed, for many of them, this is the critical source of burnout. As one activist expressed it, "You keep pushing yourself. There's no limit. It's like an anorexic getting thin — you're never quite thin enough. When you're an activist, you're never working hard enough. So you're exhausted and feel like you've got nothing left to give."

The solution to chronic exhaustion is to build resilience, by improving physical health and strength, getting sufficient rest, and learning how to relax during strenuous times. While taking a break from work can be helpful, another especially effective technique is a temporary work change called a "downshift." You downshift to some less demanding task, like routine paperwork or sweeping the floor, before returning to the more challenging jobs.

Being too available means being unable to set limits and say "no" to the never-ending requests for your time and effort. For a lot of activists, these requests are internally generated. One former peace activist described the hardest part as "the voices that I carried with me — 'you're not doing enough, you have to do more. There's no time to stop. There are poor people, there are starving people, there are homeless people'. That constant feeling that I didn't deserve a life until everybody got a life." The solution is to create uninterrupted time, some protected freedom from demands and a chance to get rested and more clearly focused on an achievable goal. You don't need to feel guilty about it, because by doing this you're actually making yourself more effective over the long haul.

2. *Lack of Control* — a mismatch between accountability for the work and your decision-making ability

Micromanagement by others, or other forms of ineffective leadership or teamwork, reduces your ability to be in control of your work, thereby weakening your commitment. The solution is to increase autonomy, shared leadership, and an understanding of the importance of all having some confidence in their ability to decide the use of their own time.

3. *Insufficient Rewards* — a mismatch between the work done and the satisfaction for the work done

People's morale and self-esteem depend heavily on recognition for what they've accomplished; yet in some places, positive "strokes" aren't a routine part of the job. There are also often insufficient material rewards, such as salary and benefits. Sometimes, if proper pay isn't an option, there are at least other perks or benefits that can be considered. Opportunities for joy and satisfaction in the work can be developed. Certainly, a group can develop meaningful forms of acknowledgement that provide praise and support for people's accomplishments.

4. *Breakdown in Community* — a mismatch between social needs and what the community offers

A breakdown in a sense of community occurs when people's social needs for support and collaboration are unmet or when the organization is riddled with hostility and destructive competition. When ongoing relationships lack trust, or have unresolved conflict, the work community will be unable to function as a collective group and may even end up tearing itself apart.

It's important for activists to attend to the relationships within their organizations. When there are literally life-and-death issues at stake, it can be tempting to focus on the success of activist work to the exclusion of the relationships you build with other activists. But these connections can be the glue that holds a group together, fostering creative and productive work. Conversely, they can be the source of endless difficulties and a drain on activist energy. A survey of peace activists in the 1990s asked participants to list the most important rewards and stresses of their activist work. "Relationships with other activists" emerged as *both* the most common reward and the most common stressor.[6]

5. *Lack of Fairness* — a mismatch between guiding principles and actual practice

People who feel the workplace is unfair are especially likely to become cynical, angry, and hostile. The solution to disrespect is to develop processes for promoting respect and civility so that people will feel committed to each other as well as to the larger goal. The solution to discrimination is to take actions that value diversity and create a climate of "zero tolerance" for behaviors that are destructive of the shared agenda for social change. Favoritism creates unfair advantages for some, which leads to alienation and cynicism for others. The solution is to ensure equity by developing clear and transparent policies and procedures.

6. *Values Conflicts* — a mismatch between your ideals of what you want to do and the reality, sometimes objectionable, of what you may have to do on the job

As an example, an activist may endorse legislation she feels doesn't go nearly far enough if she believes this is the only approach that will succeed. For activists, their values are what attracted them to their work in the first place and what sustain their motivation even when there are imbalances in the other five areas. Value conflicts can seriously erode this core commitment to the point where activists will quit the movement, saying, "I didn't leave it, it left me."

Pursuing Passion

Long-time activists often point to the positives that sustain them, rather than focusing on the negatives that challenge them. Focusing on their passion can be of central importance. As one activist put it, "I felt in love. I felt passionate about the issue. It was a passion I hadn't felt in a long time. It seemed to come from within....There was very little burnout. There was a craving." However, when burnout erodes that passion, many activists look for alternative ways to reconnect with their core values and to find new sources of inspiration.

Part of this rethinking often involves converting the major end goal, which may only occur in the distant future, into a series of more specific milestones that can be realistically achieved in the short term. There is nothing to build up a sense that you *can* achieve something like actually achieving something. In practical terms, that means accomplishing steps on the way.

Alternatively, some activists have shifted their focus to translating their goals into immediate steps that can be implemented in the immediate present. As described by Rebecca Solnit, "Recent strains of activism proceed on the realization that victory is not some absolute state far away but the achieving of it, not the moon landing but the flight....The term 'politics of prefiguration' has long been used to describe the idea that if you embody what you aspire to, you have already succeeded. That is to say, if your activism is already democratic, peaceful, creative, then in one small corner of the world these things have triumphed."[7]

Successful activists also recognize the cyclic ups and downs of their work over time, and are flexible about how they deal with them. Said one activist, "I've never struggled against the feeling of burnout. If I felt burned out, I just let myself feel burned out. I didn't have any moralistic attitude toward it, or fight it. I'd feel, 'Oh, I'm burned out, I'll just sit here for a while. Let somebody else do it.'" According to another, "I've relaxed a lot more. When I was younger I was convinced that I needed to drive myself every single minute. The planet couldn't stay on its orbit if I wasn't pushing it. Now I feel that I can go to the sauna, and I'll still hate imperialism in an hour and a half. And the delusion of grandeur, that it all rests on my shoulders, is more responsibility than anyone can accept. Both those things have changed in the last ten years. And that's helped me to stay an activist."

Burnout is a signal of imbalance, of too many negatives outweighing the positives in your life. It's a warning to slow down and calm down, and to take some time out for rest and restoration, if you hope to continue to fight the good fight. One former peace activist summed it up this way: "Don't forget to live. You've got to do that and be responsible, rather than throw yourself into the fire and be consumed."

References

1. Greene, G. (1961). *A burnt-out case.* New York: Viking Press.
2. Gomes, M. E., & Maslach, C. (1991, July). *Commitment and burnout among political activists: An in-depth study.* Paper presented at the annual meeting of the International Society of Political Psychology, Helsinki, Finland.
3. Gomes, M. E. (1993, May/June). The nature of commitment: Preventing burnout among environmental activists. *AHP Perspective, 3,* 16-17.
4. Solnit, R. (2004). *Hope in the dark: Untold histories, wild possibilities.* New York: Nation Books.
5. Leiter, M. P., & Maslach, C. (2005). *Banishing burnout: Six strategies for improving your relationship with work.* San Francisco: Jossey-Bass.
6. Gomes, M. E. (1992). The rewards and stresses of social change: A qualitative study of peace activists. *Journal of Humanistic Psychology, 32,* 138-146.
7. Solnit, R., pp. 86-87.

Suggested Readings

Maslach, C. (1982/2003). *Burnout: The cost of caring.* Cambridge, MA: MalorBooks.

This is the original analysis of burnout among people whose work was motivated more by passion than by pay, so it may be of particular relevance for activists.

Potter, B. (1993). *Finding a path with a heart: How to go from burnout to bliss.* Berkeley, CA: Ronin Publishing.

Based on the author's extensive workshops, this book provides many individual strategies for dealing with burnout.

Solnit, R. (2004). *Hope in the dark: Untold histories, wild possibilities.* New York: Nation Books.

This is a thoughtful essay on creative approaches to activism.

From the authors: This research was supported in part by a National Institute of Mental Health Fellowship to Mary E. Gomes. We would like to thank Patrick Reinsborough, director of SmartMeme Strategy and Training Project, for his thoughtful comments on this chapter.

DEALING WITH THE DISTRESSED

Rachel M. MacNair

"The idea that God gives people what they deserve, that our misdeeds cause our misfortune, is a neat and attractive solution to the problem of evil at several levels, but it has a number of serious limitations . . . it teaches people to blame themselves. It creates guilt even where there is no basis for guilt. It makes people hate God, even as it makes them hate themselves. And most disturbing of all, it does not even fit the facts."

— Rabbi Harold S. Kushner, 1981 [1]

A Danger of Doing it Poorly

Their friend, Job, had just been through a terrible time. All his property was stolen, all his children died in accidents, and now he was covered with boils and sick. It's not easy to visit such a friend as that; the temptation to ignore such pain must have been strong. Yet they came. They sat with him. They listened to him carefully as he vented his frustration. These are all very helpful things to do for someone in trouble.

Then they blew it. Big time.

Instead of agreeing with Job that his dire circumstances were unfair, they tried to argue with him that they somehow had to be fair. They thought bad things only result from having done something bad, so he must have unknowingly done something very wrong. If he were as good as he thought he was, he would still be prosperous. They thought they were defending God.

In the first recorded historical story dwelling on the theme of unfair affliction, written around 2,500 years ago, God ends up appearing in a whirlwind and telling the friends to cut that out. God was not being defended. They were just making things worse, and needed to apologize.

Job's friends were following a way of thinking psychologists now call the "just world view": Good things happen to good people, bad things to bad people, and everyone gets what they deserve, at least in the end. It's a belief that can leave people sitting by rather than opposing violence. How do you oppose unfairness if you don't recognize it, and sympathize with its victims accordingly? More to the point for the practical matter of your own dealing with others, especially other people in your activist group or that your group is trying to help, it's an attitude that can interfere with getting the work done peacefully or done well.

It's easy to be tempted with it. The "just world view" serves as a psychological defense. Did a woman get raped? She was wearing suggestive clothing; I don't wear suggestive clothing, so I'm safe. Are people poor? It's not because they were cheated or exploited or had bad luck, but that they' re lazy. I'm not lazy, so I'm safe. You can see why people want to think this way, and you could find yourself slipping into it at times.

Listening

Most of the time, a sympathetic ear is tremendously helpful. Studies have established that expression can help because inhibiting can be extra work and stress, and because processing grief and thinking things through can help with gaining other perspectives.[2] This is true as long as the perspectives are helpful — not obsessing, not self-absorbed, and not using the just world view to blame people who are either not to blame or whose blame is now beside the point (as with a drunk driver accident that hurts the driver).

There are all kinds of ways to add meaning to the suffering, and finding meaning does help. Sometimes the meaning is character development for individuals. Sometimes it's a determination to work to see to it that the problem doesn't happen to others. Being punished is generally a poor meaning, and often inaccurate or overblown. More positive meanings have been shown in many psychological studies in many different ways to reduce pain. Getting a shot from a nurse who intends to prevent you from getting sick is easier to take than someone coming and jabbing you in the arm with a needle for no reason.

At other times, words are not helpful. As Job's friends sat with him in silence for several days, so sometimes a presence is what's needed — with or without hugs and holding, depending. The important thing is to listen to the needs of the person who's in distress.

This is not a matter of your being a therapist — you may want to refer people on to therapists in extreme cases — but a matter of the smooth functioning of your group. It will help keep others going. When you need for them to do it for you, then it will also help you keep going.

The Eccentrics

You've set up your group to be loving and caring to one another. All of a sudden, you find that someone has joined who is, shall we say politely, eccentric. In some cases, there will be an actual diagnosis of mental illness with medication. In others, it's simply a person whose thought processes do not appear to be very helpful.

Why did this happen to you? Simple — you set it up to be very likely. You're a loving and caring group. You've been remarkably successful at maintaining yourselves that way. Of course you attract that kind of person. All kinds of religious groups and other helping groups have the same problem.

What to do about it? Know that it's normal, and cheerfully accommodate. It's not a mark of anything wrong — in fact, it's a sign you're doing things right.

The Traumatized

What happens when the distress someone feels goes well beyond a grief that can be expected to pass with time? When someone has been severely traumatized, they may be stuck well after the event with symptoms of Posttraumatic Stress Disorder (PTSD). This would be especially true of war refugees and torture victims, which a peace group may be working with. In that case, it's still well to listen, but more treatment will be needed. It's at this point that professionals may be needed.

Symptoms include nightmares and dreams about the trauma, flashbacks during the day, unwanted thoughts about the trauma that won't go away, irritability, jumpiness to reminders of the trauma or to loud noises, feeling detached or estranged from other people and other kinds of avoiding and feeling emotionally numb. There can be sleep problems and thrashing in bed, hypervigilance, trouble concentrating, and a feeling like there's really no future.

If the trauma is recent, these may go away with tender loving care and time. If it's been a while, it may be chronic and the person may be stuck. There can also be a delayed reaction so that symptoms appear months or even years after the event. Besides PTSD, there can also be panic or anxiety attacks, alcohol and drug abuse, and a sense of disintegration. Any talk of suicide, of course, calls for immediate action.

There is another form of PTSD that peace workers should be aware of: Perpetration-Induced Traumatic Stress (PITS). This is the form that comes when killing was the traumatic event. The person was not helpless in the situation, but active in causing it. Evidence seems to indicate this is more severe than PTSD symptoms for victims or rescuers, and with a pattern of more intrusive imagery, higher irritability in the form of temper outbursts, and the sense of disintegration.[3]

Senator Robert Kerrey was in the news in the spring of 2001 for admitting to killing civilians as a soldier in Vietnam decades earlier. Here is someone who was clearly successful, not suffering from a full-fledged disorder. Yet he talked about intrusive thoughts and dreams in such a way as to make it clear he did have symptoms. This is common. For everyone with a diagnosis, there are probably many who are functional but still have distressing symptoms.

Many combat veterans make their way to the peace movement. Unlike the military, which has an interest in killing being a job rather than a spark for negative mental consequences, we have a clearer view of the source of the problem. In some ways, we can therefore offer help more in tune with reality. The same is true for other groups that engage in socially-approved killing, such as those who carry out executions.

Psychologists figured out decades ago that, despite then-current assertions, there is no instinct for humans to kill. After all, the vast majority of us never do. Knowledge of PITS goes beyond this. It's not merely that killing is not part of human nature, but that it's *against* human nature. People working for peace can be more effective in healing the damage from war and other violence when we understand that — the victims are on both sides of the weapons.

Peace work includes healing the aftereffects of war. Our caring communities can aid the recovery of those who have committed violence by offering emotional relief, support, and opportunities to become involved in activities of human betterment. Trauma symptoms such as emotional numbing, estrangement from other people, and explosive temper outbursts can lead to committing more violence. Working to heal the trauma is working to prevent violence in the future.

We can help halt the downward spiral of violence by promoting the healing of those who have committed it before. It's one more way we can create upward spirals for peace.

References and Suggested Reading

1. Kushner, H. S. (1981). *When bad things happen to good people*. New York, NY: Avon Books.
2. Pennebaker, J. W. (1990). *Opening up: The healing power of confiding in others*. New York: William Morrow and Company, Inc.
3. MacNair, R. M. (2002). *Perpetration-Induced Traumatic Stress: The psychological consequences of killing*. Westport, CT: Praeger Publishers. For Internet discussion, see www.rachelmacnair.com/pits.

PARENTING IN THE PEACEFUL HOME

Susan M. Sisk and Larissa G. Duncan

If there is no peace in the world today, it is because there is no peace in the family. Help your families to become centers of compassion . . . and so bring peace.

— Mother Teresa

Being a peace worker can involve a variety of activities — for example, participating in anti-war demonstrations, writing letters, volunteering in a homeless shelter, and serving as a mentor for at-risk youth. You may have many avenues for working for peace, some of which you might not previously have considered in that light. In particular, as suggested by the quote above from Mother Teresa, your role as a member of a family may be one of your most important opportunities for working for peace. But do you find you're too busy, too focused on the outside world to sit down together at the dinner table with meaningful discussions about your values, beliefs, and advocacy work with your own kids? Naomi Drew, author of *Peaceful Parents, Peaceful Kids: Practical Ways to Build a Happy Home*, says that the first key to peaceful parenting is the idea that "Peace begins with me."

If this is so, how can you, as a parent, promote peace at home and create an environment that fosters the development of the next

---

[Editor's note: This is one of two chapters on parenting. This one focuses on the peaceful home as something individual peace activists want to have. Chapter 27 covers parenting as a specialized form of outreach, with children as a specialized audience.]

generation of peace activists? How can you use your role as a parent to promote your own growth as an effective peace worker? Our answers have these basic points: social responsibility, dialog, and reflection; acceptance and compassion for others as well as oneself; and mindfulness.

Social Responsibility

Psychologists Lawrence Kohlberg [1] and Carol Gilligan [2] suggest that ethical discussion can enhance moral reasoning and nurture an individual's development of such principles as justice and caring — two key dimensions of social responsibility. Other research on the social development of children suggests that their awareness of the social world and capacity for prosocial behavior emerges far earlier than we previously had thought. [3]. Research has shown that youth from around the globe are more likely to express working for the common good as a life goal when their families emphasize an ethic of social responsibility. [4]

If you find yourself thinking (again!) that you just don't have the time to give after fulfilling work and family commitments, then rethink the way you "spend" your time. If you invite your child to join you in planning and participating in a community service project, reframe your idea about spending time to include the idea that, instead of spending time, you're "buying" the opportunity to promote your child's gaining of compassion, civic engagement, and a sense of being able to do things. The projects you choose don't have to be complex. Of course, they should be age appropriate for your child: taking flowers to a nursing home, preparing a home-cooked meal for a sick or disabled neighbor, picking up trash at the park, or participating in community-wide service events such as Make-A-Difference Day or National Youth Service Day. Service to family members, such as reading to a younger sibling, also provides a sense of connectedness and purpose for your child. Do a web search with your child to discover the many websites that offer ideas about other ways to be of service in the community.

Part of the service learning process is to reflect on the service that was done and consider what the experience was all about. It's helpful for kids to reflect on what they saw, whom they met, and why there was a need for such service in the first place. This act of reflection serves as the bridge between experience and learning. Your children's prosocial behavior can be stimulated by gaining a sense of connectedness to others and the sense of meaning that can come from contributing to something larger than oneself.

The basis for reflection as a practice in helping youth learn is grounded in the work of John Dewey, who believed reflective thinking was a way to discover specific connections between actions and consequences. He believed reflective thinking would help students learn from experience and improve their problem-solving skills. Almost seventy years ago, he suggested that education should "lead to personal growth," "contribute to humane conditions," and "engage citizens in association with one another."[5]

Your role as a parent is an opportunity to educate your child regarding social responsibility. One of the ways that you can support the reflection process is to start a shared journal with your child. You can take turns recording shared and individual experiences, reactions, and observations, as well as responses to each other's entries. You could even do this with younger children by having them discuss the activities and how it made them feel and then supporting them in drawing a picture of the event and their feelings.

Acceptance

The more confident you feel, the more likely you are to be assertive, take a stand, and speak up against injustice. Aren't those also the characteristics of a peace worker? But to do or be those things, your child has to feel safe and confident. Studies have shown that children raised in an environment that communicates acceptance and reasonable rules are more likely to have higher competence and better self-esteem. [6] The most basic condition for ensuring a child's feeling of self-worth is getting across unconditional positive regard. Loving your children unconditionally means that, regardless of your expectations, you accept them for who they are, not what they do or don't do. Unconditional love is being able to "see" with your heart.

If your child feels you can "see" her or him with your heart, this will create a sense of belonging and connectedness between you and your child. Being connected promotes trust and the ability to love and accept others.

In the preface to Thich Nhat Hanh's book *The Miracle of Mindfulness*, there's a story about the School of Youth for Social Service in South Vietnam in 1974. This school drew young people "deeply committed to acting in a spirit of compassion" who went out into the villages to rebuild houses, teach children, and set up agricultural cooperatives. But there was so much mistrust in the villages because people had taken sides during the war. The youth who graduated from this school, however, refused to take sides and instead, "believed that both sides were but the reflection of one reality, and the true enemies were not people, but ideology, hatred, and ignorance."[7]

Teaching the skill of acceptance to our children involves helping them discern the distinction between a person's intrinsic worthiness and the external trappings such as skin color, politics, religion, economic status, or possessions. By teaching that our similarities make us human and our differences make us individuals, we help our children to be more likely to honor diversity and practice acceptance.

Compassion

Shortly before his death in 1968, Thomas Merton, a Trappist monk said, ". . . compassion is based on a keen awareness of the interdependence of all these living beings, which are all part of one another, and all involved in one another" (www.mertonfoundation.org). Sharon Salzberg agrees; she's the cofounder of the Insight Meditation Society in Barre, Massachusetts and author of *A Heart as Wide as the World*.[8] She says compassion is a powerful force that can transform our own lives and make a difference in the world. Teaching our children about compassion will be accomplished simply by allowing them (depending on their age and development) to witness or participate in acts of caring and kindness in the community.

Responsiveness and sensitivity to others are also elements of compassion. According to Merriam-Webster's Collegiate Dictionary, eleventh edition, *compassion* is defined as "sympathetic consciousness of others' distress together with a desire to alleviate it."

It's much easier to quote others on the subject of compassion than to try and truly define compassion as an emotion or as a behavior. The Dalai Lama humbly declared, "I often tell people, 'My compassion is just empty words. The late Mother Teresa really implemented compassion!'"[9]. Mother Teresa stressed that small, everyday acts of love can mean as much as large projects and that everyone can do the most important thing, which is to care.[10] Sometimes all someone else needs is to have a place in our hearts.

Self-Compassion

Self-compassion is a prerequisite to extending compassion and acceptance to others. According to Dr. Kristin Neff, self-compassion involves feeling forgiveness or softening toward ourselves and a decrease in the usual judgmental or critical attitude we take toward ourselves. [11] If you begin to feel compassion for yourself, then you can feel a greater empathy for others. As we all experience, it's very difficult to reconcile your idealized self with your real-world self who is often tired, overcommitted, or uncertain. If you haven't lived up to your image of the ideal parent up to this point, move your consciousness into the now and forgive yourself for not being perfect, patient, omniscient. Remember — you can't start over, but you can start from here.

Mindfulness

Mindfulness, as described by social psychologists Kirk Brown and Rich Ryan, is "present-centered awareness and attention."[12] According to the cofounder of the University of Massachusetts Stress Reduction Clinic Dr. John Kabat-Zinn, mindfulness includes open-heartedness and a nonjudgmental attitude in addition to "moment-to-moment awareness." He says "It is a systematic approach to developing new kinds of control and wisdom in our lives, based on our inner capacities for relaxation, paying attention, awareness, and insight." The old 1970s mantra of "Be Here Now" and mindfulness share common elements in that they both refer to the practice of keeping one's consciousness alive to the present reality. Mindfulness has been described as the ability to remain focused on the reality of the present moment, accepting and opening to it.[13] We believe cultivating this in your daily life will allow you to relax into the moment and fully engage with your child.

Much of the time we're either distracted by our own thoughts or preoccupied with what we're going to say next. Well, guess what? Your child is acutely aware of the fact that your attention is somewhere else! Really good listeners are "mindful," because they're right with you in the present moment, relaxed and open. If you are listening, *really* listening, this conveys acceptance to the speaker.

Surveys show that parents and children say they like to discuss topics beyond their daily activities, such as hopes for the future and other interests, while sitting at the dinner table. In fact, both parents and kids identify talking to each other as the most important family activity. Some studies report that as high as seventy percent of families with younger children have dinner together at least five days a week [14]. Time for family meals may decrease, however, as youth become teenagers. Studies show that time spent with family decreases by more than half for European-American youth in the U.S. from 5th to 12th grade. [15].

With your multiple demands as a parent and a peace worker (in addition to working to support yourself and your family!) has your family dinner hour devolved into the fast-food ten minutes? It's only too common that parents and children subsist on meals hastily eaten between activities. No, we're not lecturing you and admonishing that you can't be a successful parent if you don't sit down to a home-cooked meal each evening. Yet, taking time out from the busyness of your life to nourish and nurture your child is the first step to creating a home that is a center of compassion and peace. Even if you only have ten minutes, as long as those minutes are truly lived in the "present moment," the quality of your interaction with your child will be improved. To quiet the noise and calm yourself, we suggest adopting practices of mindfulness.

Incorporating mindfulness practices into your life can allow you to both care for yourself and improve skills that can lead to more effective parenting. Mindfulness practices can be formal or informal. Formal practices include taking quiet time for contemplation or stress-relieving activities such as meditation and yoga. Informal practices can involve really being in the present moment with everything you do in daily life. This can include a stance of openness, curiosity, and nonjudgment when experiencing challenging thoughts and feelings.

Parents we work with have reported that practicing mindfulness has helped them to become more peaceful, take time to care for themselves, really listen to their children, and get along better with their spouses and co-workers. They thus become more compassionate and effective in all spheres of their lives.

Conclusion

If you have more frequent conversations with your children and try to communicate a welcoming attitude, it may be more likely your children will develop more social competence and social consciousness. In turn, your children may gain an easier time showing pro-social behavior and developing social skills to help them connect with others. It's widely believed that children develop responsiveness and sensitivity to others through everyday experiences in relationships with their parents. If you make one of your goals as a peace worker to engage in conversations (dialogs, not lectures!) with your child that communicate an interest in your child's well-being, you'll be contributing to a more peaceful world for future generations. Not only that, your child will be more likely to be receptive to your values of peace and social responsibility.

As suggested earlier, sitting around the dinner table is the perfect opportunity to introduce topics that gives you the chance to share your values, worldview, and ideas about social change with your children. Engaging your children in volunteer activities can provide them with positive, proactive experiences that enhance their acceptance of diversity while promoting a more peaceful world.

A critical component of parenting as peace activism can be accomplished in only a few minutes every day. Please consider investing fifteen minutes each morning and fifteen minutes each night to nurturing yourself. If you spend just this small amount of time to practice mindfulness and self-compassion, you can enhance your ability to be an effective peace worker — both inside and outside your home. Let the cultivation of peace within yourself ripple out to your children, your family, your community, and the world.

References

1. Kohlberg, L. The Philosophy of Moral Development: Essays on Moral Development (Vol. 1). San Francisco: Harper and Row, 1981.
2. Gilligan, C. (1982). *In a different voice: Psychological theory and women's development*. Cambridge, MA: Harvard University Press
3. Denham, S. (1986) Social cognition, prosocial behavior, and emotion in preschoolers: Contextual validation. *Child Development.* 57(1), 194–201.
4. Flanagan, C. (1998). Ties that bind: Correlates of adolescents' civic commitments in seven countries. *Journal of Social Issues. Special Issue: Political development: Youth growing up in a global community,* 54(3), 457–475.
5. Dewey, J. (1938). *Experience and education.* New York: Macmillan.
6. Maccoby, E., & Martin, J. (1983). *Socialization in the context of the family: Parent-child interaction.* In P. H. Mussen (Ed.), Handbook of child psychology (Vol. 4, pp. 1–101). New York: Wiley.

7. Hanh, T. N., (1996). *The miracle of mindfulness*. Boston: Beacon Press.
8. Salzberg, S. (1999). A heart as wide as the world. Boston: Shambhala Publications.
9. The Dalai Lama. (2001). *An open heart: practicing compassion in everyday life*. Boston: Little-Brown.
10. Mother Teresa. (1997). *In the heart of the world: thoughts, stories, & prayers*. Novato, CA: New World Library.
11. Neff, K. (2003). Self-compassion: An alternative conceptualization of a healthy attitude toward oneself. *Self and Identity, 2*, 85–101.
12. Brown, K. W., & Ryan, R. M. (2003). The benefits of being present: Mindfulness and its role in psychological well-being. *Journal of Personality and Social Psychology, 84*(4), 822–848.
13. Kabat-Zinn, J. (1990). *Full catastrophe living: using the wisdom of your mind to face stress, pain and illness*. New York: Dell.
14. Moore, K.A., Chalk, R., Scarpa, J., & Vandivere, S. (2002). Family strengths: Often overlooked, but real. *Child Trends Research Brief*. Washington: Child Trends.
15. Larson, R.W., & Verma, S. (1999). How children and adolescents spend time across the World: Work, play, and developmental opportunities. *Psychological Bulletin, 125*, 701–736.

Suggested Readings

Drew, N. (2000). *Peaceful parents, peaceful kids: Practical ways to build a happy home*. New York: Kensington Publishing Corporation.

    A parenting guide written by an expert on the intersection between conflict resolution, peacemaking, and parenting.

Kabat-Zinn, J., & Kabat-Zinn, M. (1998). *Everyday blessings: The inner work of mindful parenting*. New York: Hyperion.

    A personal account of parenting coauthored by one of the world's leading experts on mindfulness-based stress reduction and his wife, a practicing therapist.

PEACE WITHIN, PEACE BETWEEN, PEACE AMONG

Miriam Freeman

I get up every morning determined to both change the world and have one hell of a good time. Sometimes this makes planning the day difficult.

— E. B. White

Nothing could be worse than the fear that one had given up too soon, and left one unexpended effort that might have saved the world.

— Jane Addams

Virginia Satir (1916–1988), a social worker and pioneer family therapist, considered her work with individuals, families, groups, communities, and the global family to be peace and justice work. Creating, facilitating, and sustaining "peace within, peace between, peace among" was both art and technology to Virginia. This chapter is based in part on her ideas for effecting change in the world at all levels of social systems as formulated in her Growth Model. The primary objective of the Growth Model is to become more fully human. Full humanness includes a sense of high self-esteem, congruent communication, and the ability to make choices using one's resources to her or his fullest potential.

Peace Within: Connecting with Yourself

For activists, as for all people, it's important to strive for internal harmony and balance, to use your whole self in living, and to practice self-care in order to care for others. A primary belief of the Growth Model (GM) is the need to be at peace with one's self before attempting to make peace with others or to promote peacemaking between and among others. In this way, the self of the activist becomes her or his primary tool for making change. I can know all of the techniques there are to know in the world, but the way I use myself in the process of social change is key to my effectiveness. I cannot make meaningful connections with others until I'm in meaningful connection with myself.

This involves being centered and balanced, acknowledging and honoring myself and all of my parts. When I acknowledge and recognize all of my parts, I experience integration and harmony. I am a whole person.

When I underuse some of my parts or ignore or struggle to keep them hidden or when I overuse or abuse them, I exist in a state of "dis-ease." My use of self is off balance and I am fragmented. I'm unable to use the potential I have available unless all of my parts are integrated. "If you tap your inner resources and nurture them, you and those you help will find what you need to facilitate more healthy functioning."[1] When you love, value, and respect yourself fully you can empower others to do the same.

The Self-Mandala

Virginia used the concept of the self-mandala to help us think about ourselves as whole persons. My whole person is the "I AM" that is made up of ten interrelated, interconnected parts. (Satir included eight parts in her self-mandala; I have added the parts of gender and race.) Your self-mandala includes your:

1. *physical part:* your body; the container for all your other parts
2. *emotional part:* your feelings
3. *intellectual part:* your cognition, critical thinking, analysis
4. *interactional part:* the part that's in relationship with others
5. *contextual part:* the person-in-environment part; the part that's in contact with your surrounding context of time, place, and purpose
6. *nutritional part:* the food and drink you put in your physical part
7. *sensual part:* your senses of sight, touch, smell, taste, hearing
8. *spiritual part:* the core of your being; the connection with the meaning of life; for some, this is known as the soul

9. *gender part:* how you identify yourself in terms of your gender
10. *race part:* how you identify yourself in terms of your race

Each of these parts performs a different task and makes a different contribution to your identity. All parts are valuable resources to you as their owner. Each part interacts with all other parts; each part influences and is influenced by all other parts. The more your parts are integrated and in harmony, the more fully human you become.

Virginia suggested that we use the mandala for self-assessment to strengthen, enhance, and sharpen our use of self in our work. I've modified the self-mandala as a framework for a self-inventory for activists.

To use this inventory, periodically explore how satisfied you are with your ten parts and their interactions. Ask yourself:

1. In what ways am I using each part of myself in my work as an activist?
2. In what ways am I nurturing or neglecting each part?
3. What contributions does each part make to my work as an activist?
4. What happens to each part when it's stressed?
5. Are there parts I keep hidden when I'm engaged in activism? If so, what effects does keeping these parts hidden have on my work?
6. Are there parts that I overuse or underuse in my work as an activist? Are there parts I abuse?
7. How can I take better care of each part? How can I nurture each of my parts?
8. What resources do my parts offer each other and me in my work as an activist?
9. What kind of whole self results from the way I put my parts together?
10. What changes do I want to make, either in the ways I use my individual parts or in the ways they interact?
11. What am I willing to do to make these changes?

Meditations

Meditations, or centerings, are another tool for connecting with your insides so that you can more effectively connect with others. Virginia created exquisite meditations, honoring the interplay among mind, body, emotions, and spirit. Some of these are available in print (see Suggested Readings below). You can create your own and tape them for your use. For some people, music enhances the meditative state.

I include one of my favorites of Virginia's meditations here. I think of this as a mini-centering because it can be used in the moment whenever you are feeling stuck or off balance, without anyone even knowing.

> Be aware of you. Be aware of where you are, of who is with you, of why you are here, of what you are thinking, of what you are feeling, of where you have come from to get here and of what it is like to now be here.

> Settle in your chair. Close your eyes if you'd like (or keep them open if you don't want others to know what you are doing!).

> Put your hand over your chest. Be aware of your breathing. Feel the air move in and out of your body.

> Now put two fingers on your wrist to feel your pulse. Be aware of the beating of your heart. Feel the pulsing in your wrist.

> Now appreciate the miracle that is your body. You do not have to tell your body to breathe; you do not have to tell your heart to beat.

> Your body takes care of you and supports you without your even thinking about it.

> Quietly celebrate the miracle of your breathing and your beating heart.

> When you are ready, return your attention to what you are doing and what is happening around you.

Peace and Justice Toolkit

Virginia believed each person has internal resources to promote health, growth, and wholeness. She created a self-esteem maintenance kit containing six tools. I've borrowed this idea for an activist's kit we can use in our work of promoting peace and social justice. We can also help others recognize they possess these readily accessible and powerful tools:

- *Detective hat.* Activists need to know their facts. Ask questions, fill in gaps in your knowledge, search for clues, be analytical, and find answers to your questions.

- *Wishing wand.* Your wand symbolizes your capacity to hope for, wish for, and believe in the possibility of a world in which peace and social justice reign in which we can join with others to stand against the destructive processes of social injustice in all forms.

- *Courage stick.* Social action means moving into the unknown. The unfamiliar is scary. With this tool you can move into this unknown territory with your courage out in front, dragging your fears behind you. You can join with others who are also carrying their courage sticks. What a powerful image of solidarity and strength!

- *Golden key.* Activism requires the ability to envision new possibilities, often opening doors that have been locked. With this golden key you can open the door to new possibilities for ways of being in the world that stand against the forces of oppression and destruction.

- *Yes and no medallion.* This tool is a metaphor for your integrity, your ability to say "no" when you want to say no and "yes" when you want to say yes. Oppression silences voices who want to say "no" but who must say "yes" to survive, or vice versa. How would the world be different if all of us could use our yes and no medallions and, with integrity, exercise our freedom to choose? You may need your courage stick when using your medallion.

- *Wisdom box.* You're able to know what's just and right for you, not for anyone else but for you. Your wisdom box informs you when you're behaving in ways true to your beliefs and values and when you aren't. I know right where my wisdom box is in my body, although I have discovered through many conversations with people that locations vary. Mine is in my solar plexus just below my breastbone. When I experience, see, or hear something that contradicts what I believe to be just, I feel like I have been punched in my wisdom box. It's a call first for analysis and possibly then for action. It helps if I put on my detective hat for this analysis and if I have my courage stick close by when it's necessary to act.

- *Heart.* With this tool you're able to love and feel compassion for yourself and for all other inhabitants of our world. (Virginia didn't include this; Jean McLendon added it.) This tool reminds you that you can be compassionate not only with people who agree with you or are on "your side," but with those who oppose you as well. This tool also reminds you of your capacity to love yourself in order to love others. What happens when you remember you have this powerful tool you can use when people are doing destructive actions? Who knows what new possibilities might emerge (especially if you also use your golden key)?

Pack a peace and justice toolkit for yourself. Find symbols that for you represent these tools and keep them in your physical presence as anchors to remind you that these tools are yours and readily available for use at any time. When you find yourself in a tough situation, or one in which you don't seem to be as effective as you'd like, or which doesn't seem to be going as you would hope or you simply are stuck, then ask yourself what tools you need to use in this moment to take you where you need to go. Remember you can use more than one at the same time. Social change involves multitasking, which requires multitooling.

Peace Between and Among: Mobilizing Others
Peace and Justice toolkit: Part II

Help others discover they too have internal resources for promoting peace and social justice. Often people aren't even aware they have these resources. Sometimes because of our life experiences with oppression we never learn that we have them, or we forget they are there, or they're too scary to use in isolation. Some people grew up in families where there were rules that prohibited use of these resources, and these rules may be continuing to restrict their freedoms. Encourage people to pack their own toolkits and to use them.

One group application for the peace and social justice toolkit is in social action training. Here is a suggested process. Within the training group, focus on an issue of concern. Open the space for a conversation about this issue. As people begin to talk, deliberately slow down the process. Frequently ask this question "what tools from your kit do you need right now to help you to talk about this?" (Or develop a strategy or a consensus or whatever the purpose of the conversation is.) Have the symbols representing the tools there for people to use and to physically pick up and hold as they speak. Amazing things can happen in this process. I've used these toolkits as interventions in working with intimate partners, work groups, families, and friends. I've never experienced it to be anything but powerful and transporting of relationships in preferred directions.

Temperature Reading

Temperature reading (TR) is a process designed to keep the emotional climate clear in any group of people who work or live together. A clear emotional climate creates space for open and direct communication so the purpose of the group can be achieved.

TR is based on the idea that there are universal themes that permeate all relationships — the relationships I have with myself, with my partner, with my family, with my colleagues, with my students. Through the process of TR, people exercise their freedom to comment about themselves and others within the context of the purpose of the group. These themes include:

- Appreciations and Excitements
- Complaints with Recommendations
- Puzzles/Questions
- New Information
- Hopes and Wishes

TR can be a very effective tool for connecting with others in work groups, teams, task forces, community organizing groups, and social action groups. I recommend that there be a facilitator for TR when the group is first beginning to learn how to use this process. When I facilitate TR, I briefly explain the concept if needed. Then I open TR with the question "what appreciations and excitements do you have today about our work together?" I give sufficient time for anyone who wants to share an appreciation or excitement to do so. Then I move to the next theme and say, "What complaints with recommendations do you have today in relation to our work together?" As the facilitator it's important for you to ask for a recommendation if one is not initially given in connection with the complaint. This may take a bit of prompting at first, but people learn quickly, and less prompting is needed once people become comfortable with the process. I continue through each of the themes, each time putting the question in the context of "our work together."

I have used this format for focus groups for program evaluation and for problem identification, intervention, and evaluation.

Sculpting

Sculpting is a powerful action-oriented intervention creating a three-dimensional picture using body postures and spacing to demonstrate a system's patterns of behavior, communication, and relationships. I've used sculpting with individuals, families, organizations, and groups. Here I focus on its use with organizations and community groups in social change work. This is a suggested process:

Ask someone to become the sculptor and to imagine that others in the group are clay. Ask the sculptor to create a three-dimensional picture, or "sculpt," of the status quo in relation to the problem or issue of concern. In other words, what is this sculptor's picture of the problem or issue? The sculptor positions people, shaping their body postures and facial expressions, and arranging them in relation to others in the sculpt. This stage is most effectively done nonverbally. For example, imagine the issue of concern is poverty. What would a picture of poverty look like? Who would be in the picture? What would they be doing? How would their bodies look? Where would each person be in relation to others in the group? A variation is to have the group work together to create this picture, arriving at a consensus for their collective sculpt of the problem.

Once the sculpt of the status quo has been created, the facilitator asks those in the sculpt to comment on what they're experiencing as a member of this status quo. What is it like to be in this picture? What are you thinking? How are you feeling? What's happening physically in your body? If there are people observing who aren't part of the picture, ask them what they're experiencing as they watch and listen. What do they see? What do they hear? As observers, what are they thinking? What are they feeling?

Now ask the sculptor to create a sculpt of the desired or preferred state in the matter of concern. What would the sculpt look like if the problem were solved or the issue resolved? Again, encourage this to be done nonverbally. A variation is to ask each person in the first picture of the status quo to now move to a place of greater comfort.

Once this new preferred sculpt is complete, again ask people to comment on what they are experiencing as a part of this new picture.

What's it like to be in this picture? What are you thinking? How are you feeling? What's happening physically in your body? Ask any observers to comment just as you did above.

Now ask the people in the picture to briefly physically return to the first picture of the current state or status quo. Then ask them to very slowly and deliberately move from the status quo picture to the preferred picture that was previously created. Ask them to pay particular attention to what they do to get from the first picture to the second. Did they need to move? How? Did they move closer to or create distance between certain others? Did they join with others in order to move? Who helped whom?

The literal actions that people in the picture took to move from one state to another now become metaphors for what needs to happen for change Suppose one person had to move from being on the floor with another's foot on her back to standing on her own two feet. How did she do this? Did she need help? Who helped and how? Or did she do it by herself? What about the person whose foot was on her back? How did this person move her foot? What happened when she moved that foot or when the other person stood up? How do these literal acts translate into figurative actions that will effect change? These actions now are used to generate tasks the group needs to implement to move toward the desired state. How will they be accomplished? Who is responsible for each task? What's the timetable?

One of the reasons I think sculpting is a particularly effective tool to use is its use of silence, movement, and touch when the sculpts are being created. In all groups there are people who will attempt to dominate the conversation and people who are reluctant to join in the conversation. Sculpting levels the playing field in terms of verbal participation. Through its use of kinesthetics and of silence, this tool has the potential to move people to a different level of understanding and experience that can generate a jump-start to action. One picture is, indeed, worth a thousand words.

Conclusion

I recommend adding these tools of the self-mandala, meditations, a peace and justice toolkit, temperature reading, and sculpting to the set of tools you already use in your activism. I believe they'll equip you well for what needs to be done now and in the future.

When my children leave home for soccer practice or a soccer game, I tell them "Do your best, have a good time, and be a good sport." I hope they remember this mantra not just for soccer but for life. These seem like sound practice guidelines for activists as well. Indeed, what else is there?

Reference

1. Satir, V., Banmen, J., Gerber, J., & Gomori, M. (1991). *The Satir model: Family therapy and beyond*. Palo Alto, CA: Science and Behavior Books, p. 338.

Suggested Readings

Banmen, J. (Ed.). (2003). *Meditations of Virginia Satir: Peace within, peace between, peace among*. Burien, WA: Avanta, The Virginia Satir Network.

Satir, V. (1988). *The new peoplemaking*. Mountain View, CA: Science and Behavior Books.

Satir, V., Banmen, J., Gerber, J., & Gomori, M. (1991). *The Satir model: Family therapy and beyond*. Palo Alto, CA: Science and Behavior Books.

Avanta: The Virginia Satir Network. http://www.avanta.net

10

Working for Peace and Social Justice? Who's Watching?

Robert E. Alberti

I please myself with imagining a State at last which can afford to be just to all [men], and to treat the individual with respect as a neighbor . . .

— Henry David Thoreau[1]

"Liberty and justice for all" is part of our pledge of allegiance in the United States. But where in the world — never mind just the United States — is there liberty and justice for all? And what government treats its citizens, as Thoreau would have it, "with respect as a neighbor?"

Thoreau told his neighbor, the tax collector, that he would sooner go to jail than pay taxes to a state that condoned slavery. That was a century and a half ago, and we're still trying around the world to create States that respect the individual. And such respect is even scarcer when the individual dissents from the views of the government in power.

Take working for peace. Protesting war. Advocating negotiated settlement of disputes. Promoting justice and individual rights. Sound like things everyone would want to do, don't they? Surely folks everywhere want peace and justice for themselves and their children, right? Yet in most countries it's a rather small and select group of progressive individuals who are actually willing to identify themselves with this work. Why do you suppose that is?

Why Not Work for Peace?

Let me count (a few of) the ways . . .

- Nobody has much free time because of the demands of jobs, family, home, and daily activities.

- Who knows just what "working for peace" means? Is it protesting in the streets? Writing letters to the editor? Training oneself in nonviolence? Running for office? Canvassing for political candidates who advocate peace and justice? Meeting with neighbors to bring change to the community? Or the state? Or the world?

- Strong "patriotic" and nationalistic political climates in most nations in recent years may make peace and social justice work seem "out of step" with mainstream thinking in many regions and nations.

- Similarly, in the current political atmosphere, with major concerns about international terrorism, peace work may be equated with dissent and therefore viewed as unpatriotic or even traitorous.

- "It's all pretty futile anyway, isn't it? Let's face it, in the end, the bad guys win anyway. I'm going to work in my garden."

> *Civil disobedience is the assertion of a right which law should give but which it denies . . .*
>
> — M. K. Gandhi[2]

What's the Risk?

Speaking out for peace is not without risk. We trust you consider it *worth* the risk, but let's examine that subject a bit.

Early in the twenty-first century, for example, issues of civil liberties once again emerged as a major story in the United States. Many people found intrusions on personal privacy authorized under the U.S. PATRIOT Act to be offensive. Further, reports of surreptitious government surveillance of private citizens — without benefit of court review or judicial authority — got lots of folks very concerned about the erosion of personal liberty. Such activities on the part of totalitarian governments in other parts of the world have been notorious for decades, of course. But the United States has prided itself on its protection of the privacy, liberty, and freedom of expression enjoyed by its citizens. Now those rights — taken for granted, albeit with notable exceptions, for two centuries — have once again been called into question in the name of "national security," this time in the face of an apparently unending "war on terrorism."

Those whose views may not meet the test of absolute deference to the current political leadership of their nation may find themselves — as did a Quaker peace study group in Florida late in 2005 — on lists of potential "security risks."

> One who breaks an unjust law must do so openly, lovingly, and with a willingness to accept the penalty.
>
> — M. L. King, Jr.[3]

Who's Watching Where You Live?

In the United States, it's the Federal Bureau of Investigation, the Central Intelligence Agency, the National Security Agency, the Department of Homeland Security. Around the world, it's MI5 in the United Kingdom, Direction de la Surveillance du Territoire in France, the Australian Security Intelligence Organization down under, the Federal Security Service in Russia, the Canadian Security Intelligence Service, the People's Armed Police Force in China, the newly organized internal security center in India. Similar agencies are using state of the art technology around the globe to protect — and let's face it, spy upon — their citizenry.

There is no doubt that the threat of international terrorism is real. And governments do have a responsibility to take prudent steps to prevent acts of aggression or invasion and violations of the safety and security of their citizens. But where are the real risks? And when does the cost of security and safety exceed the benefits? Ben Franklin put it well:

> They that can give up essential liberty to obtain a little temporary safety deserve neither liberty nor safety.

Those of us who have contributed to this book have concluded that working for peace is clearly worth the risk of showing up on somebody's list of dissenters. Such risks may be minimal, or of great consequence, depending upon the "national security" inclinations of the current government leadership. Every person, of course, must decide her or his own level of tolerance of risk and anxiety. You may not want to put on the line your career, or your livelihood, or your family's stability, or your reputation in the community.

What Can You Do About It?

If the potential risks of social activism are a concern for you, there are a number of practical steps you can take to help yourself deal with these issues:

- *Remember that you're in good company.* No less a supporter of civil liberties than the United Nations itself reminds us that we have every right to freedom of expression on vital issues. (See the excerpts from the UN's *Universal Declaration of Human Rights* in the sidebar.)

- *Stay well informed.* Follow reliable news sources, and search the Web for updates.

- *Speak out against violations of civil liberties.* Call, write, email, or visit your government representatives; work to elect to office those who will defend individual liberty; sign petitions; support organizations that actively promote civil liberties (for example, in the United States: the American Civil Liberties Union, People for the American Way, and the American Library Association).

- *Involve yourself at your own level of commitment.* Consider the many alternative ways to take part in peace work, and decide what action fits you. Actions by peace workers around the world have ranged from *self-destructive* (immolation, lying down in front of trains), to *self-assertive* (T-shirts, bumper stickers, sit-ins, passive resistance to arrest, voluntarily spending time in jail, marching peacefully; e.g., Women in Black, Mothers for Peace), to *self-contained* (financial contributions, letters, behind the scenes support for the protests of others). Active effort at any level helps!

- *Take affirmative steps to deal with your own anxiety about becoming involved.* (See, for example, Chapter 2, "Cultivating Inner Peace," or Chapter 34 on humor).

Excerpts from the United Nations'
Universal Declaration of Human Rights

Article 12

No one shall be subjected to arbitrary interference with his privacy, family, home or correspondence, nor to attacks upon his honour and reputation. Everyone has the right to the protection of the law against such interference or attacks.

Article 19

Everyone has the right to freedom of opinion and expression; this right includes freedom to hold opinions without interference and to seek, receive and impart information and ideas through any media and regardless of frontiers.

Article 29

1. Everyone has duties to the community in which alone the free and full development of his personality is possible.
2. In the exercise of his rights and freedoms, everyone shall be subject only to such limitations as are determined by law solely for the purpose of securing due recognition and respect for the rights and freedoms of others and of meeting the just requirements of morality, public order and the general welfare in a democratic society.[4]

Those of us who work for peace and social justice are idealists, but we must live in the real world. As in most dimensions of life, *balance* is a worthy strategy. Find your place in the larger scheme of peace work, consider the risks involved, assess your own risk tolerance, take the steps necessary to deal with it, and make working for peace a challenging and rewarding part of your life.

References

1. Thoreau, H. D. (1849). Resistance to civil government. In E. P. Peabody (Ed.), *Aesthetic Essays*. Boston: Editor.
2. Gandhi, M. K. (1996). *Gandhi's Words*. M. K.Gandhi Institute (Retrieved from http://www.indiaspace.com).
3. King, M. L. (1963). *Letter from a Birmingham jail*. Philadelphia: American Friends Service Committee.
4. United Nations. (1947). *The Universal Declaration of Human Rights*. New York: Author.

Online: Use your favorite web browser or do an Internet search on "civil liberties," or "individual rights," or "privacy," or "government surveillance," or some combination of those topics.

PART II
PEACE GROUPS
GETTING ORGANIZED

You must have an organization which will permit
interweaving all along the line. Strand should weave
with strand and then we shall not have the clumsy task
of trying to patch together finished webs.

— Mary Parker Follett, the early 1930s

Motivating Others to Work with You

Neil Wollman

People become active in working for peace for many reasons. A series of interviews with peace workers revealed five principal factors: *modeling* (repeating the actions of others), *being affected by the media* (small group film showings, books, commercial movies), *belonging to a group in which activism is encouraged, being motivated by a historical event* (napalming in Vietnam, the bombing in Hiroshima), or *responding to an important personal event* (identifying with a victim of war, traveling overseas, experiencing childbirth).[1] Though the last two occur spontaneously, you can encourage political activity by using the first three, and some additional ones below.

Factors Relating to the Volunteer

Moods and feelings

Research has found that people will be more likely to help when in certain moods or having certain feelings, such as feeling guilty or being in a good mood. Even if you don't feel comfortable in purposely making others experience these things, at least be aware the chances for receiving help are greater if you make your request when they're already feeling good or guilty.

Moral obligations

People are also more helpful when they experience certain moral obligations. Most of us feel we should be socially responsible and help those in need. Use this principle by expressing the needs you're experiencing, the justness of your position, and the good deed your listener(s) would do by contributing in some way to your need.

When you do this, keep in mind people tend to help more when they're alone than when they're in a group. People in groups may have a "diffusion of responsibility." This is a tendency for individuals to rely on others in the group to fulfill the need. Thus when you appeal to a group, it's important to state that *each person's* contribution is necessary. Saying this to an individual listener is also desirable, for whenever you can emphasize individual responsibility, your chances of succeeding increase.

Another moral obligation is termed *reciprocity* — the belief we should help those who have helped us. This effect is less likely to hold if someone feels you did her or him a favor only for pressure in returning one, but even then it might hold. When you use reciprocity to get some help on a peace project, be aware the help you gave previously to the person needn't relate to the kind of help you're requesting now — though chances are even better if they *are* related. Yet the amount of help you request should approximate the amount you gave before.

When you address a special interest group (or an individual member of a group) try to find that particular moral appeal to which most members will likely respond. For instance, when you talk with adults in "child-related" groups (PTA, Boy Scouts and Girl Scouts, youth athletic clubs), stress protecting youth. Stress the terrible nature of permanent war injuries with handicapped-related groups (military veterans' organizations, groups tied to a crippling disease). Do research beforehand to find out a group's basic moral beliefs — whether it's a political group or a service club. Then tie your appeal for money, signatures, volunteers, or whatever, to some aspect of peacework that relates to those moral beliefs.

Attributions

In whatever way possible, suggest to potential volunteers that they're the type of individuals who give assistance to others in need. This suggestion could result in their "attributing" that characteristic to themselves. If this happens, they'll likely become so in reality. This type of attribution effect has been shown in several studies. One early experiment found that telling children they were tidy individuals was an effective way to improve their neatness — in fact, it even worked better than trying to convince them that they *should* be neat.[2]

The attribution effect will be greater if you can get the person to do even one small action for peace. Perhaps the volunteer can write one postcard, or talk to one neighbor about peace, or work for half an hour in a peace group's office. By doing so, the volunteer will further take on the self-image of a helper and be more likely to do such things in the future.

One further attribution-related effect: a volunteer you can convince to urge other people to work for peace will become an even more dedicated worker. Research shows that publicly endorsing a particular action makes the endorser more likely to take that action herself.

Factors Relating to You and Your Peace Group

Research has shown we aid those who are truly needy, who are similar to ourselves, and whom we like (psychology often seems to verify the obvious!). Because people lead busy lives, they won't help unless you can establish a genuine need. Appeals should point out the needs of your group and the important human needs your group is trying to fulfill.

There are many ways that the principle of similarity can be employed. When your group is asked to talk with particular professional, religious, racial, or special interest groups you could send someone who's similar to them in one or more of these ways. Show by word and deed the resemblances between yourself and your listeners. When you address certain women' s groups, point out how you and many others in your peace group are concerned mothers. Make a few comments about sports when talking to groups likely to have many sports fans. Dress and otherwise appear similar to those you contact.

That we help those we like isn't an astounding fact, but you should keep it in mind. No matter how good your cause or specific message, a disagreeable personal style won't help.

Factors That Increase the Desire to Help
Rewards

A well-researched theory states we'll give assistance only when the benefits expected from helping outweigh the expected costs. Such potential benefits can take many forms: hoping to feel good about yourself, wanting to help with something you believe in, expecting to receive praise or finances. Costs might include the possibility the help would do no good and that time and resources would be lost. If someone gets something beneficial after helping, she or he is more likely to help in the future — even for totally new kinds of requests.

How might you use these ideas? First, try to make your appeal so those you approach will expect psychological or material benefits from their helping. Then do whatever possible to deliver those benefits. What you tell a potential volunteer depends on what you have to offer and what sorts of things are appealing to that person. Some volunteers find it rewarding to work behind the scenes for praise or inner satisfaction; others want to deal directly with the public and get a minimal salary. Some want to be assured they'll feel good by helping out or that their costs in time and effort won't be great. If you know what someone will find appealing, offer it (if you can).

Otherwise, give some options regarding what contributions are needed and what sorts of compensation are available. Obviously, giving people options from which to select is a quick way of finding out what they most want.

One of the best compensations for peace work is knowing actions will have an effect. So if at all possible, make known the success of specific peace campaigns and/or how a volunteer's assistance has helped and will help in the future.

It helps if volunteers concerned about peace first take on small assignments with a high probability of success, such as collecting signatures on a petition. The person will likely get some signatures, feel successful, and accept additional assignments. The volunteer may be encouraged to work on projects of gradually increasing difficulty if she or he continues to receive self-satisfaction, praise from others, and perhaps even media coverage.

If you have volunteers working long term, there's one more thing. What's rewarding at one point may not be so in the future. The long-term peace worker should be offered a variety of challenging tasks with opportunities for varied rewards.

Modeling

There's a psychological principle that states that we learn new behavior by watching others (models) take particular actions. We can also learn simply by hearing about others' actions. If models are rewarded for their actions, we're even more likely to perform them.

These findings apply to peace work in several ways. You can talk to potential volunteers about others who've previously donated time or sources. The modeling effect can be enhanced by mentioning models the listeners identify with or respect, such as friends, governmental leaders, or celebrities. Though it works best if those models aided your specific peace group, it can still work if they didn't. The important thing is they've been involved in the basic kinds of activities you want volunteers to do.

There's also another approach to modeling: First, schedule activities for regular group members and others to do demonstrations, fund raisers, leafleting, letter writing, etc. Then, for the modeling effect, publicize the event afterward so that the helping actions are emphasized. You can do this through stories and pictures in newsletters, leaflets, posters, advertisements, and, if you plan it right, news coverage. With modern technology, you can even hire a videographer for an hour or two and rent satellite time to make the footage available to media outlets that didn't show up — outlets nowadays like to have their coverage handed to them so that it's less work, and you have the advantage of having more control over how it's presented (see chapter 27).

Finally, have potential volunteers actually witness acts of working for peace: schedule activities in places visible to the public, invite friends and acquaintances of group members to your activities, and publicize your political events to draw an audience.

Door Tricks

The "foot in the door" effect is that if you need to ask someone for a lot of help on something, first make a small request that will be granted. The volunteer will then be more likely to continue helping with the bigger project. On the other hand, some research has indicated that the "door in the face" technique may be even more effective. First make an unreasonably large request. When it's rejected, ask for a smaller favor — the one you really wanted in the first place.

You may find these tactics too manipulative to use, but that's your choice. It should be obvious that any means you use that potential volunteers see as purposely manipulative may not work.

Recruiting Group Members

If someone joins your peace group, don't expect him or her to necessarily become heavily involved. People join groups for many other reasons than just furthering the group's goals — to increase personal interactions, meet psychological needs, and gain status. Expect different types and levels of involvement depending on the reason(s) for joining. Involvement may well change as membership continues and circumstances change.

If you want to increase your group's membership, you can probably do so by adding things not directly tied to promoting peace, such as extra social activities, group goals besides peace, or an increase in group status by recruiting prominent community citizens who may be minimally interested. However, first consider how the new membership and activities will affect your peace work.

One creative way of reaching new people combines and modifies the "house meeting" concept taught by organizer Fred Ross and the "peacemeals" strategy of Wendy Forman. Have each group member choose five or ten friends and invite them over for a meal (each meal should have five to ten guests and should be hosted by a separate group member). During the meal the host/hostess presents the peace concerns of the moment and encourages each guest to become active to some degree. The guests could even write letters to Congress or donate money that very evening. Each guest should then be encouraged to invite her own friends to similar meals. It doesn't take much mathematical figuring to realize that if you successfully follow this procedure through a few cycles of meals, you've gotten quite a few people involved.

This being the twenty-first century, it would also be obvious that email lists, web pages, and other Internet resources provide a major means of outreach. Large demonstrations have even been organized in a matter of days, much more quickly than they could have been in days of yore, so the same method could be used to find volunteers for all kinds of projects.

On that optimistic note, I will conclude and wish you good luck in recruiting.

References

1. Mehr, H. M. , & Webster, M. (1984, December). Peacemaking works. *Association of Humanistic Psychology Perspective*, 21.
2. Miller, R., Bnckman, P., & Bolen, D. (1975). Attribution versus persuasion as a means for modifying behavior. *Journal of Personality and Social Psychology, 31*, 430–441.

Suggested Readings

Fisher, J. D., Nadler, A., & De Paulo, B. M. (Eds.). (1983). *New directions in helping: Vol. 2, Help seeking*. New York: Academic Press.
    This book describes research on helping that has been conducted out in the "real world," not in the laboratory.

Note: Studies on moods and feelings, altruism, helping behavior, and modeling are commonly covered in social psychology textbooks, so a perusal of most any introductory textbook should be good for further reading. A good example:

Myers, D.G. (1999), *Social Psychology* (seventh edition). Boston:McGraw-Hill.

EFFECTIVE GROUP MEETINGS
AND DECISION MAKING

Donelson R. Forsyth

Single individuals do much to advance the cause of peace, but much of the work — the decisions, advocacy, planning, and organizing — is handled by groups. In groups we pool our knowledge and abilities, give each other feedback, and tackle problems too overwhelming to face alone. Group members give us emotional and social support and can stimulate us to become more creative, insightful, and committed to our goals. When we work with others who share our values and goals, we often come to understand ourselves, and our objectives, more clearly.

Not every group, however, realizes these positive consequences. Often we dread going to "committee meetings," "council sessions," and "discussion groups." They waste valuable time as discussions get bogged down in side issues. Jokes about drawbacks abound; meetings are "cul-de-sacs to which ideas are lured and then strangled," or sessions where "people keep minutes and waste hours." But groups need not be time-wasting interpersonal traffic jams if members remain mindful of four key processes that can make or break groups: leading, communicating, resolving conflict, and solving problems.

Leading

Leaders have two basic responsibilities: helping the group accomplish its purpose and satisfying the social and emotional needs of those in the group. Unfortunately, these two duties are often incompatible, particularly during the early stages of a group's life. When the leader must remind members of their responsibilities and push the group to make difficult choices, members may stop looking to the leader for support. The best leaders, therefore, try to maintain a healthy balance between "getting the job done" and helping members "enjoy themselves." Your leader will have to decide what's most appropriate for your group, but there's one rule of thumb to follow: provide a good deal of task supervision and less emotional support for recently formed groups and more emotional support for older groups (eventually a well-established group will need little if any task structuring).

Obviously leaders can become overburdened if they have to deal with both task supervision and interpersonal needs, especially since they may be incompatible. Leaders, too, if saddled with too many of the group's managerial duties can lose their visionary, planning perspective, and in consequence the group can waste time on unimportant matters. Leaders should therefore share leadership tasks with other group members and members should be willing to take on these duties rather than assume only the leader must lead. For instance, if several members are arguing, others may mediate rather than wait for the regular leader to step in. Similarly, the person who recognizes a communication problem or a point that needs summarizing may temporarily take a leadership role and perform the task. By distributing leadership, everyone can participate more and the leader's responsibilities are reduced.[1]

All group members, but particularly the leader, should prepare for and facilitate collective endeavors:

- *Planning the process:* Leaders should resist the natural impulse to delve into the group's key issues immediately. Instead, they should ask the group to spend time planning how members will work together.

- *Creating an agenda:* Leaders should structure group meetings by developing an agenda and assembling necessary materials (such as handouts and charts), contacting those group members who are supposed to attend, and selecting a decision-making strategy (discussed later in this chapter). Although most meetings are structured so they start with a statement of the meeting's purpose followed by discussion and decision-making, you may decide to modify these procedures. Try to use the time together to make decisions, rather than merely deliver information.

- *Monitoring the discussion:* Keep an eye on both the content of the group's discussion (points raised, ideas offered, questions resolved) and the process (who's talking most, what conflicts are developing, and who's not participating).

- *Guiding the group's discussion:* Improve group communication by summarizing and pulling together information, paraphrasing or restating decisions or action plans upon which you've agreed, and making certain no one person dominates the discussion. Also, keep track of time spent on topics and encourage resolution when necessary. It takes practice to learn the appropriate time for resolution.

In some circumstances, leadership can be distributed another way. When your group accomplishes certain tasks and moves onto other ones, the new focus may lend itself to a change in leadership. If you don't feel the need for a permanent leader for your meetings, a useful attitude toward the role of leadership might be, "Who do we need in this situation to get this particular task done?"[2] Keeping one permanent leader lends stability to the group process and develops at least one experienced leader; sharing leadership encourages new ideas and allows many members to reveal talents otherwise hidden. This sharing approach also assumes that different circumstances create different leadership needs.

Communicating

Good communication lies at the heart of effective group performance. Active, frequent participation by members, in and of itself, improves performance, but quality counts as well: Speaking frequently when one has little of value to add only slows the group's progress. If discussion shoots off on tangents, if members ignore one another's comments, or if ideas are only sketchily presented, members will go home feeling very little was achieved. Effective communication requires constant attention, but it will become easier if you follow certain guidelines.[3]

- *Preparing.* In some cases you can walk into the meeting room without having given a single thought to what the group will be discussing, but in most cases members should have spent time preparing for the meeting so they can contribute meaningfully to the discussion.

- *Expressing yourself.* In most meetings members communicate orally, and as the air fills with voices the content and intentions of each speaker's ideas can be lost in the noise. Members must therefore be careful to communicate carefully, usually in brief, clear statements. When ideas are particularly complex or novel, ask others if they follow the points you are making.

- *Practicing self-control.* When people note their pet peeves with group discussions many are quick to complain that members often seem to speak to hear their own voices. The group gets too far off the track, and members often speak up well after an issue has been resolved. These problems can be avoided if you speak only when you need to speak and add your own suggestions, statements, and questions at the "right" point in the discussion; timing can be critical.

- *Listening.* Actively listen to what others are saying. Too often people seem to consider meetings a chance to talk endlessly about their pet ideas. Listening is at least as important as talking for a group to work efficiently and effectively. Ask for clarification of statements you don't understand. Follow the discussion carefully, remembering points that have been made while anticipating profitable directions to follow.

- *Drawing in all the group's members.* People meet in groups to capitalize on the talents of skills of the collective, so draw silent participants into the discussion through questioning; be alert to nonverbal signals that someone wants to speak but is holding back or can't seem to get into the conversation.

- *Offering "process remarks."* Members should, as needed, comment on the flow of the group's meeting as well as the content. Acknowledge positive, constructive statements or suggestions that are helping the group accomplish the goal of the discussion. Some of these comments may, as noted below, deal with conflicts emerging in the group.

Resolving Conflict

Even though your group is working to promote peace in the world, small "wars" may occasionally break out within the group. Conflicts arise from disagreements over basic goals, minor arguments over a particular issue, personality conflicts, and power struggles, but nearly all can be traced back to competition among the members. Time, resources, and rewards are limited, and in some cases members feel that others' gains are their losses. Conflict therefore becomes less likely when group members adopt a collectivistic orientation that stresses the group's needs over those of the individual.

Even though people are repelled when tensions flair, evidence indicates most groups need some conflict to maintain members' interest. If your group has no conflict, it signals that members are apathetic and that you're examining unintriguing issues. But members shouldn't ignore tensions when they disrupt the group's cohesiveness and productivity. If members gloss over the problem, it may escalate or surface later in a stronger and group-damaging form.

It is not certain, however, that the group's time will be well spent trying to discuss every source of disagreement that arises. When the conflict pertains to matters at hand that must be resolved, discussion is warranted. But when the conflicts arise from clashes of personality or personal dislikes, the group should focus on the work to be done rather than the relationships among members.[4]

Problem Solving

When you need to make a decision or solve a problem, such as organizing a demonstration or letter-writing campaign, raising funds, or prioritizing goals, your group should make its choice deliberately and mindfully. Although groups reach their decisions in many ways, a functional model recommends moving through four basic stages: Orientation, Discussion, Decision, and Implementation (ODDI).

- *Orientation.* Groups should invest some time in examining the issue itself, being careful to review the fit between the issue and the group's mission. This phase involves exploring the nature of the problem, identifying goals sought, and inventorying the group's talents and available resources. The stage is a good time to consider any ethical concerns that may arise and the solutions to the problem.

- *Discussion.* When groups talk over a problem, they (a) pool the information needed to formulate a decision, (b) identify possible alternatives for action, and (c) debate the relative advantages and disadvantages of options. If, for example, a group is considering a demonstration, it may be that certain days are bad for members, or that the town won't give permits for certain kinds of demonstrations, or that one member's brother has some loudspeakers the group can borrow, or that there is a celebrity in town who might help out. This information is examined by discussion.

- *Decision.* The group should reach closure on the issue by making a decision. Some methods for making choices are discussed below.

- *Implementation.* After making a decision the group should develop a concrete form of action. Determine who in the group is interested and able to do further planning, implementing, and evaluating of the action. The group may wish to form such a temporary "committee" after the decision step and have it handle implementation.

Making Decisions: Some Techniques

Many groups adopt, without much thought, parliamentary procedures (such as *Robert's Rules of Order*) when making decisions, but efficient groups consider both group and nongroup methods for making choices.

- *Delegation.* Your entire group doesn't have to decide simple routine matters, like where to hold meetings, what kind of stationery to order, or when to mail out a newsletter. Although groups often enjoy discussing such minor issues, face-to-face meetings should be spent discussing larger issues. The leader or a designated group member, after consulting with others, should make decisions when it isn't important for all members to accept a decision, when the issue involved is clear cut, and when an individual member or a committee is competent to make the decision. Delegation is also appropriate when members know little about the issue involved; for example, if you decide to invest in a new computer for the office, seek an expert's advice. Though you might feel you can solve any question through group discussion, your group members may be merely pooling their ignorance and could make a poor decision.

- *Averaging individual inputs.* For some decisions you might have members individually rank a number of available alternatives, and the leader would then determine the group decision by tallying the rankings for each alternative. If, for example, the group wants to award a community resident for peace efforts, members can individually rank the nominees, and the leader can then total the rankings for each nominee to determine the winner. An averaging approach minimizes interaction, so it should generally be combined with group discussion both before and after the averaging.

- *Voting.* "Let's put it to a vote" is an often-heard comment in groups, with members using a show of hands or a voice signal to indicate approval or disapproval. Although voting can be an appropriate method, when a vote is close some members may feel defeated and alienated, and consequently be less likely to follow through on the decision. Furthermore, voting can lead to internal politicking as members get together before meetings to apply pressures, form coalitions, and trade favors to ensure passage of proposals they favor. Be sensitive to these possibilities, and realize that the voting technique could be the cause. A voting or "averaged inputs" technique becomes more appropriate when the time to decide is limited, when the need for unanimous group acceptance decreases, and when the likelihood for conflict in making the decision increases.

- *Discussion to consensus.* Many groups prefer to discuss matters until a choice gradually emerges so that everyone has a chance to participate and be heard, and no one feels like a loser after the decision is made. Consensus doesn't mean that everyone is unanimous, which would be very difficult much of the time, but that everyone at least goes along with the final decision. Sometimes group members would prefer a different decision but are happy enough if the rest of the group wants something else. Sometimes individuals will even allow the decision of the rest of the group if only their objection is noted in the minutes. Remember, though, that getting all members to agree on a solution is generally time consuming, and if the leader feels a need to rush the discussion, uncertain members may feel their concerns were ignored. Furthermore, unless you stay attuned to the group's processes, decisions can be railroaded through the group by manipulative maneuverings, leader domination, and pressures for individual members to conform to the general group opinion. Each member has potential veto power over the group's decision and can require the group to listen to uninformed suggestions, irrelevant remarks, and stubbornly held, but rejected viewpoints. Decision making by consensus is most appropriate for matters that require acceptance and support by all (or most all) group members in order to properly implement resulting policy.

- *Brainstorming.* Group members often like to brainstorm to come up with creative solutions to a problem. Brainstorming encourages unrestricted expression of ideas and discourages criticism and evaluation and so is best suited for generating several possible solutions to a problem than to make a final decision. Also, unless your members are highly motivated and practiced in creative decision making, brainstorming may be no more effective in producing good solutions than "averaging inputs" or than the combined output of individuals working alone.

Group Traps: Pitfalls to Avoid

Group meetings can potentially bring out the best in individuals by helping them work together to produce outputs they never could on their own. Meetings can also stifle the creativity and drive that would otherwise emerge if individuals worked alone. Be wary of problems when working collectively, including polarization, social loafing, and groupthink.

- *Polarization.* Groups don't always exert a moderating effect on members. Instead, groups can trigger a more extreme, or polarized, reaction. If individual members are already leaning a little bit for (or against) a possible solution before a discussion, the group as a whole will move more in that direction during discussion. If at the beginning of a discussion many individual members have lukewarm support for some measure, the arguments presented will generally be in favor of the measure; further positive discussion ensues, and members become more favorable toward the issue. Sometimes this stronger support will reflect members' true beliefs (if the arguments really convinced them) but sometimes it won't (if members felt pressured to conform more in the direction the group seemed to be heading).

The latter possibility is best minimized by the group regularly encouraging open expression of ideas and independence in voting.

- *Social loafing.* When people work in groups they sometimes expend little effort. Knowing others will pick up the slack, or fearing they're working harder than others, people engage in "social loafing."[5] Help group members escape from this trap by letting them know each is making a valuable contribution to the group effort and regularly identifying the inputs of each individual member.

- *Groupthink.* In some cases highly cohesive groups can make very poor decisions as they become increasingly isolated from external pressures and information. This syndrome, known as *groupthink*, is most prevalent in highly cohesive groups working under time pressures to make important decisions where it's frowned upon for anybody to "rock the boat." It involves self-censorship of dissenting ideas, refusal to tolerate disagreement among members, mistaken beliefs that the group cannot fail, belittling of those outside the group, and a tendency to rationalize away problems and shortcomings. To avoid groupthink, a leader should: encourage independent thinking and full discussion of all sides of an issue; appoint a "devil's advocate" whose job is to point out what's wrong with the proposal, a person with the task of seeing how the group may be heading to make a fool of itself; stress that the group is capable of making an unsound decision; and consider breaking the full group into smaller discussion groups, or have independent groups work on the same problem and report back at another meeting.[6]

Conclusion

Group meetings can potentially bring out the best in individuals by helping them work together to produce outputs they never could on their own. Meetings can also stifle the creativity and drive that would otherwise emerge if individuals worked alone. The ideas presented in this chapter can help you take advantage of a group's strengths while avoiding its weaknesses.

References

1. Pearce, C. L., & Conger, J. A. (2003). *Shared leadership*. Thousand Oaks, CA: Sage.
2. Hughes, R. L., Ginnett, R. C., Curphy, G. J. (2006). *Leadership* (5th ed.). New York: McGraw-Hill.
3. Keyton, J. (2002). *Communicating in groups* (2nd ed.). New York: McGraw-Hill.
4. De Dreu, C. K. W., & Weingart, L. R. (2003). Task versus relationship conflict, team performance, and team member satisfaction: A meta-analysis. *Journal of Applied Psychology, 88,* 741–749.
5. Parks, C. D., & Sanna, L. J. (1999). *Group performance and interaction*. Boulder, CO: Westview.
6. Janis, I. L. (1982). *Groupthink: Psychological studies of policy decisions and fiascoes*. Boston: Houghton-Mifflin.

Suggested Readings

Forsyth, D. R. (2006). *Group dynamics* (4th ed.). Belmont, CA Wadsworth.
   A comprehensive review of theory and research relevant to group processes. Although empirically focused, it includes chapters dealing with applications to group performance, leadership, and decision making.
Keyton, J. (2002). *Communicating in groups* (2nd ed.). New York: McGraw-Hill.
   This book thoroughly examines the interpersonal side of groups, with chapters dealing with communication, experiential learning, increasing awareness, and leadership.
Thompson, L. L. (2004). *Making the team* (2nd ed.). Upper Saddle River, NJ: Prentice-Hall.
   A practical guide to creating and using team approaches to enhance productivity.

CHANGING WITHIN TO BRING CHANGE OUTSIDE: PROMOTING HEALTHY GROUP DYNAMICS

Shawn Meghan Burn

Social change groups must organize themselves well before they can organize others. They must create a healthy group structure that supports their work and keeps people motivated.

Develop Effective Norms

Norms are the group's standards, the normal behavior in the group. They're shared expectations about how the members of a group ought to behave and guide the group's behavior. Norms also contribute to group cohesion since they may distinguish the group from other groups and represent the group's identity by signifying members' collective values and assumptions.

Norms often arise in groups without discussion. This is fine if the group's norms help foster commitment, satisfaction, and productivity. But this isn't always the case. Instead, groups may develop such norms as starting meetings late, permitting some members to dominate, and not following through on agreed-upon tasks.

The evolution of undesirable norms may be prevented and treated by having explicit discussions. Such discussions make appropriate behavior in the group "stand out" and create a public commitment to it, therefore making it more likely to occur. Most groups need to consciously agree on the norms and values they want to guide the group, develop practices, and take action when norms are violated. Occasional discussions about the group's norms and whether they're working are also useful; new norms may be adopted, outdated norms discarded. Although groups frequently avoid taking the time to have explicit discussions about norms, this is usually a mistake. In the long run, groups with healthy agreed-upon norms are more productive than other groups.

Norms of Cooperation and Inclusion

Effective groups have norms of cooperation that promote sharing materials and information, communicating about tasks, and supporting one another in achieving goals. Such groups are more productive than groups with norms of competition between members. People work harder and are more satisfied. Members feel safe sharing ideas and saying things that indicate they care about the group, the task, and other members. Feedback is constructive and there is a supportive climate of mutual respect and flexibility in regards to problem solving.

In a classic article, Gibb identified member behaviors that influence whether a group's internal communication climate is supportive or defensive.[1] A lot of these have to do with how members respond to other members. In a defensive group climate, members erode trust and cohesion by responding to ideas they don't like with negative judgmental reactions. The put-down members feel criticized and defensive. For instance, after one member makes a suggestion, another might say, "That's ridiculous, that would never work." Responses may also be nonverbal — eye-rolling or head-shaking. This could lead members to retreat from the group or to vociferously defend their idea, even if they originally weren't that committed to it. In the supportive group climate, bad ideas may be rejected but this is done neutrally, without suggesting that the person who offered the idea is an idiot. The receiver simply responds with a description of what she or he thinks, feels, or has observed. For instance, saying, "I like your idea in theory but I don't see how we could implement it in time" is a way of rejecting the idea while maintaining a feeling of support. In the supportive climate, members feel valued and appreciated even when the group does not adopt their ideas.

A defensive climate is also likely when members attempt to manipulate or control the group. For instance, a member may condescendingly suggest that he or she knows what is best for the group and others do not. A member may try to bully the group by dominating the group's discussion until it caves in. Some members intimidate the group by yelling or appearing physically threatening. Many members will resist the manipulator's efforts, taking up much valuable group time. Some members will retreat out of fear of the controller. In the supportive climate, no one member is trying to impose his or her will on the group. There is a sense that the group is working together to solve a problem.

Similarly, defensiveness is also likely when some members aren't open to the ideas of others and act as though they have all the answers. Obstinate certainty is belittling and aggravating. We need to trust that the group is one where we'll be heard and our input valued. In the supportive climate, attitudes are provisional, open to change depending upon other members' input.

Dominating members who "overparticipate" can contribute to a defensive climate, but so can "underparticipators" whose behavior may be interpreted by others as not caring about the group, its task, and its members. Members who never say anything, are not paying attention in a meeting, locate themselves in a corner of the room, or withhold participation unless practically begged, all detract from the group. When a member appears indifferent to what others say, it signals a detachment from the group that interferes with cohesion. In a supportive climate, members are involved and present, not just physically, but interpersonally. It is obvious that members care about other members and what they say.

It's hard to overstate the importance of a supportive communication climate for member commitment to the group. A supportive communication climate is also consistent with the goals and values underlying the social change group. Helping the group make this connection can be used to get a specific commitment from members to supportive communication norms.

It's also important for the group to deal with group members who violate such norms. This means privately speaking with members, gently pointing out the effects of their behavior on the group's work. There are also ways to deal with defensive behaviors during discussions. Participants may need to be reminded to express disagreement respectfully ("Emotions are running high here and I want to remind everyone to express disagreement without making any personal attacks," or "I want to remind the group that we need to all make an effort to try and understand others' perspectives"). Potentially destructive participant comments may be rephrased before too much damage is done. For example, "We see you're upset David, but I'm worried that the way you put your message is interfering with others' understanding of it. Are you just trying to say that you're concerned that this tight deadline will make it hard to get the city permits in time?"

Norms that promote equality of participation are consistent with the values of groups working for peace and justice. Ironically though, such groups often unconsciously replicate the power and status hierarchies in larger society — members from traditionally dominant groups often dominate the group and its leadership. To avoid hypocrisy and improve group effectiveness, social change groups must consciously work to include all members of the group. Members should not have to fight for equality and justice within the group; it should be a given. The group must override the tendency to assign roles on the basis of gender, age, or ethnic stereotypes, rather than individual talents. It must remember that member diversity can enhance group performance by increasing the range of knowledge, skills, and contacts that strengthen problem solving.

Constructive Controversy

It is important that the group not confuse cooperation with a failure to disagree with one another or share divergent perspectives. This is why effective groups encourage dissent and constructive controversy. Social change groups may value peace and harmony so much they avoid disagreement. Groups may discourage dissenting views because resolving conflicts takes time or because past experiences have been destructive. But avoiding dissent and conflict is often a mistake, harming the group in unintended ways. Members with dissenting views or unresolved conflicts may leave the group if they feel there is no room for consideration of their concerns. Poor decisions may be made if members hesitate to question what appears to be the majority opinion. Unresolved conflicts can be the elephant in the room whose presence makes interactions among group members strained and fearful.

Conflict can be beneficial because it focuses attention on problems that need to be solved, clarifies how we need to change, illuminates what matters to us, and helps us understand other people and their values. Ideally, conflict is the way the group arrives at a unified direction from divergent points of view. It is also a way for members to establish trust. It lets them know they will be accepted despite differences and permits greater intimacy and collaboration. Groups are strengthened when members disagree in a climate of friendship and support and cooperate to reach agreement. In a successful group, conflict increases trust and cohesion and consensus about group goals and structure.

Conflict may also enhance a group's decision making because it leads to a more complete consideration of the issue. A group that fears internal conflict may adopt the first plausible suggestion in order to reduce debate among its members and may make an inferior decision.

The bottom line is that constructive conflict is good for the group. However, groups may need reminding that conflict and dissent are important for group effectiveness. They may need guidance in establishing norms consistent with constructive conflict. These norms may include:

1. Expressing disagreement respectfully, and rationally, without personal attacks.
2. Making an effort to truly understand the differences between varied positions.
3. Identifying the core issues underlying differing perspectives and coming up with solutions that satisfy these.
4. Keeping an open mind.

Group Cohesion

Cohesive groups stick together, remain united in their objectives, and weather setbacks better than noncohesive groups. Members like other members and the group itself and are proud of the group's ability to work as a team. Group cohesion may be especially important in groups of volunteers, since a positive group experience can motivate members to stay. Members of cohesive groups also appear more likely to do things for the group that go "beyond the call of duty," thereby enhancing the group's performance.

To be effective and productive, groups may need time and training to become cohesive. To increase commitment to the group, leaders should help members identify individual needs they may satisfy in the group and increase the group's ability to meet them. People frequently look to groups to satisfy a need to belong, so satisfying this need usually enhances commitment. When group members feel they are known and valued as individuals, and feel safe to be themselves, they provide other members with the same courtesy (once again illustrating the importance of a supportive communication climate). Feeling that the group is committed to them, they become more committed to the group. This combination of knowing and accepting others and being known and accepted by them builds cohesion. This may happen over time, but it may also be promoted by social interaction such as parties or group activities that require group members to share things about themselves.

Cohesion is also fostered by a group's success. Sharing success with others brings people closer together. Groups can create smaller, reachable goals along the way and celebrate these as accomplishments.

Goal Setting

Even a cohesive group may be ineffective if members are not clear what their goals and plans are. This is why it is important to use group goal setting. Group goals are goals that group members perceive as having been consensually agreed upon by group members. Group goals improve group performance because group members work faster and longer on the task. They focus more attention on it and are less distracted by irrelevancies. Many studies have demonstrated that group goals enhance productivity.[2]

Many group productivity problems may be traced to problems in the group's goals. Sometimes groups are unclear on what their goals are and don't know what they're supposed to accomplish. Group productivity problems may also arise when members don't agree about the goals or make different assumptions about what the goals are. Talking about group goals not only ensures that group members are "all on the same page," it also increases commitment to their achievement. Preferably, goals should be talked about until consensus is reached and everyone feels a sense of ownership and a commitment to cooperation. Group discussion and agreement also ensures that goals are communicated as group norms — expectations regarding appropriate behavior.

Many groups are ineffective because although they agree on the general goal, they don't set a series of smaller, specific goals leading to the larger goal. It's well established that goal setting works best when the goals are specific and difficult, yet realistic. "We will do our best" and other general goals don't motivate group performance the way specific goals do. A performance plan outlining a strategy for reaching larger group goals (with target dates for the completion of tasks) is far more effective than simply vowing to work harder or setting a goal without thinking about the specific strategies for reaching it. The group should monitor its progress, celebrate completed tasks along the way, and "tweak" its performance plan when needed.

Meeting Structure

Group meetings are intended as vehicles for group members to share information and ideas, plan, coordinate, and make decisions. Meetings in which participants are involved can increase commitment to group goals and provide important information and contacts with other group members. Unfortunately, meetings often fail to live up to their potential.

Common complaints are that they are too long and too boring, dominated by a few influential people, poorly organized and/or led, called too frequently or not frequently enough, diverted by members with hidden agendas, subverted by members whose behaviors are destructive, and not focused on important issues. These potential pitfalls can be averted through preparation and thoughtful structuring. With effective meeting norms, clear meeting goals, and good meeting leadership, meetings can be meaningful encounters in which people work hard, produce important outcomes, and leave with positive feelings about the group and its work.

Productive and satisfying meetings depend on establishing meeting norms for getting tasks done and having positive relationships. Groups need meeting norms that encourage arriving on time to the meeting, beginning the meeting on time, participating appropriately (not too much or too little), handling conflict and disagreement constructively, and using discussion and decision-making methods that prevent domination and ensure all pertinent information is heard and processed.

Unfortunately, it's common for unproductive meeting norms to develop. For instance, once some members come late without consequence, others begin to do so as well. Or, if the group waits for latecomers, the meeting start time and ending time tends to become later and later. Groups can also develop negative meeting norms such as going off on tangents and using meeting time for socializing instead of task accomplishment. They may also develop norms where high status members say what they think and everyone else just goes along.

For a new group, it's useful to explicitly discuss norms for the group's meetings at the outset. What time will the meetings start and end? What is the group's policy regarding missing meetings or late arrivals? How does the group want to handle disagreement? What meeting behaviors are desirable and acceptable? What behaviors are undesirable and unacceptable? How are decisions to be made — by consensus, or by majority vote? Does the group want to run the meetings according to standard meeting rules such as Robert's Rules of Order? Who will set the agenda? Who will take meeting minutes or notes so the group can track its progress and have a record of agreements?

Existing groups may benefit from thinking about their meeting norms. Otherwise, inertia may lead the group to continue its familiar but dysfunctional patterns. Sometimes a meeting is needed (!) to discuss why the group's meetings are unproductive and what can be done about it. Explicit discussion of the meetings often makes members more conscious of their own behavior and how it fits in with the agreed-upon norms. Consequently, members behave better.

Group meetings are also a case where goals are important for group productivity. Groups that have specific objectives get more done than groups that have only general goals for the meeting. Specific meeting goals focus the group's work during the meeting, keeping members on track and less distracted. Ideally, meeting goals appear on a written meeting agenda with the date and a list of specific objectives, prioritized by urgency. It's often a good idea to specify an approximate amount of meeting time to be devoted to each agenda item to help keep the group on track. Enough time should be allotted for each agenda item such that alternatives can be carefully considered, most group members can participate, and some decisions can be made or some tasks accomplished. If you're responsible for the agenda, it can help to consult with group members about objectives, perhaps by sending out the agenda ahead of time for feedback. This also ensures attendees and leaders are prepared for the meeting.

Productive meetings are usually led by leaders who serve both task and emotional functions. Meeting leaders are task oriented when they run the meeting efficiently. This means starting and ending on time, preventing the group from getting off topic, and keeping the group focused on meeting goals. Meetings that run late are one of the things responsible for people's hatred of meetings. A task-oriented meeting leader has a well-organized meeting agenda and conducts the meeting so that the most important business is taken care of within the allotted meeting time. Members can't explore new topics before completing the agenda. Unless it's clear that the importance of a new topic overrides the agenda topics, the leader assertively redirects the conversation back to the topics at hand. For instance, a meeting leader may interrupt a group tangent by saying something like, "We're getting off topic and we only have thirty minutes left to take care of these pressing agenda items. I'll make a note of these other issues and I promise we'll discuss them at a later meeting or at the end of this meeting if we finish all of today's work with time to spare."

Keeping the meeting on track also means controlling group members who distract the group from its meeting tasks. For instance, some members repeat themselves or go off on long-winded tangents. A task-oriented meeting leader should interrupt these members and say something like, "I think we're clear on your position, but in all fairness, we should hear from others" or "What you have to say is interesting but it's off-topic and we have a lot we still need to accomplish. For the rest of our meeting we need to limit discussion to things directly related to our work today."

Meeting leaders are socially and emotionally oriented when they encourage participation, manage conflict and disagreement constructively, and promote positive relationships between meeting attendees. Task-oriented meeting leader behavior is important, but a meeting leader should not be so task-oriented that little space is left for members to share and process opinions and information. Meeting leaders need to do things to make sure that member participation is largely equal and members feel listened to. This means leaders must do things like control dominating group members such as the one who constantly interrupts others. The leader can interrupt the interrupter with a statement like, "Wait a minute, let's let her finish her thought" or after the interrupter finishes, the leader might say, "Suzanne, you were in the middle of your thought when James spoke up, but we want to hear what you have to say; could you finish sharing with the group now?"

Ensuring more equal participation also means soliciting input from a variety of members. A skilled meeting leader invites participation from a number of meeting attendees. For instance, a leader can ask those who haven't participated to contribute by saying something like, "Deon, we haven't heard from you and I think I can speak for the group when I say that I am interested in what you have to say."

Leaders can also structure the meeting to solicit equal participation. For example, a leader can ask all participants to make a one to two minute statement about their position on the issue or to make a list of ideas and then share their favorite one with the group.

The nominal group technique (NGT), derived from brainstorming, is also effective for ensuring equal participation and generating creative ideas.[3] The main difference between NGT and traditional brainstorming is that NGT group members brainstorm individually, without interaction. A polling technique is used to ensure all ideas are shared afterwards. These differences help to eliminate production blocking (e.g., once people start throwing out ideas we start thinking about those and have a hard time thinking of other ones) and the tendency for verbally dominant members to cause less dominant members to retreat. Since the technique requires that all members participate and ideas are voted on privately, inequality in participation due to status differences is also reduced. Because each individual works alone and yet is ultimately accountable to the group, social loafing is lessened. There are four basic steps to NGT:

1. *Silent generation of ideas.* Working silently and independently, participants write down their responses to a question. This question should be simple and specific and if possible, pilot tested to make sure participants understand what is being asked.

2. *Round-robin recording of ideas.* The leader calls on each member to share one idea at a time and writes these where everyone can see. Discussion of ideas at this time is not permitted. The leader continues to call upon the participants until all ideas have been recorded or until the group determines that it has produced a sufficient number of ideas.

3. *Serial discussion of the list of ideas.* The participants discuss each idea on the list. Ideas are clarified and evaluated.
4. *Voting.* The participants identify what they believe are the most important ideas and privately rank order their preferences. The votes are recorded, and the voting pattern is discussed. The highest ranked idea is chosen.

NGT has been extensively used in business and government, and some research suggests that it is superior to simple brainstorming when it comes to the generation of quality ideas. My students report that the technique is less exciting than traditional brainstorming but that it ensures equal participation and consideration of a greater number of ideas. Group members who don't think quickly on their feet say they're able to come up with more ideas using NGT.

Conclusion

Enhancing group dynamics in the social change group calls for a "mindfulness" about the group and its process. Group effectiveness is fostered when group structures and behaviors promote supportive communication and group cohesion. Groups need norms to prevent some members from dominating while others don't participate. They need to develop a commitment to one another, the group, and its goals. They need constructive controversy.

But all this is not enough. For groups to be effective, they must also have group structures and behaviors that are task oriented and direct the group toward goal achievement. Groups need specific goals and performance plans. They need efficient and effective meetings. They need to be reminded at times to get back on task.

These seemingly opposite dimensions, a relational focus and a task focus, in fact serve each other. Effective groups design (or redesign) themselves so that there is a good balance.

References
1. Gibb, J. R. (1961). Defensive communication. *Journal of Communication, 11,* 141–148.
2. Weldon, E., & Weingart, L. R. (1993). Group goals and group performance. *British Journal of Social Psychology, 32,* 307–334.
3. Delbecq, A., Van de Van, A., & Gustafson, D. (1975). *Group techniques: A guide to nominal and Delphi processes.* Glenview IL: Scott Foresman.

How to Know When It's *Not* Time to Get Discouraged

Rachel M. MacNair

Many's the time I've sat with friends who were most worried. They're quite sure that after all their work, things are getting worse. The social action groups they're in seem to be getting worse too, and why is the opposition more unified than they are? I've listened to this for decades now, in many different times and movements. In fact, if you look throughout history you'll find those worries are very long-lasting indeed.

This is actually not based on an objective evaluation, but on normal psychology. When these concerns are expressed, I offer my friends the following insights. Now I offer them to you as well, in the hope that when you or your friends or members of your group seem to be sliding down into frustration, you can realize not only that this is normal, but *why* it's normal.

The Worst of Times

Dynamic speakers assure us this is the worst time they've ever seen in all their lives. I suspect you've seen that if you've been around any social movements long enough. It won't matter what time you're reading this. People will be interpreting current events that way.

Now is complicated. We see all the nuances. The nuances have dropped from our memories of the past, giving it a much simpler story line. Just look at the difference between daily newspapers and history books. That shows how it gets digested over time. We also know how the past turned out. We're still anxious about what will happen now. Events can be discouraging. That's expected. We can prepare with the knowledge they might become encouraging later. They're more likely to if we keep working. Yet the gloom that comes with an assurance it's worse than it was before goes beyond this. It becomes a common form of irrational thinking.

Is now really worse than the 1940s, with a major world war and millions of people being killed, many in planned genocides, and a real danger of victorious fascist empires? Is it worse than the 1950s, when racism and McCarthyism ran rampant and a nuclear arms race was in full swing? Is it worse than the 1960s, when nuclear annihilation was a constant threat, the American war in Vietnam was raging, and the FBI and CIA were virtually unchecked on their spying on peace activists?

Note how badly I've oversimplified whole decades. The complicated reality included that all through that time, there were activists working hard to get us to where we are today. If it's worse now, then all that work and pain was for nothing. That's not a call to greater action. That's a suggestion to give up and go home. It's an unfair, untrue suggestion but one that comes from not understanding that the worsening view is in the psychological nature of viewing the close (now) and the far away (past), rather than an objective comparison of the facts.

There are direct comparisons. The response to the Japanese bombing of Pearl Harbor among Americans was fairly universal hatred for the Japanese, including Japanese-Americans, with thousands isolated into camps. The United States then entered and widened a world war. Near the end, two nuclear weapons were exploded on civilian populations.

The response to the September 11, 2001 attacks showed a marked contrast. The president went to a mosque and declared any unkind actions to Muslims to be unpatriotic. Hate crimes spiked but then were back down in a matter of months. In the second of the two relatively small wars that ensued (compared to World War II), opposition was huge. The largest coordinated world-wide peace demonstration occurred in February, 2003, largely unmolested by government squelching tactics Though efforts at squelching were documented, they didn't hold a candle to the experience of yesteryear. I found myself explaining calmly my anti-war reasoning to strangers in airports as ordinary conversation; I can't imagine having done the same in the 1970s.

Still, the two wars did happen. Many people were killed. There were many unjust incidents of repression against activists. Over a thousand people were incarcerated with great sloppiness about innocence, and there were abuse scandals in the prison at Abu Graib. Yet note the contrast. There were publicized scandals on prison abuse. There didn't used to be. That wasn't because the prison abuse didn't exist before. It's because the media didn't pay attention before. Why now?

I believe it shows the peace, civil rights, and civil liberties movements have indeed made tremendous progress. If we compare the reaction to the 2001 attacks with the ideal reaction we'd like to see, it falls far short. But if we compare it to previous reactions, we find that hard work has paid off. This is important. We need signs that hard work pays off in order to keep at it. Why avoid doing that, when such signs are honestly there?

There's more of a problem than people simply getting discouraged and quitting. Some people get so despairing by continuing to play the gloom-and-doom tapes in their heads that they take desperate, violent actions or say hateful things. They get panicked. The energy of their fury and negativity ends up doing great harm to their cause. Apathy and violence are both contrary to the ways of peace, and the gloom that encourages both is all the more a problem when it's not even accurate.

Paradoxes

Joel Best took notice of gloom not based on facts and proposed four paradoxes to help account for it.[1] In his case, he compared social indicators from the year 1900 to the year 2000. Life expectancy increased everywhere. High school graduation rates soared throughout the world. The vote was severely restricted and is now vastly expanded to both genders, all races, and in many more parts of the world.

There are still problems if we compare now to the ideal instead of to the past. Life expectancy would be better without mess-ups in medical care, education still has huge problems, and the powers-that-be still interfere with proper voting. There's plenty left to do. Yet would we not all feel better and be less gloomy if we acknowledged the leaps-and-bounds progress? Best's four paradoxes are as follows:

- *Perfectionism.* The admirable ability to have ideals of perfectionism that drives us to action also drives us to despair, if we see the failure to achieve rather than notice progress. Some social conditions require incremental improvements, and we spend time noticing how far there is to go rather than looking back at how far we've come.

- *Proportion.* When large problems are solved, they stop overshadowing smaller problems. We get a sense that these smaller problems are sprouting up all over. They aren't new problems hitting us; they're old problems that were dwarfed by more urgent concerns before. We notice subtle forms of racism more when we're no longer dealing with massive lynchings. We can be upset about military recruitment in schools when we're not trying to stop the latest war. We get a sense of more problems arising when actually the problems just gained a chance to be a priority because larger problems disappeared.

- *Proliferation.* Successful social movements are contagious, so people start thinking in new ways because of them. Hence, they discover new problems. Skills to promote new claims are already in place, along with the technology of cable channels and the Internet.

- *Paranoia.* When we build up institutions well, their fall becomes a greater catastrophe. Doomsday scenarios of losing something we have pop up that made no sense before we had it. Hence, the panic that occurred over the idea of an impending Y2K bug.

Does all this lead to more eagerness to be active? Some of it does, but an overall sense of pessimism is more likely to be discouraging. Yet once we understand how we're not only making progress but there are ways that making progress actually interferes with our seeing the progress, we can better see the progress. Gloom will no longer tear apart groups as people get depressed and leave. The chance of making progress is, in reality, quite great. The millions of hard-working people who have gone before us have shown us this.

Factions and Arguments

You may have noticed that the peace movement, and practically any other social movement, is full of opinionated people. There's no help for it. Those are the kind of people who get attracted to be active.

It's also true that people in every movement fret they are so divided while their opposition has its act together so admirably well. This comes from what psychologists call the *outgroup homogeneity bias*.[2] Your own group, the "ingroup," (just like your own time) is close to you and therefore you see all the nuances and differences. You know who is and isn't trustworthy, punctual, liable to lose her or his temper, and so on. For the "outgroup," the people who aren't so close (just like the past), distinctions drop and they're seen as more similar to each other than they are.

A simpler way of saying this is that your opponents don't air their dirty laundry in public any more than you do. So how are you to know what their dirty laundry is?

I say with confidence that, whatever your movement, you have noticed plenty of heated conflicts. I also assure you that your opponents have the same problems. How do I know? Because every large group of active people does. The only way to get out of it is to be very small or to snap-to and take all orders from a boss. Those methods are hardly foolproof. If you intend to have a large, vibrant, growing, democratically ruled movement, expect a multitude of disagreements. Obviously, you want to deal with them constructively, but their presence is no cause of alarm — it's normal.

Schools of Thought

When there are personality clashes and heated debate over finer points, conflict resolution skills apply. But certain broad philosophical arguments are common in movements, breaking it into factions. Many get distressed, thinking divisions are harmful and unity is needed. Yet the most successful method for unity is to glory in the divisions — or better, view them as multiplications instead.

People don't need to work in the same organizations. In fact, setting up one grand organization would be a recipe for failure, since opponents need only defeat one organization and they're done. With many groups, if one dissolves, the movement still has many others.

What's needed for unity is not one great command structure, but that people work in harmony. We all need to have standards of nonviolence and honesty, but once those are clear, we can expect sincere people of conscience to have differing views on what's most effective. If you work on what you think is best and let other people work on what they think is best, then we don't need to argue about what's best. Consider these schools of thought:

- *reform vs. root cause*

There is a parable of villagers seeing babies floating in their river. They immediately gear up to fish the youngsters out and help them. The radical proposes a different solution: go up the river and find who's tossing the babies in and get them to stop. That makes sense. But what do we do meanwhile? Suppose it takes time? Do we let current babies go? Maybe seeing that people care about the babies will be part of the root cause solution by reaching the consciences of those throwing babies in. Both approaches are needed.

- *street people vs. straight people*

Street people think it's immoral to wait for legal channels and it's time to take nonviolent action. Straight people want to be respectable and are afraid that success will never come without it. The first group communicates urgency that the second group needs in order to get anywhere. The second group does the follow-up, in lobbying and so on, without which the first group gets dismissed as a bunch of nuts. With both, the movement is more holistic.

- *purists vs. pragmatists*

Purists are aghast at compromise. Pragmatists would rather get something than nothing. Purists can put on pressure to keep compromises from being watered down so badly as to be meaningless. Pragmatists can make themselves look more moderate in contrast to purists — and purists set the bar higher for what being moderate is. More is done with both than can be done with either one alone.

- *single issue vs. everything's connected*

A single issue is clear, and people who disagree on other things can still get together on one. Multiple issues can go into a coherent web and build community. Victory on a single issue can build to greater progress when multiple issues were organized around a basic theme: peace, civil rights, antipoverty, feminism, consistent life ethic, environmental protection, nonviolent problem solving, and so on. Different situations call for different approaches, and both can be useful at different times.

- *newcomers vs. old-timers*

Newcomers make a movement grow, bringing in new ideas and enthusiasm. Unfortunately, at times they lack the perspective experience brings. The old-timers know what has and hasn't worked in the past. Sometimes newcomers don't catch that there is past experience on which to draw, since they weren't there for it. Contempt between these two groups can be painful. Unlike the above groupings, which may do best in different organizations, groups do better when both of these are here. Having only experienced people gets the group in a rut without growth, and newcomers alone can be naïve and ungrounded.

The approach that both sides can be right works well if, instead of splitting up in acrimony, they split up in harmony. With members working on what makes most sense to them, there's no need to figure out what's better. Two or more approaches are better than one approach alone. And coalitions can be formed when practicalities require unity on specific points.

Therefore, there's no reason to be discouraged when groups "break up," if the result is that you have two or more groups where people get to work on what matters most to them, rather than one group where people spend too much time arguing or doing political maneuvering in factions. Sometimes, letting people work separately for at least part of the time is the best way of transforming conflicts on how to do things into a win/win for everyone, as long as people still work together where there is agreement and that is effective. This has all the strength that long experience shows comes with diversity.

References

1. Best, J. (2001). Social progress and social problems: Toward a sociology of gloom. *The Sociological Quarterly, 42*, 1–12.
2. Forsyth, D.R. (1995). *Our social world*. Pacific Grove, CA: Brooks/Cole.

STORYTELLING:
A WORKSHOP FOR INSPIRING GROUP ACTION

Niki Harré, Pat Bullen, and Brad Olson

People are spurred into action not so much by knowing the right facts and numbers as by hearing stories and developing a worldview that makes sense of the confusion and contradiction in their lives.

— Paul Loeb, *Soul of the Citizen*

Why Storytelling?

Our chapter describes a workshop for telling and listening to stories we hope will inspire you and your group to more fully live your values. Together, you may hit upon new ways to take collective action, grounded in your common visions. The storytelling method described here is a modification of the story/dialogue method developed by Ron Labonte and his associates.[1] Our hope is that it can be used to foster more ethical, community-based action in the world.

We've found this workshop to be a powerful way of quickly creating a sense of intimacy and trust between people. It's an excellent tool for newly formed groups, groups with several new members, or groups with cliques that need restructuring. Because of the formal process that requires everyone to speak (and prevents anyone from speaking too much), this method genuinely provides space for everyone to be heard. This encourages democracy within the organization and reduces the risk that a single view dominates or becomes the group's position simply because it's being stated by someone perceived as powerful.

The method

Ideally, two sessions are beneficial. In the first, people are told about the method and given a theme on which to base their stories. They write these on their own time. In the second session, people tell their stories to each other in small groups and generate collective insights. Allow a good two hours for this second session. The workshop can work with anywhere from five to fifty participants.

1. The theme

Participants should craft their stories around a theme. You can use any theme, but one that works well is:

What are my values? Where did they come from? How do I live these values? How am I supported in living these values? How could I live my values more fully?

If your workshop is focused on inspiring political action, you may wish to further elaborate to your participants that you're interested in their values aimed at creating the good society/a peaceful world/environmental protection — whatever concept best suits your group.

You may wish to give participants a worksheet with each of the questions that make up the theme spaced out over one or two sides so they can jot down notes for each. If you use the value theme, some people may feel guilt or despair because they believe they're not living their values. None of us lives up to all our expectations. You could write a story around all the ways you're not living your values, but by focusing on the positive, you reaffirm your commitment to the things you do. All stories have equal value as all help us understand what it is to be alive in this world at this moment in history.

2. Sharing stories

As mentioned, it's best if the stories are shared in a second session, having given participants time to collect and connect their various life experiences. But if a single session is all that's allowed, you can give participants twenty minutes or so at the beginning to sketch out a rough story before sharing it with others. When you gather for the storytelling, organize participants into groups of about five. We recommend selecting the groups in a random fashion, so if you want four groups, number people 1, 2, 3, 4 and then gather the 1s in one location, 2s in another, and so on. This helps ensure people talk with those they don't know as well, creating more interconnections within the larger group.

There may be some people who decide they don't wish to tell a story. You can find this out before you organize the groups and then put the nonstorytellers in different groups. The workshop will still work fine regardless and there are many ways for those who choose not to tell their stories to contribute.

Once the groups are organized, each should appoint one or two note-takers. There are two rules to ensure that a sense of trust and safety is built (not destroyed) by this process:

1. Details of the stories are to be kept confidential to the group. Group members can talk about the abstract insights created in the discussion to anyone who will listen, but they should never reveal the details of other members' experiences outside the small group.

2. People should be sensitive to the fact that these stories are personal — and precious to people. They may reveal vulnerabilities, so must always be treated with absolute respect. It's never productive to speak negative judgments about someone else's life choices or experiences.

Each group should follow the procedures outlined below. You may ask one of the note-takers to ensure these rules are followed and all voices are fully respected.

1. Organize a speaking order. Those who most want to tell their stories go first.

2. The first storyteller tells her or his story. It's important not to interrupt. You may want to limit storytellers to a set time to ensure all stories can be told.

3. Once the story has been told, listeners can ask for clarification.

4. After that first story, members should, in a set direction, starting to the left or right of the speaker, say how this story *is like* and *not like* their own experiences. Everyone gets a turn, and no one should interrupt a speaker. We recommend that the note-takers write down the gist of what's being said, making special note of emerging themes — for example, common reactions to a particular story.

5. Next, the group can discuss what can be learned from the story. If you hope to generate action agendas from this process, then

this discussion could focus on ways in which the story suggests individual or collective action.

6. Once the group moves on to the next story, steps 2–5 should be repeated until all the stories have been told.

7. The group then organizes the ideas from the discussions of each story into three to four insights that can later be shared with the workshop as a whole. You may want to instruct groups to focus their insights on a particular aspect of the theme. If you were using the "values" theme, insights could focus on "ideas for living our values more fully" — that is, action agendas. Although the insights will, for the most part, be written, groups can also present insights in other forms, for example, diagrams or short skits. (We've seen it done!)

3. Insight sharing

After the groups have generated their insights, these can be presented to the larger group. From this point, your group could generate collective action agendas based on the insights and what participants have learned from the process.

Stories of Everyday Activists

We believe the storytelling process naturally fosters action and provides momentum toward collective goals. Discussion of commonalities strengthens cohesion in the group, and discussion of positive differences often inspires people to take on new actions. The formal structure of the workshop purposefully avoids abstract critiques of the world that tend to be nonproductive and instead keeps the stories at a personal, action-oriented level. It challenges members to live their lives according to their values. Most important, the process is fully affirming, creating for participants a sense of being part of a value-based community that is slowly but surely improving our world.

Because of our positive experiences with this method, we're in the process of creating a collaborative project to use storytelling to better understand our collective values and to generate resolutions for action. These resolutions may surround small acts (carrying around a cloth bag when shopping) or larger acts (running for office in a local action group).

Our newly formed collaborative has developed a website for this purpose: www.everdayactivists.org. Our website includes sample worksheets, a set of instructions for running the workshop, stories of everyday activists, and a place for people to post their own stories. We encourage groups that use the storytelling method to comment on their experiences and any action outcomes that their involvement generated. In this Internet medium, we hope to communicate with one another and anyone else interested in becoming part of this social experiment. We'll also be running workshops and are happy to talk to people who want to run their own.

At its heart, social change is generated by value-guided collective action. We believe the world needs institutional change through grassroots momentum. The beauty of storytelling is that everyone can choose, from the possibilities generated, the ones that feel right for them and their situation. When our values and situations match just enough, maybe we can move forward together and find out what happens.

Reference

1. Labonte, R., Feather, J., & Hills, M. (1999). A story/dialogue method for health promotion, knowledge development, and evaluation. *Health Education Research, 14*, 39–50.

Suggested Reading

Everyday Activists. http://www.everydayactivists.org

THREE EXAMPLES OF SUCCESSFUL SOCIAL ACTION GROUPS

Susan M. Koger, Carol J. Merrick, John W. Kraybill-Greggo, and Marcella J. Kraybill-Greggo

Never doubt that a small group of thoughtful, committed people can change the world. Indeed, it is the only thing that ever has.

— Margaret Mead

[Editor's Note: This chapter is three sections, each by different authors, of a fine variety of experience — groups showing the use of psychological principles. All three examples come from presenters at the May, 2005 conference of Psychologists for Social Responsibility.]

Example #1:

Susan M. Koger

Community Efforts to Reduce Pesticide Use

We activists have lofty goals and it's easy to get discouraged, particularly when we're faced with continuous news about violence and warfare, environmental destruction, species extinctions, and various forms of injustices. But just like any task that seems overwhelming at first, there are a few simple keys to success.

Building the fire of effective activism.

- *Create a spark.* Figure out your priorities. Which issue feels most important or "closest to home" for you personally? An honest interest, passion, and a healthy sense of being challenged can all spark one's enthusiasm.

- *Add kindling.* Identify a support system, including other individuals who share your concerns.
- *Build the firewood framework.* Brainstorm together to develop a series of achievable goals. Then specify the steps required to realize your goals. Identify the special and unique skills each individual brings to the group, while discouraging the development of "leaders" and "followers" as that tends to centralize responsibility and accountability.
- *Enjoy the fire's light and heat.* Remember to celebrate and express appreciation whenever you see some success — however small or insignificant it may appear.[1]
- *Be patient, and don't overreact to drafts and precipitation.* Recognize there will always be unanticipated obstacles. Learn to laugh at yourself and at the setbacks you will inevitably experience.
- *Periodically reevaluate the fire's framework, make adjustments, and add new pieces as needed.* Activism is a dynamic process: Energy ebbs and flows, other priorities intrude, group members come and go. A successful movement responds to these shifts with openness and enthusiasm, rather than resistance or resentment.

A *case study: the perils of pesticides.*

As long as we're polluting the planet's air, water, and soils, we're polluting the vision of a healthy, sustainable, and peaceful world. Pesticide pollution is a major threat to the health of humans, natural ecosystems, and the economy. Pesticides are chemicals that are intentionally released into the environment, specifically designed to kill things: weeds, bugs, rodents, molds, and so forth. Thus, they're inherently toxic. They can directly damage the nervous and immune systems, lungs, and reproductive organs and can cause birth defects, developmental disabilities, and cancer.[2,3,4] Minority and low-income populations are often at greatest risk for exposure to toxic chemicals, especially migrant farm workers.

I became particularly concerned about widespread pesticide use when I saw a neighbor spraying Round-Up in his yard while he carried his three-year-old son in a "snuggly" on his back. As a physiological psychologist, I suspected such chemicals could be dangerous for a child's development, so I began researching.

Serendipitously, I also met a charismatic staffer (appropriately named Pollyanna) from The Northwest Coalition for Alternatives to Pesticides (NCAP) at a local Earth Day celebration. She was there to collect signatures on a petition for the Salem Oregon City Council, showing public support for reducing pesticides on city properties, including parks.

Pollyanna informed me that a group had been meeting to coordinate the circulation and presentation of the petition and offer testimony, and I volunteered to help. The group gathered over 200 signatures, met with the city's environmental commission to enlist their support, scheduled meetings with individual city councilors and the mayor, and ultimately received unanimous support for the proposal to institute integrated pest management (IPM) techniques, beginning with city parks. We then worked with the parks department as they drafted their proposal and scheduled a ceremony to express our appreciation for their good work when it was adopted. We have since been working with other city departments as they develop their policies in consultation with the parks department, as well as organizing public education and outreach events. We applied for and received a grant from the city's Department of Public Works to assemble educational materials to distribute to the public. We hosted an educational forum and attended various local events to display information, while collecting signatures for our mailing list.

I believe this collective has been very successful for several reasons.

- *Sparks*

Initially, we were inspired by the group's founder. But more importantly, each of the individuals involved holds a strong personal commitment. We are teachers, parents, scientists, doctors, farmers, protectors of watersheds, and proponents of organic agriculture, as well as environmentalists.

- *Kindling*

We all support each other and share a common goal.

- *Framework*

Each of us were respected and treated as critical contributors to the process, rather than as simply "followers." Every member contributed to developing the group's mission and agenda and took ownership for realizing it.

- *Enjoying the light and heat*

We regularly celebrate our successes — sharing popcorn at a meeting or gathering for a potluck. We also issued a press release when the city council approved going forward and organized a ceremony to acknowledge the parks department when it adopted the policy. With permission from the city council, we invited the key parks department personnel and created the "Ladybug Award," presented by the mayor to the parks department director, with several local children wearing ladybug costumes (handmade by one of our volunteers). We gave the parks department director a framed photograph of the event, which he displays proudly in his office.

- *Patience and humor*

While we're fortunate there haven't been too many setbacks, it's been over three years since this campaign began. It takes time to change the world! In the meantime, we've had a lot of fun and have enjoyed a spirit of camaraderie.

- *Reevaluating and adjusting*

While several of us have been consistent group members, others have come and gone. In fact, our "leader" left to attend graduate school. I'm confident her ability to engage all of us from the outset accounts for the fact that we're still "going strong" a year after her departure.

Need a psychologist?

Given that many if not all so-called "environmental problems" result from unsustainable or destructive human behaviors, it isn't surprising that psychology — the science of human behavior — can contribute to effective advocacy for their solutions. For example, even though some of Freud's theories have been largely discredited, he was right on in his discussion of our use of defense mechanisms to diffuse anxiety. How many of us have used "denial" when we just couldn't deal with the problems society's facing? Or have "rationalized" away our own responsibility for making things better? Certainly, a better alternative is to use "sublimation," where we channel the energy created by our anxiety into productive action.

Psychologists have identified various techniques for effecting behavior change, including fostering more environmentally responsible behaviors. In general, these techniques can be categorized as *information*, *social forces*, and *internal forces* (see chapter 33). We've used several of these strategies in our outreach campaign.

Information:

- *Offer incentives.* A clear incentive for reducing pesticides is lessening potential harm to children's brain development as well as to overall human and environmental health.

- *Provide procedural information.* Giving citizens clear and specific information about less or nontoxic alternatives enables them to make behavioral changes more easily. Many organizations publish informative and accessible guides to reducing pesticide use (see www.pesticide.org).

- *Change attitudes.* Many people erroneously assume that products that are widely available in stores are subjected to thorough toxicity testing and proven safe before marketing. It's important to persuasively counter the attitude that pesticides are safe, particularly for children's exposures. In fact, products are treated by regulatory agencies as "innocent until proven guilty" — not an effective strategy for protecting health.

- *Present educational programs.* We organized an educational forum, "Not in My Backyard," which was partially grant funded. It was free of charge and open to the public and attracted thirty-two people. A representative from NCAP reviewed the hazards of pesticides; I reviewed the hazards to children;[5,6] a local landscaper shared ideas for avoiding pesticides; and a city parks staff member discussed that department's integrated pest management strategy. Several local environmental groups were also invited to table at the event, and we provided organic refreshments donated by a local health food store.

Social Forces:

- *Change social norms.* It's currently the norm to strive for a weed-free yard and to view bugs and rodents with disgust. Our group emphasizes that weeds, bugs, and other critters are normal, and it's healthier and even more effective in the long run to eliminate habitats for unwanted species rather than to try to eliminate the species themselves. Trying to destroy particular species can result in pesticide-resistant strains and the destruction of beneficial or predator species. The increasing availability and popularity of organic produce reflects the growing understanding that such items are healthier. Our group hopes to extend the norm of buying organic to avoiding chemical pesticides. One of our campaigns involves the sale of yard signs advertising "pesticide free zones" (see www.pesticidefreezone.org). As more community members display these signs on their properties, "pesticide free" will become the norm!

- *Secure commitment.* One of the most effective ways of changing people's behavior is by asking them to commit to a change. NCAP's "Healthier Homes and Gardens" plan includes a commitment to try pesticide-free solutions for pest and weed problems that people can make online (www.pesticide.org/ HHG.html) or by mailing in postcards, which are provided at tabling and educational events. Displaying a "pesticide-free zone" sign in one's yard is also a public commitment to refrain from using pesticides.

Remember, our group's initial efforts focused simply on gathering signatures on a petition. This can be seen as a "foot in the door" technique: if people get us to agree to taking a small action, they can often get us to take a larger one. After signing the petition, it's expected that those individuals will be more receptive to considering their own use of pesticides and perhaps ultimately become willing to take a more active community role.

Example #2:

Carol J. Merrick

Attracting Public Attention and Volunteers' Interest

Nonprofit organizations face a challenge in attracting public attention and encouraging people to volunteer. Northwest Vegetarian Education and Empowerment Group (VEG) began in the fall of 2003 in Portland, Oregon. Our mission is to educate and empower people to make vegetarian choices for a healthy, sustainable, and compassionate world. A vegetarian diet, or at least occasional vegetarian meals, is a simple, everyday peace action.

A key element we used to attract public attention as we organized was identifying and taking advantage of publications, radio, and TV programs that offer free publicity. We began our group with a potluck and advertised in many progressive media outlets. Calendar listings in many neighborhood publications and newsletters have been helpful. The mission of any organization is crucial, so at our first leadership retreat, we thoroughly discussed name possibilities and mission statements.

At Northwest VEG's first public gathering, we created a mailing list and established an email network. Later we acquired a voice mail phone number so people could contact us. Activities that attracted people to our events included a monthly potluck, a dine-out, and a Thanksgiving celebration. The following spring, we helped to organize our first public outreach event, The 2004 Meatout. It was a joint venture with another activist group that shared our values. Gathering donated food, we served 900 people in Pioneer Courthouse Square in Portland. This gained mainstream media attention, including a front-page article in the Metro section of the *Oregonian*.

Not long after Northwest VEG formed, we developed a website with a "contact us" feature. The website has effectively informed our members and friends not only about our organization's events and membership promotions, but also resources concerning food issues, local veg-friendly businesses, and other similar groups. For instance, we have an animal sanctuary in Oregon we endorse and promote.

Five months after we organized, we started printing a newsletter. It's distributed to our members and friends by email and in limited quantities by hardcopy to various public locations. We strategically place the newsletters and our brochures where people who are "friendly" to our mission might frequent, such as specialized grocery stores, libraries, bookstores, and restaurants. In addition, we distribute the publications at our events where we encourage people to sign our mailing list.

Hosting speaker events attracts the public's attention and fulfills our mission. Several times we've invited a number of activist groups to table for free at our events, to network, and to create more interest, thereby attracting a larger crowd. To publicize our events, we've appeared on radio programs to highlight issues, such as genetically modified foods and the possible health and environmental hazards connected to them. We distributed and posted a flyer. Besides bringing attention to our event, the poster highlights our group, so we become more recognized in the community. That means we've still accomplished something, no matter how many or few come to the event.

With our limited funds, we only occasionally buy advertisements. We try to place them in reasonably priced periodicals that connect us with a group or community that's more responsive to our mission, such as a college population. Weekly or monthly publications are better priced than the daily mainstream newspaper. One of the nonprofits in our area produces video and audio tapes. Often we invite them to our events free of charge to give them the opportunity to film or tape the event.

Finding volunteers is an ongoing challenge. The number of activities and projects we undertake is limited by money and volunteers. When we began, it was crucial that we have six to twelve dedicated core members to form our board. We felt this board needed to have strong, shared leadership, ground rules on how to operate, and ways to be accountable to our membership. Much of our focus the first year was to develop what we needed.

Our volunteer coordinator works with event coordinators and the leadership group to help find volunteers, but she's not the only one who recruits people. All board members are looking for people who have the interest, time, and passion to further our mission. We try to find short-term and long-term positions for people in projects that they favor. When members join we send them a survey to find out their interests and encourage them to become involved.

We have several people willing to call members and friends to ask for their participation or remind them of the commitment they made. At our potlucks and other events, we have a clipboard that describes projects and events where we need help. Our newsletter also amplifies and promotes finding volunteers. People often need to hear about projects several times and in different ways before they decide to commit their time. We endeavor to honor people's time commitments and encourage, not pressure, them. We network with other nonprofits to educate our vegetarian community about other interesting projects. When we have a special event that's cosponsored by one or more nonprofits, we often get short-term volunteers for the event from other organizations.

We show appreciation to our volunteers by recognizing them and organizing a party celebration each year. We've also held new member gatherings to welcome people to our community, during which we provide food and connections for people, especially if they're new to our area.

There's always more we could do to find volunteers. This includes phoning and talking to new members so we can find projects that interest them. We feel the best ways to attract members and volunteers are by sponsoring interesting, educational, and unusual activities and events. This year, we organized Portland's first Compassionate Living Festival with speakers, food samples, and cooking demonstration. We hope to build upon our successes in the coming years.

Example #3:

John W. Kraybill-Greggo and Marcella J. Kraybill-Greggo

Learning Structural Change:
An Immersion onto the Navajo Nation

Having worked with college-age students for a combined twenty years, we've frequently observed students' strong desire to "change the world," expressed in class and through community service projects. For some, this desire forms the core of who they'll become and how they see themselves in the world. For others, the lack of change results in discouragement or even cynicism. However, what we often found in both groups is the tendency to perform actions of charity rather than social change.

There's a continuum of moving from charity to justice that ranges from, say, taking food and clothing collections on one end to doing a deeper analysis of issues and advocacy for social change on the other. Some will participate in charity because they believe it's important to do something, yet not necessarily questioning the underlying structural factors, social and economic injustice, or oppression that contribute to the existence of the problem in the first place.

A program in 2004–05 inspired students to move beyond performing charity and consciousness raising to viewing themselves as change agents, developing advocacy and activism skills. This program included an eight-week planning and preparation phase, a midpoint immersion onto the Navajo Nation, and four weeks of reentry group meetings for deeper analysis of social issues and advocacy and activism planning.

Planning phase.

The planning phase is crucial in establishing the mission and purpose of any project. Is it within an organization or is it a grassroots community effort? This will make a difference in its direction. Under whose auspices the project is will impact the availability of supportive or in-kind resources, the presence of preexisting networks with stakeholders, and how the project is perceived by others. This may also result in varied logistical considerations.

The Navajo project involved brokering connections with appropriate college officials to gain approval and also with service providers and local Navajo on the reservation to develop project tasks and a time line. Once on the Navajo Nation, new tasks were developed based on interactions with and input from local community members and service providers.

Regardless of whether a project is within an organization or purely grassroots based, those who are directly experiencing an issue must have primary input on how it's addressed and how social change is advocated. Some organizations are more comfortable with entering into those types of shared relationships, while others are reluctant to let go of decision-making power. If a social change project is conducted by an organization, the planning phase is the critical juncture for establishing direct dialogue with the administration on the expectation for shared decision making with those who are the target of the change effort.

Preparation phase.

The length and structure of the preparation phase depends on the nature of the project and its setting — local community based vs. an immersion experience. The group preparing for the Navajo immersion met for eight weekly meetings during the fall of 2004, whereas other groups working locally might meet more frequently each week for fewer weeks. However, a primary goal of preparation will be similar regardless of meeting schedule: working toward developing trust and cohesion in the group.

The group facilitators encouraged members early in the preparation phase to talk about their motivation for participating, to share what they've done previously in addressing social issues and what they'd learned about themselves in the process, and to explore their personal commitment and definition of social justice. Norms for safe discussion were set early and members were told that it was expected they would likely become aware of their own biases. They might struggle in resisting their own sense of being "experts" while "joining" with others most directly affected. At times they might doubt that the world they thought existed actually did, resulting in some crises of meaning. Time was allotted regularly throughout all phases of the project to allow members to share with the group what was happening for them in terms of their shifting level of self-understanding or awareness of personal biases or assumptions and simply to react to all that was happening.

Another goal of preparation is for group members to understand the issues and context underlying the project before the experience phase. The themes addressed for the Navajo project, beyond participating in group-development and trust-building activities, were Navajo customs, culture, spirituality, and indigenous healing and helping systems, social justice education, and social issues and problems on the reservation. There was an ongoing emphasis on being more culturally competent and sensitive.

In enhancing group members' understanding of Navajo customs, culture, and spirituality, they were exposed to Navajo healing traditions, traditional stories, poetry, music, food, and rituals and to the Navajo creation story at Spider Rock. The group was also joined one night by an expert on the Navajo. Members were given an array of readings throughout the preparation process.

Social justice education included defining social justice through experience and what each member sees as the vital parts of the "social contract" between a society and its members. What should all members of a society have a right to? The group also spent time discussing the social justice literature and reviewing the continuum of moving from charity to justice. All members spent time trying to determine where they would place themselves on the continuum and why.

In understanding social issues on the reservation, group members were provided with census and other government data (federal and Navajo) and other information on the dimensions of poverty, unemployment, alcoholism, domestic violence, housing issues, children's issues, and environmental issues as well as on the responses by the Bureau of Indian Affairs (BIA), Indian Health Service (HIS), and the tribal government of the Navajo Nation.

Later, while on the Navajo Nation, group members met frequently with community members, health and human service providers, and church leaders to learn more about these and other issues.

Projects using this program model would want to highlight specific issues experienced in the community where the project is based and include community members, service providers, and those with expertise in the preparation process. It's important to keep in mind that the preparation can't cover all possible topics. The immersion itself will surface a greater depth and breadth of issues.

Immersion.

In late 2004 through early 2005, the group split time between living in two different communities on the Navajo Nation. While there, members experienced a cultural immersion in many aspects of life on the reservation. After meeting with community members and service providers, members analyzed social issues and participated in several service projects with various community organizations. Throughout the experience, members grappled with consciousness raising and attended ongoing group reflections for further discussion and understanding.

The social issues on which members listened to the perspectives of community members included poverty (a rate of nearly 50% vs. 12.5% nationally), growing methamphetamine production and use, concerns over public housing and increasing gang activities, coupled with the desire for expanded recreational programs and environmental issues around dumping and water rights.

Reentry.

Upon returning from the Navajo Nation, the group met for four weeks to share reentry experiences and emotions, discuss how the Navajo maintain cultural richness, beauty, and resilience in the face of multiple social problems, reflect on personal meaning and development, assess the evolving view of self as change agent, and identify possible venues for social action and activism. The issues that several group members chose to follow up on from a deeper analysis and advocacy perspective were primarily on the environment, leading some to contact policymakers.

Further assisting group members with putting together their ideas of the experience more fully and analyzing issues more deeply was the opportunity to have a panel discussion and interactive presentation at the very end of the project. Over seventy-five faculty and staff members and students attended. The presentation enabled members to succinctly synthesize many of the issues for the audience, share new awareness about themselves and the world, and discuss the need for possible social change. The venue provided group members the chance to educate and raise the consciousness of others while advocating for the need to address specific issues on the reservation.

This final step brought group members full circle: they had prepared for the reservation having had some beginning understanding; they then experienced immersion where they listened and learned from those living on the reservation; and now they had reentered their old lives and were able to speak to others about issues in a way that joined the voices of those whom they had listened to, calling for social change.

Only time will tell if the project will contribute to a changed world. But for those who participated, the world they now see and the way they see themselves in it has changed.

References

1. Weick, K. E. (1984). Small wins: Redefining the scale of social problems. *American Psychologist, 39*, 40–49.
2. Landrigan, P. J. et al. (1999). Pesticides and inner city children: Exposures, risks and prevention. *Environmental Health Perspectives Supplements, 107*(3), 431–433.
3. National Research Council. (1993). *Pesticides in the diets of infants and children.* Washington, D.C.: National Academy Press.
4. Weiss, B., Amler, S., & Amler, R.W. (2004). Pesticides. *Pediatrics, 113,* 1030–1036.
5. Koger, S. M., Schettler, T., & Weiss, B. (2005). Environmental toxicants and developmental disabilities: A challenge for psychologists. *American Psychologist, 60*, 243–255.
6. Schettler, T., Stein, J., Reich, F., Valenti, M. & Wallinga, D. (2000). *In harm's way: Toxic threats to child development. A report by Greater Boston Physicians for Social Responsibility.* Cambridge, MA: Greater Boston Physicians for Social Responsibility.

Suggested Readings

Example #1:
Winter, D. D., & Koger, S. M. (2004). *The Psychology of environmental problems* (2nd ed.). Mahwah, NJ: Lawrence Erlbaum Associates.

Community-Based Social Marketing. http://www.cbsm.com

Example #2:

The Vegetarian Resource Group. http://www.vrg.org

Physicians Committee for Responsible Medicine. http://www.pcrm.org

Society & Animals Forum (formerly Psychologists for the Ethical Treatment of Animals). http://www.psyeta.org

Example #3:

Fourré, C. (2003). *Journey to justice: Transforming Hearts and Schools with Catholic Social Teaching*. Washington, D.C.: National Catholic Educational Association.

Freire, P. (1970). *Pedagogy of the oppressed*. New York: Continuum.

Gil, D. (1998). *Confronting injustice and oppression: Strategies for social workers*. New York: Columbia University Press.

PART III
PEACEMAKING
TRANSFORMING CONFLICT INTO CREATIVITY

If there is no struggle there is no progress. Those who profess to favor freedom and yet depreciate agitation . . . want crops without plowing up the ground, they want rain without thunder and lightning. They want the ocean without the awful roar of its many waters.

— Frederick Douglass, 1857

USING CONFLICT CONSTRUCTIVELY

Robert Pettit

If you do not specify and confront real issues, what you do will surely obscure them. If you do not alarm anyone morally, you will yourself remain morally asleep. If you do not embody controversy, what you say will be an acceptance of the drift to the coming human hell.

— C. Wright Mills[1]

As a peace worker, you may feel uncomfortable when conflict arises in a conversation, demonstration, or other encounter you have with those of opposing viewpoints. You may feel guilty for having been a party to conflict, that you're betraying your commitment to peace if all is not forever harmonious between you and those who disagree with you. You may hesitate to speak or act boldly for fear of confrontation.

Misgivings about conflict may handicap your effectiveness as a peace worker. Nevertheless, in a world in which inequality, injustice, racism, sexism, violence, and militarism are so ingrained, we who actively work for peace and justice are bound to encounter resistance. The pursuit of peace paradoxically entails confrontation and conflict.

You need to master your misgivings about conflict — learn how to civilize it, make it creative and constructive, keep it humane. Conflict can be a tool that can work to your advantage. It's a powerful tool for social change. Not only should you not fear it, sometimes you should welcome it — even foment or escalate it.

You can be insistent without being abusive. You can stand toe to toe with adversaries and press your case in the face of intimidation or coercion. You can meet the challenges of confrontation rather than shrink from them. You can grow into a more forceful and effective advocate for your ideals.

Misconceptions about Conflict

If you want to master the use of conflict in your pursuit of peace and justice, first dispel some common misconceptions about conflict:

Misconception: Harmony is the normal state of affairs, and conflict is abnormal.

A brief survey of history — from abolitionists to labor organizers, civil rights demonstrators, and war protesters — shows conflict has been necessary time and time again to redress grievances. Conflict is just as "natural" to any social system as stability.

Misconception: Conflict is pathological, simply a result of misdirected anger.

This misconception reduces real grievances to personality problems or emotional disorders. When you're confronted with real injustice, anger and frustration aren't inappropriate.

Misconception: Conflicts are just disagreements, simply "failures to communicate."

Certainly, clear communication helps dispel misinterpretations in a conflict. But if goals are incompatible, no amount of "better understanding through communication" will resolve the conflict. In conflicts between participants of unequal power, it's no surprise the more powerful party wants only to talk . . . and talk.

Misconception: Conflicts are harmful and should always be reduced, resolved, or eliminated.

Our culture views conflict as primarily negative. We're told, "don't argue," "be nice," "stop fighting." But this is often a "pro-establishment" bias of whoever holds the power. It's why every corporate president stresses teamwork and morale, while minimizing or ignoring disagreement and discontent; why the political party in power always discourages dissent and encourages "patriotic" support for our president. Those in power want to keep things the way they are.

The Nature of Conflict

A free society can't exist without conflict. A conflict-free society would be a totalitarian society. The very meaning of "free" is the liberty to press conflicting views and rights.

Conflict can be constructive and creative as well as destructive and degrading. If handled with skill and mutual respect, conflict can produce better alternatives than could either conflicting party alone. Since none of us has a monopoly on truth or virtue, it's only through serious exchange — even conflict — that we learn and grow.

Conflict can be beneficial for your group. Conflict with outside forces can intensify your members' convictions and commitment, help members come to a common understanding of your group's identity and purpose, and rally members to comfort and support one another. Conflict with a common foe on a particular issue may offer the opportunity for alliance with groups not otherwise committed to your cause. Conflict between your group and those who oppose you may be helpful for both groups: it may establish a relationship where none existed before, and it may help establish rules and norms to govern further relations. It may only be through conflict, furthermore, that your adversary can gauge the strength of your resolve and finally come to deal with you seriously.

You need to be able to distinguish realistic and nonrealistic conflict. Realistic conflicts occur when there are real differences over goals; nonrealistic conflicts merely vent frustration or aggressive impulses. Realistic conflicts — like strikes and protests — can be productive, since they seek identifiable goals. Nonrealistic conflicts — like senseless riots or emotional shouting matches — tend to be destructive and meaningless, mere tension relievers. Since most conflicts probably contain elements of both, concentrate your efforts on the realistic conflicts over goals while trying to defuse the nonrealistic emotional elements.

Conclusion

In Chinese, the written character for "crisis" is made up of two symbols: one for "danger," the other for "opportunity." So it is with conflict. Its potential for both danger and opportunity is great. It is what we make of it

Reference

1. Lee, R., & Marty, M. E. (Eds.). (1964). *Religion and social conflict*. New York: Oxford University Press.

PROMOTING PEACEFUL INTERACTION

Paul W. Keller and Charles T. Brown

During his stay in South Africa, Mahatma Gandhi did battle over racial injustice for years with General Jan Smuts, that country's Minister of Finance and Defense. Yet Gandhi fought in a way that kept the two talking to each other while fundamental changes took shape in that society, and the two men came to understand and respect each other.[1]

It seems strange, but peace workers often have difficulty getting along with people. They can be so determined to make everybody nonviolent that they will knock their opponents' heads together to do it. Sometimes they even struggle among themselves so intensely that their peace groups are destroyed. In short, instead of creating peace and uniting people, they often create conflict and alienate people by their actions.

Why? How do people inspired by such high ideals so often turn off the very persons they would like to persuade? What is it that builds barriers between peace workers and the rest of the world? What are the characteristics of those human contacts, such as Gandhi's, that *nourish* both parties in the face of conflict?

The most important step in improving how we deal with each other is to become aware that conflict is not a static thing — it is dynamic. It is a flow of events between two people, a dance that may be relatively harmonious one moment and suddenly turn into sharp disagreement or dissent the next.

Consider an example: You begin talking with someone you have heard disagrees with your point of view. He seems quite open and agreeable, and you are surprised at how easy and nondefensive the conversation seems. You think to yourself that there may have been a mistake here. Perhaps the disagreement was only imagined. But then the other person becomes noticeably cooler, and you begin feeling negative about what he is saying. As the negative feelings increase, you find a growing mistrust of the other and a need to "wheel out the big guns" and arm yourself. You stand on the edge of an all-out battle.

What happened? Was it inevitable that it happen that way? Perhaps not, for it is quite possible that better communication would have prevented this exchange from turning in such a negative direction.

Four Keys to Better Dialog

Peaceful interaction becomes possible if you become more aware of the things you are thinking, doing, and saying during the course of a conversation. To do this, turn on four powerful monitors: (1) the *self-talk* monitor, (2) the *empathy* monitor, (3) the *nonverbal* monitor, and (4) the *punctuation* monitor. They can help you gain increasing control over your behavior in conflict situations.

The self-talk monitor.

One peace worker, after exploding during a phone conversation with a government official and abruptly hanging up, exclaimed, "I can't stand that man! He drives me up the wall." In conflict situations like this that lead you to negative feelings, the normal reaction is to assume that your emotion is caused by the other person and that you are powerless to change it.

Such a view has problems. Two people can react quite differently to the same stimulus. A word, a tone of voice, or a particular look can drive one person "up the wall" but affect another person positively. This difference in response is, clearly, not caused by the stimulus, but by the silent statements these persons make to themselves about the stimulus.[2]

In the situation cited above, the peace worker may be thinking ideas like these about the official: "Officials should be rational and fair at all times," "If I don't convince him, I'm a failure," "He doesn't like me, and unless everybody likes me, I am not worthy." This kind of self-talk is not very rational. Once you recognize that, you can modify your emotional reactions by developing more reasonable expectations and by thinking more rationally. You cannot control the other person, but you can begin to control what you think and do in response.

If you are saying to yourself, "They are exploiting me," and if events show they really are, then your anger is justified. But even in this situation your self-talk can reflect a problem-solving rather than aggressive motivation — "I feel exploited. I wonder how I can best help you to understand that," rather than, "You are exploiting me. You should be punished."

By refraining from blaming the other in your self-talk, you can better maintain a sense of calm and control that will help keep the conflict constructive.

The problem is that the self-talk monitor is seldom turned on. You may listen to the words you say out loud but ignore the words you say to yourself.

That is the bad news; the good news is that you can change if you want to. You can change by examining your self-talk until such review becomes habit. For some people, it helps to write down what they said silently, and to do this soon after a conflict situation. For others, talking with someone about the self-talk works well.

In any case, by recognizing your self-talk after an exchange, you soon become more conscious of the silent assumptions and thoughts that precede your emotional reactions and spoken words. With the self-talk monitor on, you will gain a new kind of understanding, as well as control of your thinking patterns and their effects on communication.

The empathy monitor.

The cliché says, "Put yourself in the other person's shoes." Left at that, it rarely gets the desired results. But once the empathy monitor is understood and used, it makes a fundamental difference in how conflict is handled. Empathy requires two things:

- *Imagination* — the ability to imagine what the other person feels, to call on one's own experience, asking, "What do I know that is anything like what this person is experiencing?"

- *Flexibility* — a willingness to focus on the other person, to feel good enough about yourself to step out of the focus of attention long enough to "live" with the other.

To become more empathic, first be aware that empathy for the other has been lost (or never existed in the first place). Train yourself, with reminders again and again, to ask yourself, "How is the other person interpreting my words?" and "What does she mean by the words she is speaking?" Or more concisely, "What does this message mean to her?"

Isn't that what we naturally ask ourselves when we are involved in an exchange? No, it isn't. Instead, and especially in the heat of conflict, we tend to ask, "What does this message mean to me?" Because we feel threatened, conflict tends to promote ego-centered thinking. Therefore, injecting the question, "What does this message mean to him?" can have a radical effect on the way you respond. It can, in fact, produce an atmosphere much more open to constructive handling of conflict.

"But," said one peace activist who had been applying this approach, "when I do that I begin to see the problem from that person's point of view, and it makes some sense, and that makes it harder for me to totally support my own position." That possibility is real. It seems easier to act on an absolute position, one that does not take into account anyone else's perception. But that is only the case if outright victory is the goal. If "truth" is the goal, as it was for Gandhi, and if "opponents" are instead viewed as partners in the search for truth, then conflict can be both exciting and rewarding. You can promote that search by employing an empathy that can reduce defensiveness and surprise your combatants with unsuspected openness.

The nonverbal monitor.

Some psychologists estimate that nonverbals — voice, gesture, facial expression, body posture, and the like — make up more than sixty-five percent of the social meaning of any conversation; less than thirty-five percent of the meaning is actually carried by words.[3] The reason is that nonverbals are often involuntary. While words can hide feelings, nonverbals are more likely to reveal them. Words are strong, but feelings revealed through nonverbals are stronger. If words say one thing and nonverbals say another, the nonverbals, in many situations, will be believed.[3] Sometime the face gives away one's true feelings, sometimes the hands, sometimes the voice. Any part of the nonverbal channel can do it When the verbal and nonverbal signals go in different directions the result is increased distance and distrust between the participants. It is not as important to know which part of the nonverbal channel is "tattling" as it is to know that when either you or the other party is sending mixed messages, it can be noticed. Train your nonverbal monitor to recognize such mixed messages.

This is especially important for peace workers. If your struggle is really for world peace rather than for ways to control or defeat others, it is important that both your verbal and nonverbal messages confirm that.

Witness an actual happening: A peace worker presented herself as open, flexible, and empathic in a meeting with a college administrator. She smiled, "listened," and nodded appropriately. However, the administrator could not escape a growing feeling of mistrust in spite of the cooperative words she spoke. Something in the visual signals she was giving him made him wary (Was it the shifting of the eyes? The tension of the body? The forced laughter?). In the car going home from that meeting she said to a colleague, "We really backed him into a corner, didn't we? I think we've got him now." In subsequent meetings the administrator grew increasingly alienated and his position hardened as he realized that her nonverbal signals indicated her determination to defeat him.

It happens that many peace workers are quiet verbally even though they are committed to strong action. They see silence as a consistent feature of their "peaceful" intent. But they overlook one of the basic rules of communication: "You cannot *not* communicate."[4] Silence is a nonverbal expression, and our silence may be interpreted by others as saying we are afraid, or feel superior, or are angry — or any number of unknown possibilities. Silence has its virtues, but it does little to build trust or encourage understanding. To be authentic, that is, to have your outward appearance to others match your feelings, is to lay the foundation for trust and to make possible constructive handling of conflict.

Much more can be said about nonverbal communication. But boiled down, here are some hints for peaceful interaction:

- Make eye contact frequently, but keep from letting your eyes "go hard."
- Be aware that touching sends a powerful nonverbal signal. The context in which it is done determines how it

will be interpreted. A hand placed on someone's shoulder can be seen as an assertion of status or as a sign of affection. Do not automatically assume that it will be taken as a sign of affection.

- Try to make the nonverbal signals you send — appearance, interaction distance, posture, gestures, tone of voice, touch — as nonthreatening as you can.
- Remember that although nonverbal messages are more trusted than conflicting verbal ones, if you want to be precise and unambiguous, your words are more helpful than nonverbals.

The punctuation monitor.

Conflict is a flow of events between two people. How that flow gets organized is important in determining how people deal with conflict. In every conflict, there is punctuation, a way of organizing the events that make up the exchange.[4] And people are led, by their different histories, to provide different punctuation. In a marriage, for example, a conflict may be punctuated as follows:

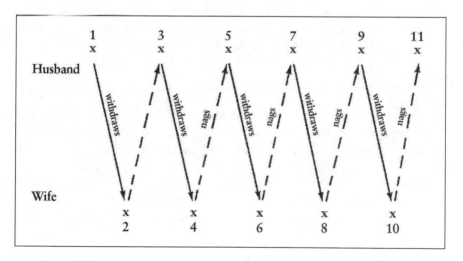

The husband sees their argument as stemming from the wife's nagging (as though to say, "Who wouldn't withdraw in the face of such nagging?"). The wife, however, sees the root problem in the husband's withdrawing (as though to say, "Who wouldn't nag a husband who doesn't say a word?") This pattern can be applied to virtually any conflict. There seems to be a universal tendency to want to point a finger and say, "You started it."

In the Middle East, the Israelis say they must attack because they are being harassed by the Arabs. The Arabs say they wouldn't be harassing the Israelis if the Israelis hadn't pushed them out of their land. The Israelis say they wouldn't have pushed the Arabs out if the Arabs hadn't pushed them out first. The Arabs say . . . and so on.

Two things become clear: (1) when you try to punctuate a conflict you discover it is impossible to find an agreed-upon beginning and (2) how each party punctuates the conflict makes a tremendous difference in his or her attitude toward the solution. If you feel the other party started it, then you probably think he or she is the one who should have to back down. Turning on the punctuation monitor, then, helps us recognize that neither side is absolutely blameless, or absolutely right, or absolutely justified. It is a reminder that each side operates with a set of blinders that shuts out important understandings

To be able to say to the other party, "I know this looks different to you . . ." is to create a different kind of atmosphere. It is the beginning of an effort to understand the other's perceptions. Such an action by one party may lead the other party to do the same.

Peace workers, who usually act out of a strong idealism, tend to blame leaders and institutions for the problems that exist. "The Pentagon is determined to plunge us into war." The Establishment, under attack, punctuates it differently. "If we didn't have to fear the terrorists, we wouldn't need war." The parties cannot seem to agree on how to punctuate the conflict, and there probably never will be agreement on that punctuation. Even so, it is good to recognize the particular punctuation occurring on both sides. Being conscious of one's own biases can help develop empathy for the biases of the other person ("I can imagine how you feel; that is the way I would feel if I were in your shoes"). The punctuation monitor provides another way to build awareness.

Conclusion

Conflict is, by its nature, hard to deal with. Skills for handling it constructively are available, but they will fail unless they are based on self-awareness To work toward awareness, follow four paths:

1. Start listening to and examining your thoughts more deeply (a self-talk monitor).
2. Ask yourself, "What do these messages mean to him or her?" (an empathy monitor).
3. Open your eyes and ears to pick up signals you have been missing in yourself or others (a nonverbal monitor).
4. Recognize the game of assigning blame (a punctuation monitor).

Turning such monitors on, and keeping them on, takes discipline, of course. It involves forming a set of habits that, with practice, become easier to use. Such discipline requires a strong motivation, but that motivation can be found in the very purpose of communication to establish community. Conflict threatens community. Divorces, wars, civil hostilities are all around us. If we would have community we must know the price. That price is dedication to promoting constructive conflict. Such dedication offers opportunities to establish a community enriched by the very differences from which it is made.

References

1. Fischer, L. (1951). *Life of Gandhi*. London: Jonathan Cape.
2. Ellis, A. (1962). *Reason & emotion in psychotherapy*. New York: Lyie Stuart.
3. Knapp, M. L. (1972). *Non-verbal communication in human interaction*. New York: Holt, Rinehart, & Winston.
4. Watzlawick, P., Beavin, J., & Jackson, D. (1967). *Pragmatics of human communication*. Palo Alto, CA: W. W. Norton.

NONVIOLENT COMMUNICATION

Roxanne Manning and Jane Marantz Connor

An enemy is one whose story we have not heard.

— Gene Knudsen-Hoffman

A major source of discord in human communication is the notion that something you did *caused* a reaction in me. "You make me so mad!" is a common expression. The notion is false, of course. No one can *make* you feel or do something. Your feelings and behavior result from within yourself: your needs, your attitudes, your beliefs, your behavioral habits. If communication is important in peace work and if we want to improve our communication with one another, we need to reframe the way we view our relationships.

Nonviolent communication (NVC) is a method of viewing human relationships that emphasizes deep connection with the needs of all the people involved. NVC trusts that when that deep connection is present, strategies to meet all needs will most effectively be found. The idea is that all behavior is motivated by the desire to meet universal, positive human needs — biological needs (shelter, food), social needs (connection, caring), and spiritual needs (purpose, meaning, hope). Conflict arises not because needs are different, but because the strategies used to meet needs are in conflict.

NVC views the behavior of another person as a *trigger* for one's feelings, but not as the *cause* of one's feelings. For example, imagine you're leaving a community meeting on race relations and you see a police officer on the sidewalk who calls the man next to him, "nigger." As you walk away, you feel angry and afraid. Later, when you learn that the police officer was talking to his brother and they both had grown up in Harlem, you feel relaxed and amused. The stimulus was not the cause of the feelings: the stimulus was the same. What differed were the needs that were stimulated. Initially, you might have needs for respect, harmony, and safety that weren't met when you heard the officer's words, which then gave you feelings of anger and fear. Later, needs for humor may be met, resulting in the relaxed, amused feelings.

NVC, developed by clinical psychologist Marshall B. Rosenberg [1] over a thirty-year period, draws from many disciplines, primarily including psychology [2–4] and spiritual writings.[5–8] The contemporary perspective most closely related to NVC is Motivational Interviewing, developed by academic psychologists, with many studies demonstrating its effectiveness.[9]

Needs vs. Strategies

To truly connect with the needs of those around us, NVC requires us to see the difference between true *needs* and the *strategies* we use to meet those needs. Needs are universal and ongoing. Strategies are specific to a person, place, or situation. This distinction is crucial.

Conflicts arise over disagreement about strategies chosen to meet a need, not over the need itself. Needs are never right or wrong. For instance, everyone shares the need for shelter. There's no disagreement over whether people should have safe places to live — the need is evident. Differences appear, however, when it comes to how they are to acquire shelter — the strategy is not so clear.

Awareness of the needs underlying each human behavior helps make it easier for activists working with people on both sides of an issue.

NVC is being taught and used on five continents to address a wide range of conflicts in diverse situations — in schools, prisons, war zone areas, and families.[1] Understanding the human needs underlying people's choice of strategies or behaviors frequently leads to transformations in how "the enemy" is understood. Then peaceful solutions that meet the needs of both parties can be found.

Miki Kashtan describes such a dramatic shift in an encounter between a right-wing Israeli settler on the West Bank and a left-wing NVC trainer. After thirty minutes of dialog the settler said, "If there were more people like you in the Left, if I ever felt such true compassion and understanding, I would, despite all the pain involved, consider moving to another place in Israel."[10]

The Language Tool of NVC

NVC includes a powerful communication tool, a language for expressing feelings and needs and responding to the expressions of others. This helps develop mutual understanding and connection.

The type of language we use is a powerful influence on the way we experience and behave toward each other. The NVC language refines and expands upon many communication distinctions that have been described in the fields of psychology and communication. The tool structures dialog between two parties around four components: *observations*, *feelings*, *needs*, and *requests*.

• *Observations*

An observation is a description. It's what you saw, heard, smelled, touched, or tasted. It's only objective data — free of judgments, evaluations, interpretations, or feelings. When you make an observation, you want it to be as specific as possible. For instance, consider the following two statements offered as observations:

1. Those welfare moms are lazy — they never want to work.
2. In the past month, I found five employers who would hire the mothers in the shelter; none of the mothers accepted any of the positions.

What reactions did you have to the two statements? The first statement includes interpretations (they don't want to work) and judgments (welfare moms are lazy). It's also nonspecific — does the speaker truly mean the moms have refused and would always refuse every job ever offered to them? An advocate for welfare change who hears that first statement might react defensively and find it hard to even bring her awareness to the needs of the speaker. Many dialogs that begin with such statements end in arguments about their truthfulness. One side will say, "I can point to five welfare mothers who work eighty hours a week." Another will say, "I can point to a bunch of them who just sit in the house and watch soaps all day."

In contrast, the second statement is very specific (five employers, clear timeframe). It also doesn't include any interpretations or judgments. Since it's factual and verifiable, both the listener and the speaker can agree on what happened. Conversation can then focus on what the speaker is feeling and needing in response, rather than on the truthfulness of the observation.

• Feelings

An expression of feelings doesn't include the stories or thoughts we may be telling ourselves, only the emotions. One way to distinguish *feelings* is to see if you are using the phrases "I feel like" or "I feel that" instead of simply "I feel." What follows "like" or "that" is often a thought rather than a true feeling. Consider possible feelings statements:

1. I feel like they're wasting my time and money.
2. I feel frustrated.

In the first statement, the speaker is actually offering a judgment. We don't know what feelings he or she is experiencing, although we might guess anger, frustration, or annoyance. In the second statement, we have a clear expression of the emotion the speaker is experiencing. We don't want to judge the rightness or wrongness of the speaker experiencing any specific feeling. Instead, we use the speaker's expression of his or her feeling in two ways — as a way to connect with the speaker's reality at that moment and as a guide to what needs might have been stimulated within the speaker.

• Needs

Needs cause our feelings. When the feeling in the previous step has been identified, you can ask yourself, "If I'm feeling this, what am I needing?" At the beginning of NVC practice, it's helpful to look at the list of needs to help see the difference between needs and strategies to meet those needs. So, continuing our example:

1. They need to take the jobs I find for them.
2. I want to understand what's going on.

In the first example, the speaker's actually proposing a strategy. Notice that specific people (they: the mothers) have been identified; this is one clue that this is a strategy, not a need. Needs can be met by anyone; strategies are tied to specific people or places. The second statement is truly a statement of needs. The identified need, for understanding, could be met in a variety of ways.

• Requests

Requests usually serve one of two purposes:

Connection requests aim to deepen the connection between you and the other person. They do this by asking for a reflection of the feelings and needs you've expressed or by asking for an expression of the other person's feelings and needs in response to what you've expressed.

Action requests ask for the other person's willingness do something that would meet the need.

Both types of requests are worded in positive action language — what you want the person to do, not what you don't want them to do. Requests are immediate and doable. Consider these request statements:

1. Can you make the women stop refusing the jobs?
2. I'd like to meet with you this week to identify the reasons the women weren't willing to take the jobs. If you're willing to meet, would you tell me a convenient time? If you're not willing to meet, would you let me know why?

The first statement doesn't meet the criteria for an NVC request in several ways. First, it's not immediate. The listener might agree to the request, but the listener and speaker might have completely different timeframes in mind; it's unlikely the speaker will be happy if the women take a job she or he finds for them two years from now. Next, the first request isn't really doable. The listener doesn't have control over the women. He or she can offer enticements and listen to them, but it's doubtful he or she can make them do anything. The first request is also not worded in positive action language. The listener is asked to prevent something from happening (the women stop refusing the jobs), rather than to make something happen.

On the other hand, the second statement is immediate. The listener is asked to agree to a time to meet or to explain the unmet needs that prevent the listener from being willing to meet. It's also in positive action language — the listener is asked to commit to an action. And, it's doable — it's within the listener's ability to fulfill this request.

Integrating the Four Components

The four components of an NVC expression are often put together in the following way:

When I *[insert observation]* I feel *[insert feeling]* because I need *[insert need]*. Would you be willing to *[insert request]*?

This format does several things. It reminds both the speaker and the listener that while the observed event may have been stimulating to watch, it was the needs that were met or not met that caused the feelings. It helps the speaker take responsibility for his or her emotions. It facilitates connection between the listener and the speaker, since it helps to remove the accusatory flavor that goes with many requests around unmet needs. The listener is able to connect with the beauty of the need the speaker is trying to meet.

Requests are then evaluated by their ability to meet needs, not from debt, shame, or guilt. This format can make it more likely that even when a request isn't fulfilled, dialog continues. Both parties remain aware of the needs on the table, rather than staying attached to any specific strategy to meet those needs.

Other NVC Dialogs

In addition to this "expression" dialog, there are two other types of NVC dialogs: *empathy* and *self-empathy*.

Empathy. When practicing NVC empathy, the second type of dialog, you're trying to connect with someone by understanding her or his feelings and needs. We do this by listening for the feelings and needs behind the statements and seeing if our guesses about the person's feelings and needs resonate with that person. These guesses serve to connect the speaker with the listener who's making the guesses.

Sometimes you might feel afraid of making an empathy guess — what if you suggest the wrong feeling and need?!? Won't that be a source of disconnection? No, because it's such a powerful experience to have someone listen attentively and really attempt to connect with the deeper motivations. Even when a guess is "off," the speaker usually just makes another attempt to explain and get the right feeling across. "No, it's more like . . ." is a common phrase. Rather than disconnection, dialog continues at a deeper level.

Self-empathy. The third type of NVC dialog means you're trying to get clear about your own feelings and needs. Self-empathy is an especially important skill for activists, who often feel overwhelmed at how much effort is required to get even minor changes in social policy.

Many activists feel frustration, despair, and burnout, often focusing on the apathy of others. By connecting with our unmet needs, we can hold in our awareness and mourn those needs that can't be met at the moment. We can also come up with specific, targeted strategies to help us meet those needs that can be met. This frees us from the overwhelming sense of powerlessness we may feel when we only consider the observations (others not showing up or committing to our cause) and our lack of control over getting others involved.

Conclusion

We've offered a brief introduction to NVC consciousness and NVC language, including descriptions of the three types of NVC dialog: expression, empathy, and self-empathy. Each of these three dialogs will be important as you work to promote social change:

- *NVC expression* makes it more likely that by connecting with the universal needs behind your requests, you can establish connection between yourself and others. That helps maintain mutual commitment to finding strategies to meet everyone's needs.

- *NVC empathy* will help you connect with the needs behind others' words, whether they're words laden with pain or spoken in anger.

- *NVC self-empathy* will help you stay connected with the beauty of the needs that are motivating you to persevere in your work, a connection that will be sustaining in those moments when progress and hope seem faint.

By focusing on needs instead of strategies and promoting an awareness and caring for the needs of all parties, Nonviolent Communication is one strategy that can help activists be more effective in working with others to achieve our goals.

References

1. See http://www.cnvc.org
2. Ellis, A. (1961). *A guide to rational living*. New York: Wilshire Book Co.
3. Maslow, A. (1998). *Toward a psychology of being*. New York: Wiley & Sons.
4. Rogers, C. (1977). *On personal power*. New York: Delacorte.
5. Buber, M. (1974). *I and thou*. New York: Macmillan.
6. Dass, R., & Bush, M. (1992). *Compassion in action: Setting out on the path of service*. New York: Bell Tower.

7. Kurtz, E., & Ketcham, K. (1994). *The spirituality of imperfection: Storytelling and the journey to wholeness*. New York: Bantam Books.
8. Wink, W. (1999). *The powers that be: Theology for a new millennium*. New York: Doubleday.
9. Miller, W. R., & Rollnick, S. (2002). *Motivational interviewing: Preparing people for change*. New York: Guilford Press.
10. http://www.cnvc.org/noenemies.htm

Suggested Readings

Connor, J. M., & Killian, D. (2005). *Connecting across differences: A guide to compassionate, nonviolent communication*. New York: Hungry Duck Press.
Rosenberg, M. B. (2003). *Nonviolent communication: A language of life* (2nd ed.). Encinitas, CA: PuddleDancer Press.
Rosenberg, M. B. (2005). *Speak peace in a world of conflict: What you say next will change your world*. Encinitas, CA: PuddleDancer Press.
Rosenberg, M. B. (2003). Speaking Peace. (two disc audio set). Louisville, CO: Sounds True.
The Center for Nonviolent Communication. http://www.cnvc.org

RESOLVING CONFLICT FROM THE THIRD SIDE

Carolyn Gellermann and Kurt C. O'Brien

You have to help resolve a dispute. If you don't intervene and something happens between the two disputants, you are accountable.

— A Semai Tribe Member[1]

*C*onflict. It's a word that elicits many different responses from people all over the world. Some see it as useful, some as destructive. Some welcome conflict, while others seek to avoid it at all costs. Sometimes conflict can be resolved peacefully. Other times it escalates into all-out violence. Regardless of our orientation to conflict, we typically view conflict as being two sided. That is, the parties involved in the conflict are looking at the dispute from their own perspective and are usually trying to figure out how to convince, compel, or in some way win over the other party to their way of thinking — a strategy that results in varying degrees of success.

What if there were another way to look at conflict, one that involved considering not just the perspective of the other party but that of the larger "whole?" What if there was an approach that caused us to ask, "What is the likely impact on the larger community? What would best meet the needs of this broader community?" Taking such a perspective is what author, mediator, professor, and consultant William Ury calls the *Third Side*. The Third Side is a way of looking at conflict, not just from one side or the other, but from the perspective of the surrounding community, as illustrated in the following Figure.[2]

156

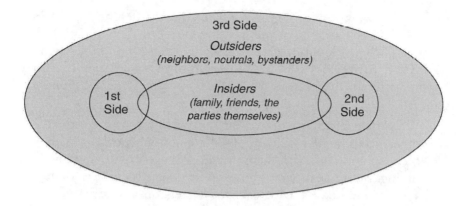

Individuals and groups active in efforts to increase social responsibility and justice are certainly familiar with conflict and all its challenges, whether it's on a personal, local, or even global scale. Seeking to expand our view of conflict so it encompasses a larger whole brings a perspective that many of us continue to ignore.

What Is the Third Side?

Joe was sitting in his car waiting for his daughter to finish her music lesson. When the children began exiting the building he heard a loud voice and looked up to see another father walking toward the cars, berating his own daughter. The girl was in tears yet the father continued his tirade. Joe was deeply concerned about this scene, but was unsure of what action he could take. He got out of his car and stood by the front fender, making direct eye contact with the father and daughter. He didn't speak a word. The father noticed Joe's presence, immediately lowered his voice, and then stopped talking altogether. Joe never knew what happened once they got in their own car, but in that moment, he had acted as the Third Side.

The above story is an illustration of one of the simplest forms the Third Side can take. William Ury has spent the better part of his life helping people around the world resolve their differences in peaceful ways. During the course of this work he not only made his own observations about how we approach conflict but also spent time studying how different cultures resolve conflict, seeking to understand what could be learned from these different approaches. Part of this research involved visiting modern day hunter-gather societies such as the Bushmen of the Kalihari desert and the Semai of Malaysia. During his visits with these cultures, he learned that they have a different orientation to conflict, viewing it as a *community* concern, not an individual or private concern.

> When two members of the Bushmen tribe are in conflict, other tribal members take immediate action, speaking with the disputants to calm them down, and even removing and hiding their weapons. These community members then spend time talking with each party, encouraging them to resolve the conflict, and reminding them that the rest of the community is dependent upon them.[3]

Coupled with his own observations, Ury formulated the notion of the Third Side as a mental model for conflict. Table 1 captures the essence of this thinking, contrasting it with how conflict is often viewed.[4]

Table 1	
FROM	*TO*
Conflict is negative and destructive.	Conflict can be constructive and positive.
Conflict is a private concern.	Conflict is a community concern.
Conflict resolution.	Conflict prevention and transformation.
Conflict is two-sided; the goal is win-win.	Conflict is three-sided; the goal is a triple win.

When the Third Side is invoked, it has the power to transform conflict as well as the individuals engaged in it. Furthermore, the Third Side creates the contagious conditions of hope and optimism as well as collaboration and cooperation. People end up feeding off this positive, hopeful energy, and new solutions unexpectedly emerge.

In fact, Ury points out that no single person controls the Third Side. It has an emergent property to it, meaning we all contribute to it, but we can't predict the actual outcome because of the complexity of the interactions. Ultimately, the Third Side requires a "change in heart and spirit," causing us to think about conflict in an entirely new way, one that offers hope for peaceful resolution.[5]

Third Side Skills

The Third Side consists of three key components: Prevention, Resolution, and Containment. Each of these areas has corresponding roles that community members can take at any time to help prevent conflict from becoming destructive or violent. Engaging in these roles, however, first requires development of specific skills that help us to manage our own emotions, understand and acknowledge the needs of others, and search for mutually beneficial solutions.[6] The biggest barrier to successfully transforming conflict is our own tendency to react emotionally, so the most important skill needed is the ability to maintain our own emotional balance. This requires us not to stifle our emotions but to control them and suspend the natural reactions of anger or defensiveness. A distanced, depersonalized perspective is needed even as we participate wholeheartedly in the conflict. One method for stepping back, collecting our wits, and viewing the situation more objectively is to ask the question "what is my ultimate goal in this interaction?" Focusing on this desired outcome can often prevent an impulsive reaction.

The next skill needed is the ability to defuse the emotional reactions of the other parties involved. This requires stepping to their side and acknowledging their feelings and point of view. It doesn't mean agreeing with them. At this stage the goal isn't to reach a Third Side agreement; it's to understand the other parties' perceptions, and hear what they're trying to say so they can also gain emotional balance and move on to logical problem solving. Summarizing, empathizing, inquiring further, thanking them, agreeing where you can, and apologizing are all useful at this stage.

When all parties' emotions are under control, it's necessary to distinguish between *positions*, which are statements or demands framed as solutions, and *interests*, which are the needs that motivate a person to take a position. These underlying hopes, fears, or concerns can often be surfaced by asking open-ended, problem-solving questions such as "Help me understand why this is important to you," "Could you explain the significance of . . .," "Tell me more about . . ."

After everyone's interests are on the table, skillful questioning is once again needed. Option-generating questions are necessary to encourage the imagination and open up possibilities for mutual gain. New ideas are encouraged by asking, "What if we tried . . .?", "What else could we do?", "What are all the solutions that might work?"

The skills of questioning and listening to both ourselves and the others involved make it possible for us to effectively take on any of the roles of the Third Side.

> *It helps to constantly test our assumptions, perceptions, and desires against the complex truths we encounter. It matters if we listen to our 'opponents', are open-minded about our assumptions, and don't get too self-righteous about our vision.*
>
> — Paul Loeb[7]

Third Side Roles

One challenge for any new concept or approach is to make it practical and real for people. The Third Side addresses this by highlighting explicit roles that people can assume when faced with situations of disagreement or conflict. These roles are based on Ury's years of observing conflict in all its manifestations and understanding when specific actions by individuals made a difference in the outcome of a potentially destructive situation. The ten roles appear below. We describe when it would be appropriate to invoke a particular role and then offer a brief description of how the role actually plays out.[8]

The Provider — Enabling People to Meet Their Needs

Use when the cause of conflict is *Frustrated Needs*

- Shares resources and knowledge
- Gives others a sense of security
- Offers respect
- Strengthens others

Conflict often arises from a frustrated need. Frustration leads people to bully others, to use violence, and to grab someone else's things. The most basic human needs include safety, identity, and autonomy. If we as Thirdsiders can help people address these needs, we can avert destructive conflict.

The Teacher — Giving People Skills to Handle Conflict

Use when the cause of conflict is *Poor Skills*

- Delegitimizes violence
- Teaches tolerance
- Teaches joint problem solving

Sometimes people fight simply because they know no other way to react when a need is frustrated and a serious difference arises. By helping people learn new values, perspectives, and skills, we as Teachers can show them a better way to deal with differences.

The Bridge-Builder — Forging Relationships across Lines of Conflict

Use when the cause of conflict is *Weak Relationships*

- Creates cross-cutting ties
- Develops joint projects
- Fosters genuine dialog

Good relationships are key to preventing conflict. Anyone can help bridge relationships across natural divides. A relationship operates like savings in the bank; whenever an issue arises, the parties can dip into their account of goodwill to help deal with it. Often not a discrete activity, bridge-building takes place all around us — sometimes without us even perceiving it — at family meals, on school projects, in business transactions, and at neighborhood meetings.

The Mediator — Reconciling Conflicting Interests

Use when the cause of conflict is *Conflicting Interests*

- Brings the parties to the table
- Facilitates communication
- Helps people search for a solution

At the core of conflict are often conflicting interests. As Mediators, we can help reconcile the parties' interests. The Mediator doesn't seek to determine who's right and who's wrong, but rather tries to get to the core of the dispute and help the parties resolve it. We may not think of it as mediation, but that's what we are doing when we listen attentively to people in dispute, when we ask them about what they *really* want, when we suggest possible approaches, and when we urge them to think hard about the costs of not reaching agreement.

The Arbiter — Determining Disputed Rights

Use when the cause of conflict is *Disputed Rights*

- Replaces destructive conflict
- Promotes justice
- Encourages negotiation

Sometimes mediation isn't enough to resolve a dispute or isn't appropriate because basic rights are being violated. Whereas a Mediator can only suggest a solution, an Arbiter can decide what's right. The Arbiter is a familiar role — the judge in the courtroom or the arbitrator in a work setting. More informally, the Arbiter is the teacher deciding a dispute among two quarreling students, the parent ruling on a matter involving two children, or the manager determining an issue among two employees. In this sense, we are all potential arbiters.

The Equalizer — Democratizing Power

Use when the cause of conflict is *Unequal Power*

- Levels the playing field
- Empowers the weak and unrepresented
- Seeks fair and mutually satisfying resolution

Every conflict takes place within the larger context of power. Imbalance of power often leads to abuse and injustice. The strong refuse to negotiate with the weak or to submit their dispute to mediation or arbitration. Why should they, they think, when they can win? This is where the Equalizer makes a contribution. Each of us holds a packet of power, a measure of influence over the parties around us. Individually, our influence may be small, but collectively, it can be considerable. We're capable of empowering the weak and the unrepresented so they can negotiate a fair and mutually satisfactory resolution.

The Healer — Repairing Injured Relationships

Use when the cause of conflict is *Injured Relationships*

- Creates the right climate
- Listens and acknowledges
- Encourages apology

At the core of many conflicts lie emotions — anger, fear, humiliation, hatred, insecurity, and grief. The wounds may run deep. Even if a conflict appears resolved after a process of mediation, adjudication, or voting, the wounds may remain and, with them, the danger that the conflict could recur. A conflict can't be considered fully resolved until the injured relationships have begun to heal. The Healer assists in this process.

The Witness — Paying Attention to Escalation
Use when the cause of conflict is *No Attention*

- Watches out for early warning signals
- Speaks out
- Gets help fast

Destructive conflict doesn't just break out but rather escalates through different stages from tension to overt conflict to violence. By watching carefully, the Witness can detect warning signals. If acted on, this can prevent escalation of conflict and even save lives. A Witness can also speak up to persuade the parties to cease fighting and sound the alarm to call the attention of other Thirdsiders who can intervene as Mediators, Peacekeepers, or other Witnesses.

The Referee — Setting Limits to Conflict
Use when the cause of conflict is *No Limitation*

- Establishes or reiterates ground rules
- Ensures a fair process
- Reminds people of consequences

If and when people do disagree, it's important to reduce the harm. That's the role of the Referee, who sets limits on fighting. Parents know this role well: "Pillows are okay, but fists are not," "No blows above the neck or below the belt." As Referees, we can change the way people disagree, replacing destructive methods with substantially less destructive ones.

The Peacekeeper — Providing Protection
Use when the cause of conflict is *No Protection*

- Interposes her- or himself between parties
- Enforces the peace
- Preempts violence before it starts

When the rules are broken and the limits exceeded, others need to employ the minimally forceful measures necessary to stop harmful conflict in its tracks. The role of Peacekeeper need not be limited to specialists like the police and UN Peacekeepers; it's an organizational function that anyone may be called upon to play. When two children fight, adults can step in the middle and, if necessary, physically pull the two apart. The best Peacekeepers never fight. They never fight because they don't need to. They accomplish their ends by intervening early and using persuasion.

Implications

Choosing to take the Third Side isn't necessarily an easy thing to do, but it's imperative if we want to reduce conflict and improve the world we live in. Those involved in advocating for social responsibility and justice know this well, for they live the Third Side and understand its benefits better than most. Paul Loeb, author of *Soul of a Citizen*, writes, "When bystanders take relatively small actions to challenge injustice, this can trigger more significant responses on the part of others."[9]

The Third Side and its specific roles offer us a common language to use and have the ability to completely change how we perceive and interact with our surroundings. When we take this perspective, a little voice that wasn't there before is suddenly present, asking, "So, what's your role in this? Do you have a responsibility to do something here?" In this regard, the Third Side is absolutely transformative. It gives us choices to consider, choices we may not have known even existed. It helps us to find our own voice.

It's the roles that provide more explicit detail for these choices and move the Third Side from being merely conceptual to being real and practical. So pay attention to these roles. Consider how you have assumed them in the past and how you can invoke them in the future. Our ability to do so just may change how this planet approaches conflict and makes social change in the future.

References

1. Ury, W. (2000). *The third side: Why we fight and how we can stop*. New York: Penguin, p. 23.
2. Ury, p. 19.
3. Ury, pp. 4-6.
4. Summarized from workshops developed to teach the Third Side and Ury, pp. 3–26.

5. Ury, pp. 7–17.
6. For information regarding the skills, see Fisher, R., Ury, W., & Patton, B. (1981). *Getting to yes: Negotiating agreement without giving in*. New York: Penguin.
7. Loeb, P. (1999). *Soul of a citizen: Living with conviction in a cynical time*. New York: St. Martin's Press, p. 51.
8. Summaries of the Third Side roles were compiled from the Third Side website: http://www.thirdside.org and from Ury, pp. 114–179.
9. Loeb, p. 63.

Suggested Readings

Fisher, R., Ury, W., & Patton, B. (1981). *Getting to yes: Negotiating agreement without giving in*. New York: Penguin.

Loeb, P. (1999). *Soul of a citizen: Living with conviction in a cynical time*. New York: St. Martin's Press.

Ury, W. (2000). *The third side: Why we fight and how we can stop*. New York: Penguin.

The Third Side Website. http://www.thirdside.org

CONFLICT TRANSFORMATION SKILLS
FOR LEFT AND RIGHT

Rachel M. MacNair

The brother and sister both take the position they want the one remaining orange. They seem irreconcilable. Yet when they look at interests, they find the brother wants the inside to eat and the sister wants the rind to make marmalade. Now we have a clear solution.

— from a classic case offered by Mary Parker Follett[1]

Positions and Interests

Ever since Mary Parker Follett first talked about it in the 1920s and 1930s, one of the basics of dealing with conflicts has been the difference between positions and interests. In the complexity of the real world, this understanding can often be worked out into some creative ways of having everyone satisfied, rather than merely settling for compromises.

Politics isn't well set up for this. In elections particularly, not only are underlying interests ignored, but positions are in packages. You have to select a package. Nor are these based on a coherent principle; it's more of a hodgepodge based on history. A principle of "less government" is proposed by those who nevertheless want stronger military, prisons, police, and the death penalty. Pro-war sentiments tend to be entrenched in both of the major packages, just more in one and not quite as much in the other. Even those of us who set ourselves loose from a mere two choices find that our unwinnable third-party options are complete packages of positions. We must choose between rigid programs rather than creative problem solving.

Though elections are obviously a vast improvement over battles for making decisions, there's a reason the word "battle" is still used to describe them. People divide up into "enemy camps."

To cope, people use "rule-of-thumb" decision-making. They pick the closest package, then ignore the rest of the positions — meaning they may help promote something they don't mean to. But because of oversimplification, stereotypes of those who selected the other package abound. The win-lose high stakes hardens positions.

Yet when we approach individual issues, considering underlying interests can dissolve the stereotypes and battle lines. We come up with more creative approaches to social problems.

Here are some examples that you might find useful and that give you ideas that can help you come up with others. We may have different positions on what the best "family values" are, but we have interests in strong families. Positions may differ on the science of creation and evolution, but all peace lovers have an interest in avoiding Social Darwinism. Though we take different positions on the death penalty, we all have interests in preventing criminal homicide and adamantly communicating its unacceptability, along with sympathy for the families of its victims. We may have a variety of positions on the market and required levels of regulation, but we all have an interest in stopping corporate abuses. We may have different positions on any given war, but we all have interests in protection.

These examples just give you a taste of the possibilities. With the principles in mind and a good listening ear, you'll be more effective in peace work. This is the most basic point about being convincing — don't just spout off what you think. Pay attention to your audience.

The Stereotypes

The "outgroup" — people in a group other than yours — are at a distance. So they look more alike to you than they look to themselves. In psychology, this is the "outgroup homogeneity bias." I remember once hearing a woman complain how inconsistent U.S. Republicans were by having moral concerns and yet being greedy. I had to smile as I remembered how many times I had heard the "business" wing of that party decry how the "social" conservatives were hurting them, and the "social conservatives" had dismissed the business wing contemptuously as "country club" Republicans. It wasn't an inconsistency; it was two different groups that can't stand each other yet cooperate politically. Even that's oversimplifying, of course, but seeing the distinction is more realistic than seeing them as all the same.

What do *right-wing* and *left-wing* currently mean? The original terms referred to wings of the French parliament. Right-wingers divided people into races or nations and thought their own was the best, while left-wingers divided people into economic classes and thought divisions should be dissolved. But what do they mean now? Are they the same as conservatives and liberals, which used to mean those who don't want change and those who do? Especially since the 1980s, those features have often been reversed. I've asked several audiences what the principle is that separates the wings, and so far nobody knows.

The peace movement has historically been seen as on the Left, which would make sense according to the original definition. Yet there were right-wingers, such as Pat Buchanan, who opposed the war in Iraq and liberals have been among those pushing wars from World War II to Vietnam to Iraq.

In a 2005 case in Florida where a court ordered a severely disabled woman's feeding and water tube removed so that she would die, the media presented it as right-wing politicians who objected. Yet Rev. Jesse Jackson, Ralph Nader, and Senator Thomas Harkin also objected, along with disabilities-rights groups such as Not Dead Yet[2] — all based on left-wing understandings of protecting the rights of the weak and voiceless.

Similarly, on abortion, there are groups such as Republicans for Choice and Democrats for Life, Catholics for a Free Choice and the Religious Coalition for Abortion Rights, Feminists for Life and the Prolife Alliance of Gays and Lesbians.[3] The peace movement has many who assume a pro-choice position is part of the program but also groups like Consistent Life, which oppose war, the death penalty, poverty, and racism along with abortion and euthanasia based on the idea that all are violence and therefore poor solutions to problems that we can deal with more constructively.

Conversely, on the death penalty, while polls of pro-life activists show the majority oppose it on "culture of life" grounds (though this isn't true for anti-abortion politicians or opponents in the nonactivist general public), I have met two such activists who don't buy that argument. They identify themselves as definitely right-wing and nevertheless oppose the death penalty on the grounds that no self-respecting pro-lifer trusts judges with life-and-death decisions!

In other words, the packages of positions are less defined for political "wings" than they are for specific candidates in elections. The first rule of dealing with any individuals or groups is that some may hold the same positions and yet have entirely different underlying interests, while some have opposite positions and yet the same underlying interests.

The most important thing is to listen first, so you know what those specific people are thinking — without stereotyping them by lumping them in with similar others. By doing that with individuals in dialog or audiences in speeches, you'll find yourself far more effective and persuasive, which makes sense since you'd be following the practicalities of conflict resolution and transformation at which the peace movement excels.

References

1. Follett, M. P. (1940). Constructive conflict. In H. C. Metcalf & L. Urwick (Eds.), *Dynamic administration: The collected papers of Mary Parker Follett*. New York: Harper.
2. Not Dead Yet. http://www.notdeadyet.org
3. See websites: http://www.republicansforchoice.com, http://www.democratsforlife.org, http://www.catholicsforchoice.org, http://www.rcrc.org, http://www.feministsforlife.org, (also http://www.fnsa.org), and www.plagal.org

MOVING FROM THE CLENCHED FIST TO SHAKING HANDS: WORKING WITH NEGATIVE EMOTIONS PROVOKED BY CONFLICT

Deborah Du Nann Winter

You can't shake hands with a clenched fist.

— Indira Gandhi

There is little need to explain to activists why conflict produces negative feelings. Anyone who has worked on social justice issues in the real world will instantly recognize that people devoted to different ideas and agendas get irritated, angry, fearful, or sad. Negative emotions usually occur as a natural part of social change. As Christopher Morley put it, "There is no squabbling so violent as that between people who accepted an idea yesterday and those who will accept the same idea tomorrow." Yet violent squabbling prevents creative problem solving, and with it, social justice.

One reason that negative feelings are so toxic is they impair accurate perception and logical thought processes. We know that people who are locked in ongoing conflict develop distorted perceptions about each others' goals and intentions. Several kinds of what psychologists call "attribution errors" follow — inaccurate ways of attributing characteristics. For one, people tend to see their own group as honest, straightforward, hard working, and sensible, but see their opponents as selfish, inconsiderate, greedy, and untrustable. This *ingroup/outgroup bias* leads to a tendency for people to interpret the actions of their opponents as deliberately aggressive but their own actions as necessary responses to a dangerous threat.

People in conflict believe they're simply making reasonable responses to danger, and yet their behavior is interpreted by their opponents as deliberately aggressive. This interpretation then causes them to take actions that seem to only be reasonable given the threat but is perceived by the opponent as aggressive. I call this attribution problem the *offense/defense ambiguity*; it leads to a vicious cycle of escalating conflict. When the offense/defense ambiguity and ingroup/outgroup bias occur, direct communication tends to fall off, producing a negative cycle. Negative interpretations are less likely to be corrected when information about each others' intentions and experiences is limited. Thus, a set of negative attributions gets locked in. I call this the negative attribution cycle because the lack of information feeds the negative views and the negative views further decrease the communication.

These three attribution problems feed on each other, so that a cycle of poor communication, negative attributions, and ingroup/ outgroup biases increase unless otherwise interrupted. Locked in these distorted ways of viewing each other, opponents are likely to solidify negative perceptions and feelings.

Activists who want to move an agenda have to watch their own tendencies toward these very human processes. We need to find ways to see "the other" as a full and vulnerable human being, especially when we are busy not doing so! We also need to help people who are busy with these negative attributions and feelings find ways to break the cycle. Without intentional structures to change the negative perception/feeling cycle, conflict progresses toward violence of one form or another, usually interpersonal and emotional, but eventually physical.

How do we unlock this negative cycle? As I reflect on my own experiences with conflict and my reading of psychology, I have come to the conclusion that what moves people out of the negative conflict cycle is the ability to accept and communicate vulnerability in themselves and others. This vulnerability is usually hidden from all (including the self) by anger, hostility, and certainty about the rightness of one's views. Rigidified positions and opinions on issues help lock in vulnerability and keep it from everyone's experience. Thus when vulnerability and uncertainty are unacknowledged and unexpressed, opposite emotions occur instead: self-righteousness and anger.

But I have also found that anger melts when a sincere message of vulnerability is communicated.

Managing Our Own Emotions

This insight has several implications. Let me begin at the personal level. The first lesson is to examine our own anger and self-righteousness. We all know this feeling — exasperation with people who disagree or fail to act on our views.

After identifying our own negative emotions, we can inquire about our feelings of vulnerability that underlie them. Personally, I worry about the next generation's well-being when I consider the loss of habitat, global warming, air and water pollution, and so on. I feel afraid about the enormity of our ecosystem threats in the face of such ineffective responses to them.

Now the trick is to hold on to this fear and vulnerability in my next conversation with someone who disagrees with me about environmental problems. I notice my tendency to assume that someone who differs with me is stupid, selfish, uninformed, etc. I tune in to my uncertainty and vulnerability and listen for what I can learn from this "other." I notice my inclination to tighten up around my rigidly held positions, as I stay focused on my own sense of vulnerability and listen to an alternative viewpoint. I express my fear, my uncertainty, my concern. I listen for those feelings in the other person. I help us both focus on those aspects of our emotions, rather than the irritation and hostility we might otherwise portray.

In a more explicit or formal conflict situation where, for example, I'm trying to promote zoning legislation that would impede landowners' chances to develop their land for real estate value, I find ways to express my understanding of my own and others' vulnerability. Say for example, I'm afraid of our land being ruined by sprawl, while I recognize the landowners are afraid of their financial futures being threatened by new zoning laws. I recognize and articulate my own and others' fear and vulnerability that surrounds the conflict. I express my feelings as "I statements," owning the feeling state as my own experience, rather than something caused by another person. In other words, I am vigilant about my tendency to blame others for my negative feelings. I refrain from impugning, as well as making the standard attribution mistakes (in group/out group bias, offense/defense ambiguity, negative attribution cycle), and maintain my faith that if we can talk to each other about our fears, we can muster the compassion for each other needed to understand our alternative viewpoints and arrive at creative win-win solutions.

At the Facilitator Level

In addition to tracking and working with our own negative emotions, activists can empower others to find creative solutions to conflicts by setting a tone and structure that encourages them to experience and communicate their fears and vulnerability. While traditional approaches to conflict resolution and mediation tend to deny the importance of feelings, I believe that when people learn how to address their feelings in nonthreatening ways solutions are more, rather than less, likely.

When facilitating group process, activists can give guidelines for communication and help the group stick to them. Some guidelines with which an activist could open a group discussion are:

1. Everyone has a legitimate point of view.
2. All people need to learn something from others who disagree with them.
3. All of us are prone to the attribution errors (in group/out group bias, offense/defense ambiguity, negative attribution cycle, discussed above). A good discussion goes beyond them to break the negative cycle.
4. When engaged in conflict, all of us are likely to have done something to promote or legitimize it. All of us can identify our own role, communicate our regret, make promises for the future, and ask for and give forgiveness.

Moving beyond hostility and anger requires emotional intelligence, insight, humility, and compassion. Sometimes these traits are absent altogether, but in most cases, I believe they're buried by negative emotions and attribution mistakes that are normal when people find themselves in conflict. Helping ourselves and others go beyond our rigidified positions, irritations, and hostilities can do a lot to promote social justice and peace in our relationships, our workplaces, our communities, and our world.

PREPARING FOR NONVIOLENT CONFRONTATIONS

George Lakey

The student could scarcely control himself. He was big, bigger than the whites who were taunting him with "Nigger!" and putting mustard in his hair. He dug his fingers into the bottom of the lunch counter stool he was sitting on. Somehow he held on. The next day he came back, determined not to come so close to losing his self-control, wanting to be more composed like his fellow students from the black college on the outskirts of town. The preceding night he'd taken seriously the nonviolence training on campus and even joined in the prayers led by the preacher. He didn't want to fail and hurt the sit-in.

A week later the abuse increased, and a woman was able to push him off his stool. He hit the floor, paused, then slowly got up and, with a noble gesture and a smile, moved a barrier, allowing her to move easily away from the counter. She dissolved into tears and was led from the store by a friend. The young activist experienced in himself a new sense of power. And the woman? A week later she was organizing a women's group in support of the sit-in.

This story, which I learned from the leader of the sit-in, reflects several elements of nonviolent confrontation:

- The goal of the demonstrators, integration as a first step toward racial equality, was difficult to achieve; previous petitions and negotiations had failed, and nonviolent confrontation was required to reach the goal.

- The conflict brought out strong emotions on both sides, as well as the unpredictability that goes with that kind of intensity.
- Deep-seated attitudes are more open to change during crisis; it's as if people, like metal, are more flexible when hot.
- Preparation increased the activists' chances to be creative under stress.

Nonviolent Action: Training and Application

As with any form of protest, nonviolent action requires specific preparation. Training usually involves experiential exercises that enable participants to "feel" their way into the planned action. Some of the tools used in training include role plays, quick-decision exercises, and strategy games. Such preparation helps not only during the confrontation, by building confidence, reducing fear of the unexpected, and learning how to focus on the situation at hand, but also beforehand, by bringing organization and unity to a group as members work together to plan and coordinate an action.

I will not go through the exercises here, as they are covered quite well in several other places: see Katrina Shields's *In the Tiger's Mouth: An Empowerment Guide for Social Action* (Social Change Training and Resource Centre, PO The Channon, 2480, Australia) and *Resource Manual for a Living Revolution* and *War Resistors League Organizer's Manual*. Or locate an experienced trainer by contacting Training for Change through its website: www. Trainingforchange.org or <peacelearn@igc.org>. The exercises deal principally with how to act toward others to reduce their hostility during confrontations; I want to concentrate instead on how to act toward yourself, what you can do to remain psychologically "balanced" during the chaos and danger of a nonviolent action confrontation.

You should be aware of a number of things as you contemplate and then become involved in nonviolent action. Nonviolent protesters facing life-threatening situations have reported afterward that they felt that even if someone were killed in the confrontation, it would be "somebody else." And like other battlefield combatants, you can expect that you will not freak out if the going gets tough. In fact boredom may be more of a problem than danger, since even the most dramatic confrontation involves a lot of tedium.

The Indian nonviolent leader Mohandas Gandhi suggested that we become fearless; one way to do that is to turn our fear into excitement. Stage performers do this with their jitters on opening night: the adrenalin courses through their veins and adds to the vitality of the performance. Sometimes lovers notice the same on their first sexual encounter with a desired partner; the nervousness adds to the excitement of making love. Gandhi recommended, in fact, that we enter a prison cell with the attitude of a bridegroom entering the chamber of his bride.

If you haven't learned how to shift your fear to excitement and therefore become "fearless," there are a number of ways to at least control it. Share in the group leadership and stay busy attending to the group's needs. This doesn't need formal appointment; just do it! Breathe deeply and remind yourself that love is present. Choose someone who needs support and give it. Relate positively with the police officer or pro-military supporter nearest you. Look at your opponent with as much good will as you can muster. Remember the folks back home who are rooting for you; decide to behave so they will be proud of you. Pray. Visualize Jesus (Moses, Buddha, Confucius, Muhammad . . .) holding your hand.

Think how you have controlled your fear in the past and draw inspiration from those times (most of us have survived some scary situations in our lives). Choose the responses to fear that have allowed you to feel in control and do what you needed to at those times.

Adversity, like standing in a freezing rain during a silent vigil, being locked up in jail, being called vicious names, or being shoved during a confrontation, does not have to result in negative feelings. You determine your feelings by how you interpret and think about the hardship (see discussion of the "self-talk monitor" in chapter 15). You can choose an attitude of self-pity, despair, or worry; you can also choose to see the hardship as a challenge, to you personally and to your cause. You can use the hardship for your own benefit, if you choose. India's first Prime Minister, Jawaharlal Nehru, contended that he was a better leader because of the time he had spent in British jails. A veteran of South Africa's jails told me that when he was being tortured, he found resources within himself he never dreamed he had.

Chaos challenges all of us who like some order in our lives and in our political action. During the Algerian War, French nonviolet activists who opposed French colonialism were frequently attacked by police. They developed a handy rule for themselves: "When in doubt, sit down." They found that the level of violence decreased (it's harder for police to keep striking someone who is seated) and they had a better sense of control over the situation — they were more "grounded." You might find other ways of attaining psychological order and composure among surrounding chaos, like deep breathing, chanting, holding a rabbit's foot, etc.

The Ups and Downs of Nonviolent Action

Nonviolent confrontation is analogous to white water rafting; sometimes it can be exciting, and other times it is just plain hard work. You will have a sense that you're not entirely in control and that there is some danger (although little compared to violent action). As in rafting, you also get a chance to bring 100% of yourself to the moment, to — as they say — "Go for it." This is the personal dimension of nonviolent action. Used correctly, nonviolent confrontation confirms the feminist insight that "the personal is political; the political, personal."

Suggested Readings

Lakey, G. (1985). *Strategy for a living revolution* (2nd ed.). Philadelphia: New Society Publishers.

    This book presents cases of nonviolent overthrowing of military dictatorships, as well as a framework for how to strategize for nonviolent action.

Pelton, L. H. (1974). *The psychology of nonviolence*. New York: Pergamon.

    This is a scholarly (but readable and practical) application of psychological theories and research to issues confronted by nonviolent activists. Topics include the nature of social power, the relationship of behavior to attitudes, and the effective use of persuasive communications.

Sharp, G. (1973). *The politics of nonviolent action* (Vols. 1–3). Boston: Porter Sargent.

    This extensive study of the nature of nonviolent struggle is in three volumes: *Power and Struggle*, which compares and contrasts the different types of power, *The Methods of Nonviolent Action*, which examines in detail 198 specific methods of nonviolent action, and *The Dynamics of Nonviolent Action*, which investigates exactly how it works against a violent, repressive opponent.

PART IV
PEACE WORK
GETTING THE MESSAGE OUT

I believe that unarmed truth and unconditional love will have the final word in reality.

— Martin Luther King, Jr.

Effective Media Communications

Matt Keener

C hances are you've already encountered the cold shoulder of the mainstream media machine. And just as you've seen how hard it is to get media attention, you've had to stand by helplessly as your corporate-backed opposition seemed to have the media at its beck and call.

Media Action Project helps "level the playing field" by researching and disseminating the best practices to those working for the greater good. We aggressively study the strategies of rich corporations for adapting to those doing cause-related work.

However, we've found there's a problem with merely passing on even the best practical "how to" advice. People tend to have five misconceptions — all result from reasonable people following what appears to be reasonable thinking, yet they undermine using media more effectively.

Misconception #1: "Doing the work" is our focus; media attention is icing on the cake.

Working for the greater good means generating media attention — better, faster, and more aggressively than the opposition. If you save a tree with no media coverage to see it *not* fall, it may as well not have happened. Sure, you'll have saved one tree, but you'll have squandered the opportunity to leverage that action to raise awareness, money, volunteer help, and coalition partners, and to put public pressure on the forces threatening the trees. By not using the power of media to publicize that one tree, you lose the opportunity to save many trees. Since most groups have limited resources, opportunities to leverage their work cannot be squandered without seriously endangering the larger cause.

Organizations that aren't consistently generating greater awareness aren't likely to be as effective in raising money, attracting skilled people as staff, volunteers, or coalition partners, or even gaining needed access and authority to do the work they've set out to do. To be effective, we must have media communications as a top priority.

Misconception #2: "All that media stuff" is great, crucial even. But fundamentally it's something other people should do, like P.R. people.

"I'm not on the 'P.R. Committee' so Someone Else is calling the press, Someone Else is writing the press release, Someone Else is hiring the photographers. That's not my job." Sound familiar?

The opposition can afford to hire media specialists and professional spokespeople. You probably can't — besides, most of the best ones are already working for your opposition. So to be effective, you have to learn to do the "media stuff" yourself.

Even if you won't be officially called on to handle media, you'll most likely be called upon periodically as an on-the-spot, informal spokesperson for your cause. When current events come up in conversation, in email when a friend forwards you a misguided political joke or petition, at your organization's annual fundraiser, or even at your kid's PTA meeting when a parent says, "So what do you do?" you're in the position of being a media spokesperson. If you've had some basic media training, these informal situations can be powerful opportunities to further your cause. If you haven't, they can be stress-causing, heart-wrenching, "I wish I had said" moments.

Misconception #3: Media communications is something you do near the end the event-planning process, when it's time to "get the word out" or "drum up publicity."

Given the sheer volume of those vying for media attention, if you aren't actively building media communications into your earliest plans, you're starting too late to be effective.

Getting media attention generally requires a long-term investment in building strategic relationships with members of the media and with your membership, so when you have something to publicize, you aren't relying on the kindness of strangers. You have a solid foundation of good relationships.

Misconception #4: Only people who lie or distort use media techniques. The truth doesn't need to be "spun."

There's a widespread feeling among activists that media techniques are inherently manipulative and therefore dishonest. This isn't without some justification — corporate promoters often use "spin" to mislead.

There's a good reason for this. If your media message is dishonest, you'll need to put more "art" and skill into selling it.

But as a result of this misconception, when a spokesperson for the greater good meets a spokesperson for the opposition in a public forum, it's often a sad and shameful one-sided slaughter. The person advocating for the truth was probably relying on the truth alone to be automatically self-evident and convincing, regardless of how ineffectively it was communicated.

Even naturally gifted, genuinely talented athletes need to practice before they hit the field. If they relied on natural ability and moral correctness rather than practicing hard beforehand, they'd lose almost every game they played.

Doesn't your truth deserve as much preparation and careful articulation as the opposition's lies? After all, even David probably spent a little time *practicing* with his slingshot before he faced Goliath.

Misconception #5: The major benefit of effective media communications/P.R. is that it's "free publicity."

This misconception is so prevalent that the P.R. industry refers to getting "free media" to contrast it with advertising as paid media.

But the reality is "free media" isn't free. It requires a long-term investment of time and energy. A better term for it is emerging — *earned media.* Generally, it's earned three ways:

1. By building relationships with the press (in advance, ideally) so you have access.
2. By making your message engaging, compelling, or attention grabbing, so your message has appeal.
3. By doing what's necessary to become a credible source, so you have authority to speak on behalf of your cause.

Media Action Project: Top Twenty Media Communications Tips

1. Build media relationships before you need them.

Don't make the classic rookie mistake of only going to the press when you want something. Plan ahead before asking them for coverage.

The first step is knowing who in the press to develop relationships with. Stay current with all media that might be relevant to your cause. When you see someone covering your issue, note the names and contact info of the reporter(s). In addition to the byline, check at the end of the article for contributing reporters. They're often junior people who'll be more accessible.

Don't cover only "friendly" press. Read the opposition's stuff, too. Their reporters often need quotes to appear "fair and balanced." They have to call someone; it might as well be you.

Send the reporter a letter or email expressing appreciation of her or his coverage of the issue. You'll likely get a good response since reporters get so little positive recognition; people usually only write or call with complaints. If you're an authority or a member of an issue-based organization, consider offering to be a source of background info or quotes for any follow-up.

Building a good Media Contacts Database can take awhile, but it's relatively straightforward. The information is available online. It's a great way for volunteers to participate, as it can generally be worked on in small chunks from any location with web access and then forwarded to a central coordinator to assemble.

2. Activate your existing audience.

People are often so focused on getting mainstream media attention they overlook the people they already have on their email list. And if they do reach out to their mailing list with emails that are vague, lengthy, or boring, they wind up alienating members or at best going straight into the "trash" folder.

Strive to build the relationship by creating opportunities for two-way communications. But be careful not to ask for too much information too early or you may turn off prospective members. Start with simple things. Collect email addresses like gold, and you can create your own media outlet with a simple monthly e-newsletter. But fair warning: most of your members receive several newsletters, and the majority go unread. Make sure your newsletter is relevant, fun, well-written, and *short*. Focus on motivating news (good news to avoid depression/burnout, and bad news to inspire ire!) and opportunities for your readers to have a positive impact on the issue(s) they care about.

Being creative and personal can help beat the newsletter blues. For example, can you sort your mailing list(s) by date of birth? Then you can send personal email birthday cards. How can their birthdays be tied to the cause? You can send out a suggestion a month in advance that they email their friends requesting that instead of gifts people make a small contribution to the cause.

Or you could create a special email with fun or motivating historical information about the issue in the year of that person's birth. (Keep things positive. A major oil spill or a grisly massacre on his or her birthday might not go over well.) This may seem like a lot of years to cover, but most groups are focused in a range of about twenty years. (And researching this is another opportunity to get volunteers involved.)

3. Recruit, train, discover and then dedicate key staff and volunteers to P.R.

Getting the word out takes resources. One of the most important resources will be human labor — skilled human labor. The requisite skills include writing skills (for press releases, web content, blogs, flyers, email newsletters, etc.), people skills (phone follow ups with press and opinion leaders), and organizational skills (strategy planning, making sure it all gets done). NOTE: You will almost never find all three in one person. Generally people become good writers because they're not so great at people skills, etc. Ideally, you want to assemble a P.R. team. This may require recruiting internally — among your present staff/volunteer base — or externally — e.g., from Craigslist (www.craigslist.com) or nearby universities.

Don't overlook anyone involved in your organization, no matter how "low-level" they may seem. Volunteers often have untapped relationships, latent potential or even experience unknown to you. The person who volunteered to run the donut table may be looking for a "neck down" break from a high-powered job as a corporate public relations professional. The college student helping to assemble your database may have a roommate who's interning for a high-powered corporate PR professional. Treat every member of your team as a valuable asset. You'll never know if you don't ask or clearly "advertise" the opportunity. And since motivating staff/volunteers is all about hooking them up with tasks that will turn them on, make it a priority to find the people in your mix who'd be really excited to be made part of your communications team.

4. Include P.R. strategies in the very first stages of event planning.

Make P.R. planning a first priority. For starters, every meeting should include someone whose sole job is to focus on press and publicity.

Start your event planning by asking, "Who's the audience we're addressing?"

Avoid making the classic mistake of trying to get your message out to everyone — "the general public." In trying to reach everybody, you often wind up reaching nobody. Identify your intended audience and know what your objectives are with that audience. Are you trying to recruit new members/participants? What type of new people are you trying to reach out to? Or are you demonstrating to current and future funders that you're effective in getting attention for the issue(s) with a specific audience?

Once you have a sense of who you're looking to appeal to, identify the media outlets servicing that particular demographic. Young adults in metropolitan areas often read the regional weekly "entertainment" newspapers. Senior citizens are more likely to read the neighborhood or community newspapers.

5. Don't overlook the two most read sections of the newspaper.

It may seem odd, but consider suggesting that more active members request that their passionate support of your organization/cause be included in their obituaries as a tribute to their contributions to a cause they believe deeply in.

Letters to the editor are relatively easy to get published and are actively read, especially by the staff of elected political officials. They see it as a key resource for tracking constituent opinion.

Getting published tips:

- Be short.
- Be witty. Try a play on words, or a fun juxtaposition.
- Be clear. Have people who don't already know what you're trying to say read it — can they find any part that isn't utterly clear?
- Add reliable facts from credible sources ("According to the American Lung Association . . .").
- Be a credible source yourself. Prominently site your authority ("As a professor of ____ at ____ . . .," "As a

psychologist who works with suicidal teens . . .," "As a single working mother . . ."). Ideally, these will be the first words of your letter.

Even if your letter doesn't get published, it wasn't a waste of time. Newspapers generally print only one out of ten to twenty letters they receive on a given subject. Sometimes they need to get ten or more letters on an issue before they'll publish even one. So yours might have been that critical ninth letter!

6. Keep a sharp eye out for messaging backfires.

If you know your target audience, the key to messaging is quite simple. Ask yourself how would this particular version of our message be read (or misread) by members of the target audience? It's simple, but not easy. The answer requires multiple analyses from multiple points of reference, requiring a fairly sophisticated skill set that you probably will ultimately need some professional help to master (self-promotion: Media Action Project can teach your organization how to do this).

But to get started, ask yourself (and have colleagues ask):

- Can your wording be misinterpreted?
- Can the opposition cleverly turn the phrasing around to undermine your message or make you look ridiculous?
- Does the wording suggest any images, metaphors, or subtle emotional connections that work against your cause?
- If so, can you reverse the significance of the connection?

Don't overlook potential backfires in photographs and graphics. Pictures, both still and motion, have a "language" of their own, just as much as words.

Take every suggestion of possible misinterpretation seriously, even if it seems silly or farfetched. Remember, you know what you're trying to say, so you're the least likely to find misreads and mistakes. An interpretation that seems implausible to you may well be the most common and dangerous misread of your material, costing you major missed opportunities and years of hard work as your message backfires.

7. Design events with the media in mind.

All too often, event planners don't take advantage of the opportunity to make their event "media friendly." But keep in mind that your primary audience for any event is not the participants but those who will learn about the event afterward through media coverage.

Ask yourself these questions:

- Is the area layout arranged to create strong visual photo and video images?
- Will participants be spread out into thin straggles or are they naturally grouped together for shots that suggest a well-attended event?
- Where's the organization's logo displayed?
- Is the logo readable from multiple angles?
- How will the signs and other key elements look on television? (This goes beyond whether your keynote speaker is wearing camera-unfriendly stripes, but that's a good place to start.)
- Will pictures and video clearly show people who look like your intended audience(s) and that they are happily and productively participating?

8. Invite the media.

So you've done your planning and now it's time to "get the word out" about some situation or event — either in advance to get more participants or after to maximize the impact beyond the participants.

The most common method is to send a "press release" to all the media contacts you've built relationships with. (Okay, so you probably didn't do that relationship-building part yet. In the future, you hopefully will, but for now, you still need to maximize the media potential of what you're planning.) So send your press release generically to various media outlets that make the most sense for your event or issue.

A press release is not an op-ed. Make clear up front what the "news" element is. The news element is always an *action*, a verb. (Remember who/what/where/when/why from high school journalism? Now's the time.)

"So and so did such and such" is a news event. Your opinion, analysis, and point of view *are not news events*. It bears repeating: News events are *actions*. The fact that your organization wants leaders to answer for misleading your country into war is *not* a news event. But if your organization sends an open letter to those leaders demanding they answer, the sending/releasing of the letter is the news event. You can, and should, use the news item as a launching pad to make your point (the opinion part). Just make sure you have an actual news action item. Even if you're releasing the results of a study, the release is the news action item.

9. Follow up.

Once you've sent out the press release, make follow-up calls to verify it was received and forwarded to the right person. Make additional follow-up calls on the day of the event or the day before or even both, depending on the situation. News organizations get dozens or even hundreds of press releases every day. Calling to make sure yours was received and emphasizing the uniqueness/importance/relevance of the event will help yours stand out. Most "greater good" organizations won't call. Most corporations will. Guess whose event gets covered? The fact that the media is either owned by or completely dependent on corporate advertising gives them enough of an advantage. Don't make it worse by giving them an excuse to ignore you!

10. Plan for the press not to arrive.

So you send out your press releases, do your follow-up calls. And the newspapers, television, and radio stations can generally be counted on to do one thing: not show up. If they do, they usually cover it poorly or from the wrong angle — visually, philosophically, factually.

And for many that's where the whole "media thing" begins and ends — in disappointment, frustration, and hopelessness. The government, the military, and big corporate interests continue to monopolize media time, getting their messages across in place of yours.

But what if you took a different approach? What if you knew the media wasn't going to show? Saving the energy of inviting them may seem like a good answer, but it's not. You've got to invite them, if only as a courtesy. The better answer would be:

11. Always have your own cameras documenting your work/events.

Whether the press shows up or not, what if you had your own professional news video crew and stills photographer cover the event, including interviews with key participants? Then you quickly made the photos and footage available to media outlets? Just because your event didn't rate high enough on their newsroom's priority for the day doesn't mean they won't run the story if you provide them with all the field work.

It's not that hard nowadays to create your own professional grade news material and make that available to the media. A video camera operator, a sound person, and an editor (or one person wearing all three hats) can be hired by placing an advertisement on the international Craig's list (www.craigslist.com). You can offer to pay reasonably well, say $30-100 an hour (or something similar in non-U.S. currency for non-U.S. locales), because if you plan things right, you'll only need them for a couple of hours. If the media did come, they'd probably shoot about ten minutes. Your hired professional could shoot three times that and still stay on an extremely tight budget.

The key is that the edited footage is made available to the media quickly, usually within hours (not days!). This requires building a database of contact info well in advance so you can send out the offer right away, both to the media that did attend and to those that didn't.

Having your own video dramatically increases your chances of getting coverage, since you've done the hard and expensive part. Creating your own material has the added advantage of letting you more accurately tell your story. You shape and choose the content of what you provide — just like the government and big corporations selectively provide what they release and don't rely on the independent judgment of journalists to spin their news for them.

Having your own footage also means you own the material. You don't have to beg, plead, and even pay for access to the footage from the TV news people. You can use it in "here's what we are/do" type videos, documentaries, and on your website for fundraising, recruitment, and morale boosting.

12. Don't forget the photos!

Whether or not you can get video, always get still photos, ideally professional quality. Hire the best your budget can afford, but even if your budget is zero, *any* photos are better than none. Use your own camera (ideally digital) to take plenty of candids and some posed group shots. A dozen snaps from your lame old "point and shoot" can be a fun addition to the website, the "thank you" letter/email to volunteers and participants, or the recruitment materials for the next event.

Photos are also great for keeping your funders informed and enticing new funders. Grant-makers in particular usually love to see photos and/or video of programs they're funding or considering.

13. Be prepared if the press does show up.

Depending on the competing news events that day, the news vans might well pull up at your event. Designate a Media Coordinator to handle the press. (This may or may not be the same person who manages your "in-house" media creation.)

The Media Coordinator should be prepared to:

- Greet and credential reporters
- Give them a brief overview/tour of the event
- Introduce them to key spokespeople
- Suggest interviewees
- Point out visually relevant features for possible "B-roll" footage, backdrops, etc.

Ideally, your Media Coordinator should also feel comfortable asking a random knot of people to reposition themselves while they continue their activity, so the cameras can get a better shot — say, of the big banner with the organization's logo in the background.

14. Sell your people on the importance of getting good media recorded.

All too often, at live events, the focus is on the live event — creating the maximum experience for people attending in person. Don't forget there are many, many more who couldn't attend but who can be impacted through strong media images. Ideally, the Media Coordinator should be able to tell the emcee, "Hey, we need to do that part again; the video camera didn't get it." If this is clearly agreed on with the emcee in advance, it's generally not a problem. The live audience is usually okay with it, as most will understand and even enjoy the fun of a certain amount of "doing it for the cameras." If they've taken the time to be there, they're likely committed enough to want to maximize its effectiveness.

15. Make sure everyone on your team knows "Media-Speak Haiku."

In most media venues today, you only get a maximum of thirty seconds to say your thing. To be effective, this means you say one thing. Since that will often be edited down, say your one thing at least three times. One thing repeated a minimum of three times in a maximum of thirty seconds means you get less than ten seconds to communicate your core message. If you look closely, you'll notice this holds true even if you're the main featured guest on a full hour-long talk show. Then you'll get about ten minutes of actual speaking time — comprised of several ten- to thirty-second sound bites.

It may seem a daunting challenge, especially when your issue(s) aren't simple. But know that you'll be either edited or omitted, so you get no choice. And with some practice (and coaching from friends and colleagues) you'll become more comfortable with it.

The secret to the effective sound bite is something we call "Media Haiku": Find different ways of saying the same thing. Connect them with "and," "so," "therefore," so your presentation seems like you're doing a logical progression (this follows that) rather than merely repeating the same thing.

Example:

The most important reason to protect the environment is for the future of our children. And a healthy pollution-free planet is the greatest legacy we can leave the next generation. Therefore, to do our duty to our children and their children, we must make the environment our number one priority.

Same thing, said three different ways. No matter what part of this sound bite they use, your message will be in it. There's simply no way to cut it out. But if they're only going to use ten seconds or less, why not hone the perfect ten-second sound bite and just say it once? Several reasons:

1. Technical problems could mean the one ten-second recording isn't usable.
2. You may garble your speech or accidentally put it in a "noneditable" context. Again, not useable.
3. A ten-second response will usually prompt a follow-up and if you just repeat, you'll come off as "uncooperative." If you give three or four variations, it will seem like you gave them a full interview. Plus, you've given the reporter the power of being able to choose the sound bite.

16. Assemble and maintain a Rapid Response Team.

Is your organization(s) prepared to respond to a request from local, regional, national, or international TV or radio news for a spokesperson to talk about an aspect of your issue(s) within an hour's notice twenty-four hours a day, seven days a week, fifty-two weeks a year? Your opposition most likely is.

Do you have a trained spokesperson at the ready within an hour's drive of a major metropolitan center to go on "live via satellite" and debate a well-trained representative of the opposing viewpoint? The opposition most likely does.

What about doing a phone interview with a newspaper, web blog, or magazine twenty minutes before its deadline? It's not uncommon for an editor to tell a reporter to add a source or two moments before deadline to make a report "seem more balanced."

Do you have a phone number for the press to call 24/7 to make such a request? Is that phone number posted prominently on your easy-to-find "Contact Us" page on your website? If a media person were to Google your organization's name and the words "media or press contact" would that "Contact Us" page be the first result? If a media person were to Google your main issues, would your organization's website be among the first ten listed?

17. Be prepared for things to go worse than expected.

What to do when you get bad press? The best approach is preplanning. Preplanning is actually a lot easier than most media experts would have you believe. The key: you have to actually do it. Otherwise, when things go wrong, crisis communications people charge small fortunes for their "in the heat of the crisis" services.

The quickest way to preplan is to ask: what are the ten worst things that could happen to your organization? Make sure not all of them are just big wins for your opposition. For example, if your organization works with kids, one of your ten is a prominent board or staff member being accused of child molestation. Or what if someone is beaten or shot at your peace vigil? Now come up with a game plan for how to respond to that crisis. What would you like to have your spokesperson say? Script it out. Send copies to a few key people for feedback. (Label it something fancy like "Crisis Communications Plan"). Try to include some lawyer types as well as communications types in your feedback group. Often in crisis communications one needs to be compassionate without taking on inappropriate legal responsibility. Revise, polish, and distribute a copy to everyone in senior positions. Ideally, have one person preselected as the lead spokesperson for crisis communications.

18. Be prepared for things to go better than expected.

Often organizations aren't prepared for the upsurge in interest, applicants, or information requests resulting from a news item or a prominent mention in the media. Before you beat the bushes to generate media coverage, be sure you're ready to handle the potential increase in inquiries. For example, after months of hard work by the American Lung Association's communications people, Dr. Phil mentioned the organization's no-cost "Freedom from Smoking" program on his show. The ALA had more requests in the next twenty-four hours than it typically has in an entire year.

19. Celebrate your media victories.

Share the news when you get media coverage. Email everyone in advance if you can. Make a high quality recording of it for future use! If the coverage makes you look good, circulate copies widely. If your cause would be hurt by the coverage, study your copy for how you can do better next time. Either way, celebrate the victory of having earned the media access; you got that part right!

20. Always be learning and improving your media communications techniques.

Keep an eye on how others are using media. Learn from other cause-related groups, corporations, and government agencies and especially your opposition.

Developing good media communications strategies takes some practice, but the first step is to actually use them! The more you use them, the more skilled you and your colleagues will become and the easier it will be. But even when you use them inexpertly in the beginning, you'll still be more effective than if you weren't trying at all.

Suggested Reading

Media Activist Kit
Email: info@MediaActionProject.org for this free kit with checklists, frequently asked questions, more detailed how-to pointers, and additional resources.

ATTRACTING AN AUDIENCE:
THE PSYCHOLOGY OF LAYOUT AND DESIGN

JW P. Heuchert

The best piece of writing is useless — unless it is read. We often spend a lot of time and effort honing our writing skills and polishing our message but then neglect to pay attention to what will get our message read: the layout and design of the written document. Just as people are psychologically and emotionally affected by the content of a message, so are they affected by its presentation. There's one major difference however: the presentation (layout and design) often determines whether readers will bother to read your message at all and whether they will keep reading past the headline. Some say 1.2 seconds is all you get to "seduce a potential (reader) with a piece of printed matter." After that, she's looked away and moved on.[1]

Reading is an effortful activity and we all tend to want to conserve energy — physical as well as psychological. It's important therefore that your publication assists your readers so they will have more physical and psychological energy to put toward reading and internalizing your message. Physical energy is conserved by making your publication easy to read (layout), and psychological energy is conserved, and even increased through increased motivation, by making your publication attractive and interesting (design).

Most people in your audience are reading "scanners" — they scan across a page, stopping here and there, and then turn the page, unless you can capture their attention and draw them into a story. You're most likely dealing with voluntary readers, and they're the best kind. Psychological research shows volunteers are often more loyal and committed and work harder for the causes they believe in. The challenge is that because they are volunteer readers, you can't force them to read — only entice them. If you do that well, they will reward you with loyalty and commitment.

The layout and design of your publication also helps, or hinders, the *cognitive* processes readers must perform — like concept formation, mental images, and cognitive schemas — which are necessary for thinking to take place. Your readers can't think about your material unless they read it first. Your job is to get them to pay attention to your text and then concentrate on reading it. Grab their attention with your layout. Then make your text accessible through improving readability and legibility by improving layout, typesetting, typographic cues, and text organization (heading, subheadings, pull-quotes, etc.).

The content of your message is mostly processed at a conscious level, but subconscious and nonconscious thinking is strongly influenced by the design and layout. Most people are aware of the research in psychology pointing to hemispheric specialization in our brains. Language is mostly a left hemisphere activity, while visual-spatial processing is a right hemisphere activity. We also know that using the strengths of both hemispheres leads to optimal functioning. Your layout and design capitalizes on right brain capabilities and supplements the language processing going on in the left hemisphere.

It's assumed that basic questions such as the content (main message), format (flyers, posters, stickers, newsletters, buttons, books, pamphlets, etc.), and medium (print vs. audio, video, or electronic) have already been decided and that you are now ready to see your message in print. Welcome to the world of stimulus overload! Your readers are bombarded with written messages wherever they turn their heads. You have to design and publish a product that stands out enough to capture their attention, pique their interest, and solicit their commitment to continue reading past the headlines. Unfortunately, using preprogrammed desktop publishing programs and templates won't allow you to "check your brain at the door" and let the machine do the work for you.[2] You'll be required to do a great amount of thinking, planning, and experimenting. Some of the following factors may help.

Basics

Humans use their sense of vision to access written materials, but this is not a static process because they also "perceive" what they see — interpret what is seen. We also evaluate, react to, remember, and try to understand what we read since our "consciousness functions not only on a perceptual but a conceptual level as well."[3] Seeing and perceiving written materials are necessary prerequisites for concepts to be formed.

Fortunately we have a number of reading habits and preferences that can be capitalized on to enhance our reader's experience with our publications. A few of them are:[4]

- *Eye flow*

Westernized humans usually read from left to right and top to bottom. Remember you want to catch the eye where it enters the page — top left on a single page. Bottom right is the exit point and often a stopping point that can be exploited. On a double page spread, however, the eye starts on the *right-hand* side page, at the top where the eye goes when the page is turned. Most time is usually spent on the right-hand page and it's therefore a more important space than pages on the left. The eye needs to be "seduced" to the left, often by graphics or pictures.

- *Dominance*

There's a hierarchy of dominance in the different design elements. Pictures (especially ones with color) tend to be seen first, headlines next, etc. Your text starting point should be in close proximity to the picture, or else the reader's eye will wander off.

- *Simplicity*

Humans tend to simplify in order to conserve energy. Help your readers by providing them with simplified designs — using basic, or pure, shapes in your layout: circles rather than ovals, squares rather than rectangles, etc. The shapes come from how your page is divided by graphics, white space, or text elements.

- *Unity*

We are soothed by unity in a publication. If there is a visual rhythm created by unity and repetition in typeface, heading and subheadings, graphics and photos (sizes and placements), etc., readers are lulled into a comfort zone akin to a trance-like state that will let them spend more time with your publication. It will also make them enjoy — and feel more positive about — your publication, your organization, and your cause!

- *Balance*

Balance is the result of an even distribution of the different elements of design. It's usually achieved through symmetry in design, which is pleasing to the human eye. Asymmetrical designs can be used to attract attention and create interest, but are more difficult to achieve.

- *Contrast*

Contrast is one of the most basic techniques to create interest in a publication. Contrasts of scale (larger and smaller elements) and of tone (dark, light, and tonal variations of your colors) are some of the easier techniques.

Design

Design creates the emotional climate within which you present your message. Just as you are soothed by a well-designed and well-organized room or building, so will your readers be comforted by a well-designed publication. Design minimizes distraction and enables them to focus their attention on the important issue: your message.

An additional benefit to pleasing (read: rewarding) design elements is that it predisposes your reader favorably to your message. Because of the principles of classical conditioning, positive associations will again be elicited when design elements (such as nameplates, logos, familiar layouts, etc.) are repeated in your other/next publications. Good design is "candy for the eyes" in that it provides visual rewards (operant conditioning) to readers who turn the pages of your publication.

Most readers are design savvy. They've been exposed to sophisticated design in most printed materials they've encountered and will therefore be irritated by poor design and consequently not bother to pay attention. When the care you've taken in preparing your publication is obvious, your message appears to be more valuable and generates more respect.

Good design shows that you and your organization:

- planned your publication and are thoughtful and rational, not impulsive "hotheads";
- selected an appropriate tool for the task at hand (putting stickers on church pews probably won't get you much sympathy);
- know your audience and their interests, reading level, and available time;
- know what's out there — what you're competing with;
- have unity in your various publications;
- have provided organization that conserves you reader's energy that can then be used for a more important purpose: receiving and internalizing your message.

Studies on the impact of design on readership and comprehension show that good design can more than double the readership (from thirty-two to sixty-seven percent) without changing a single word on the page![5] The choice of fonts can increase comprehension from twelve to sixty-seven percent, while using dark screens could *reduce* comprehension to almost zero.

The first thing you need to do is decide who your audience is for this particular publication. You may have to create several variations if your audiences are very different. Then decide what you want to include this time, where your publication will be distributed, and when you need to have it done by. Now you're ready to think about how it's going to look.

Creating a look:

The "look" of you publication is a complex psychological process determined by what you present the reader with, as well as by what the reader has previously experienced (the reader's frame of reference). Thus, a bright neon paper color may attract a certain crowd but may be experienced negatively as screaming by another. Complex drawings and small print in various fonts may be interesting to folks with the time and motivation to decipher them, but an incidental reader may not bother. A newsletter dense with type may be skimmed over, while one with too much white space and simple graphics may be considered frivolous. A wide variety of colors may attract children's attention but could be rejected as "cheap commercialism" by adults. It's therefore important you know your audience and tailor your publications to capture and hold their interest. Good design is like a good resume — it gets you the interview that allows you the opportunity to talk to your audience. Bad, careless, cluttered design — no interview, no shot at the audience!

The "look" of your publication is determined by fixed elements, repeated in the publication, and repeated over several publications. For newsletters, for example, your nameplate (the title of your publication) is the first and most noticed aspect of your publication. Since the nameplate reflects the core of your identity, considerable thought should be given to choosing the name. Generally you'll want to emphasize the essence of your cause in a few words, usually not more than three in the main title and a few more in a subtitle. Using only a few words means you can print them quite big and bold so they catch the eye. You may want to emphasize the most important word, or put it in italics or a heavier typeface. By mixing a bold font (Bookman) and using italics, the title

Peace *Action*

will focus the reader's attention on the two important aspects of your publication, peace *and* action. In addition, the placement of the light, italicized word "action," suggests activity and movement after the relative stability of the solid word "peace."

Horizontal lines above and below your nameplate will frame it and anchor it on the page, or you can use a background screen for the title, or reverse print (in white on a darker background). Exclude "extra" words such as "the" and "newsletter" from the title; it should be obvious your publication is a newsletter.

Size considerations:

When deciding on the size, keep your reader's interest in mind. Large publications (tabloid newspaper size) are generally hard to hold and store, while letter size ($8\frac{1}{2} \times 11$ inches) publications are standard for printers, copiers, and mailing (saving you costs) and can easily be handled and stored in files and filing cabinets. Small pamphlets may be easily discarded on the street, while letter-size pamphlets may be kept since discarding them will be inhibited because it may feel like littering.

White/empty space — valuable freebies:

When we think of publications we often think mostly of what's printed on the page. But what isn't printed is often also important — the white/empty space that surrounds and frames our text. Readers get discouraged and overwhelmed when they face a page crammed with words. It's better to cut some of your text and have your text read than to include all your text and have no one read it because it's overwhelming or intimidating.

Provide relief by using ample white borders, space at the top and bottom and right and left. Allow enough white space between columns, heading, subheadings, and paragraphs. Wide margins with hanging indents further accentuate the breaks in your text, particularly with only one column. The space between columns can be smaller if you use flush-left alignment.

Be careful, however, not to use too much space, or to use first line indentations with a narrow column. Two or three columns per letter-size page are ideal. Too much space will have your article fall apart at the seams and make it seem disjointed.

Fonts:

Fonts are the type of lettering you choose. There are hundreds of fonts available. Don't go for the look as much as for *legibility* and *readability*. There are two broad categories of fonts: *serif* and *sans serif*. Just as we hear words as units, not individual sounds, people also *read* words as units, rather than individual letters. Serif fonts all have a little foot, or hook, at the bottom of the letter. For example, the serif font (Times New Roman)

first draft will be more readable than the sans serif font (Futura) first draft, especially at the normal size: first draft vs. first draft.

Serif fonts visually join the letters to each other and make the word a whole, and thus more readable. People can read serif fonts faster, more comfortably, and with more comprehension. However, san serif fonts are more *legible*, easier to discern, and stand out more. Generally speaking then, the body of your text should be in a serif font, and your headlines and subheadings in a sans serif font. Using the Condensed Heavy, or Condensed Black, version of the sans serif font you choose can also make your headings and subheadings more prominent.

The size of the type you use is important in the sense that you want to get your audience to read and keep reading. If they have to squint, they stop; if it's too big, it will seem like you're shouting. If you have a general audience, 12-point fonts are usually good, while you may want to bump it up to 14 points for an older audience. When using 8-point or smaller (yikes!) fonts, use a san serif typeface.

While there are many beautiful, fancy fonts available, bear in mind you want to attract and keep a reader, not an admirer. Therefore, stick with a few basic fonts. Times New Roman is probably the most economical in terms of legibility, readability, and characters per inch.

Pictures and other graphics:

The old adage of a picture being worth a thousand words is still as true as it ever was. Pictures and other graphics are usually the first things that are looked at. In addition to telling stories, photos, cartoons, and drawings often save space because words describing the picture will take up more space. Pictures also convey emotions that are hard to capture in text, provide interesting "hooks" — ways to grab attention — and provide respite for tired text-reading eyes.

However, avoid the temptation to use fancy borders, thick lines and other distracting graphics. Remember your aim — getting readers to focus their attention on your message, not on the frills.

To determine whether you need illustrations or photos, consider what they add:[6]

- Giving information: maps, diagrams, etc.
- Creating realism: an accurate picture of what something or someone looks like.
- Stimulating emotion: pictures of babies raise emotions that words can hardly do.
- Establishing an identity: a logo stimulates a slew of responses and emotions.
- Raising interest: break up boring text with an illustration or picture.

Identity formation:

Social psychologists remind us of the importance of our various identities, such as personal, gender, ethnic, national, group, and religious identities. The tendency to value our social identity can be used to get and hold our reader's attention. The content of our publication will usually do this through appealing to our common interests. It will encourage reader participation through reports about the reader's activities, letters to the editor, members' news, etc. However, graphic elements can also be very strong symbolic and emotional unifying elements through the judicious use of logos, photos, and other graphics. If a picture is worth a thousand words, a picture of oneself in print is worth a million words! Use your organization's logo (or create one — better yet, have a competition to get your readers to create one); publish photos of your members doing things; repeat your graphics (layout and design) in publications, business cards, and stationary, on t-shirts, coffee mugs, and stickers. You'll strengthen your group's social identity through the subliminal process of social identity formation.

Layout

Layout is both an art and a science: an art because you create a visually stimulating piece and a science in that the process can be learned by following some basic rules. The aim is to "lead the viewer's eye around the piece and entertain it with repetition (pattern and texture), contrast (scale, tone, and color), and direction (created through the interaction of shapes and lines)."[7]

The medium is the message. Your choice of a traditional, classical layout gives implicit clues to create the image of stability, trust, respect, and a common sense approach. By using a more contemporary layout, you create the image of being more progressive and adventurous and perhaps of being willing to take risks

Grabbing Attention

Headlines are usually the first *text* element people look for, and see, on a page. A catchy headline is important, but it also needs to be very readable. Short headlines are quicker to read and will be chosen first. Readability is improved by making the words more of a unit by reducing the letter spacing (through tracking and kerning), leading (reducing the space between lines), and starting flush left. You shouldn't hyphenate in the heading, nor capitalize every word, nor break the sentence at awkward places. Overly long headlines can often be broken into a shorter headline with a subheadline above or below the big headline, for example:

Our organization in disarray —
President resigns!
or
President resigns!
Our organization in disarray.

The above versions not only maximize attention grabbing but also have different meanings and interpretations.

Increasing Commitment to Reading

Subheadings, pull-quotes, and initial caps help your readers focus attention on the task at hand: reading your message. The more you do to make your message available, the more successful your publication will be. Subheadings when new topics are introduced every few paragraphs serve two purposes: they organize, summarize, and focus the material *for* the reader, so *the reader* doesn't have to expend energy on that; and subheadings encourage readers to give your article another try if they tire after getting halfway through the first paragraph.

Pull-quotes are short sentences, quotes, or sentence fragments from your text that are placed inside your article to highlight a certain issue, to draw attention as a "hook," or to break up long columns of text. Pull-quotes can be:

- in a column of text,
- between columns with text wrapping around it,
- as side heads (in a broad white margin on the left of your text).

Initial caps are larger initial letters and can be raised, like at the beginning of this sentence, or dropped — pushed down into the second and third lines.

Initial caps draw attention and break up long text — especially if a subhead cannot be used because a new subject is not introduced; and raised caps create extra white space between paragraphs, which is sometimes desirable.

The length of the lines also influences your reader's commitment to reading. Most people find it most comfortable to move their eyes twice for each line. If your lines are longer than about forty characters, their eyes may have to move a third time, so they lose their place because the left side moves out of their peripheral vision. They get eye fatigue and ultimately give in and move on to the next piece without finishing. Adjust your column width to keep your line length at an optimal level given the size of your type.

Flush-left alignment (as opposed to full justification or the "boxed" look) leads to more natural sentence lengths and letter spacing, thus increasing readability.

Using Color

Color has emotional value for most people. Different moods are elicited by different colors. This can be used to attract attention (READ THIS NOW!) or set a tone (we're hip/classy/artsy/conventional/businesslike). Color can add impact to your design, but it can also be very distracting if overused. Generally speaking, it's more soothing to the eye (read — less irritating) to use only one or two colors, supplemented by shades or tones of those colors (which gives you multiple colors without the cost or irritation). Reverses and screens are also very effective ways of emphasizing, or setting apart, a piece of text. Be very careful with screens, however, because they don't always reproduce well. Text should usually be printed in black, or a very dark color, in order for it to be readable (except when reverse printing — always with ample font sizes!). If color printing is too expensive, color can still be used very effectively by printing or copying black text on colored paper.

Conclusion

Designing and deciding on the layout elements of a publication is an exciting and rewarding process. It will consume a lot of your time, but thinking psychologically about your activity and your audience will make your publication more successful. It will make you feel far more engaged in this highly creative art and science.

References
1. Whitbread, D. (2001). *The design manual*. Sydney: UNSW Press.
2. Morgenster, S. (1993). Timesaving design techniques: With templates you need not always start from scratch. *Home Office Computing, 12*(2), 28–29.
3. Turnbull, A. T., & Baird, R. N. (1975). *The graphics of communication* (3rd ed.). New York: Holt Rhinehart and Wilson.
4. Whitbread.

5. Parker, R. C. (1995). *Desktop publishing & design for dummies*. Foster, CA: IDG Books.
6. Quilliam, S., & Grove-Stephenson, I. (1990). *Into print*. London: BBC Books.
7. Whitbread.

Suggested Readings

Whitbread, D. (2001). *The design manual*. Sydney: UNSW Press.
Parker, R. C. (1995). *Desktop publishing & design for dummies*. Foster City, CA: IDG Books.

ADDING PEACE TO THE CURRICULUM — PRESCHOOL THROUGH COLLEGE

Linden L. Nelson

Averting war is the work of politicians; establishing peace is the work of education.

— Maria Montessori

Creating a peaceful world requires developing peaceful people. Therefore, peace education is an essential part of working for peace. Broadly defined, peace education includes all efforts to facilitate development of peaceful people.

Because attitudes about conflict, violence, and peace originate in childhood and may be resistant to change, peace education should begin with young children. As children progress through school grades and beyond, they must adjust to a culture that supports violence in many forms and learn to deal with conflicts of increasing complexity, from interpersonal to international. So, peace education should continue into adult years. Learning to be peaceful is a lifelong task, and the need to develop peaceful people applies to the entire life span.

Peace education takes place in schools, churches, families, community learning centers, counseling centers, clinics, prisons, and the workplace. It may occur anywhere, and learners may be anyone including children, graduate students, United Nations peacekeepers, police officers, etc. Nevertheless, this chapter focuses on school and college programs because they offer the best opportunity for educating the majority of people and because schools and colleges have been assigned the task of preparing children and young adults to become cooperative and responsible citizens. Many of the resources described here, however, may be useful for peace education in other settings as well.

Goals of Peace Education

The primary goal is to develop peaceful people. What do we mean by "peaceful people?" A peaceful person may at least be defined as generally cooperative and nonviolent. The question then becomes, "What enables and motivates a person to behave in cooperative and nonviolent ways?" People are likely to act peacefully if they: (1) possess required knowledge and skills, (2) value peaceful behavior and its outcomes, and (3) believe they're capable of creating peaceful outcomes by their own actions or by working with others.

Knowledge and Skills

To be cooperative, one may need to understand another party's interests and perspective, know about nonviolent strategies for resolving conflict, and use communication skills for problem solving. Given the time limitations teachers are likely to have, it's important to identify and teach basic knowledge and generic skills. Basic knowledge for the high school level might include principles about tendencies toward bias in perception of others (prejudice, ethnocentrism, dehumanization); factors in escalation and de-escalation of conflict; causes and consequences of cooperation, competition, and violence; the role and dynamics of emotion in human relations; the importance of reconciliation following conflict; effective communication, problem solving, and decision making; conflict resolution strategies (negotiation, mediation, arbitration); and nonviolent methods of social influence (positive incentives and reinforcement, friendly initiatives, nonviolent activism and resistance).[1]

Values

Knowledge and competencies aren't enough. One may know how to cooperate yet decide to compete. Militaristic leaders are not necessarily deficient in problem-solving ability or in knowledge of negotiation principles. One study found college students' scores measuring problem solving for international conflict resolution didn't correlate with their opinions about use of military force (vs.

cooperative actions).[2] Peace educators must do more than teach facts, concepts, and skills. To develop peaceful people, we must instill peaceful values.

Some citizens will object to the notion that schools should instill peaceful values if they're framed as anti-war or anti-military. Yet few are likely to argue that peace, justice, democracy, and equal opportunity are unimportant. The central values of peaceful people are widely respected. If the goal is framed as developing "moral character," "democratic values," or "the values of peace and justice," there's likely to be consensus about the importance of this educational objective. Valerie Braithwaite identified a cluster of ten correlated values that she labeled "international harmony and equality values."[3] They are:

- A good life for others (improving the welfare of all people in need)
- Rule by the people (involving all citizens in making decisions that affect their community)
- International cooperation (having all nations working together to help each other)
- Social progress and social reform (being ready to change our way of life for the better)
- A world at peace (being free from war)
- A world of beauty (having the beauty of nature and the arts: music, literature, art)
- Human dignity (treating each individual as someone of worth)
- Equal opportunity for all (giving everyone an equal chance in life)
- Greater economic equality (lessening the gap between rich and poor)
- Preserving the natural environment (preventing the destruction of nature's beauty and resources)

This captures fairly well the value system of peaceful people and has potential for wide acceptance describing objectives for public schools in the realm of values. While there's less evidence on the effectiveness of teaching values than for concepts and skills, there are a few relevant findings. Values are probably acquired largely through modeling, with evidence that a high level of student-teacher interaction facilitates students' adopting their teachers' values.[4] Curricula should provide activities that require discussion about values among students and between teachers and students. Students' values are likely to be influenced in a peaceful direction by group norms that develop during discussion about negative consequences of violence and the benefits of peacemaking and peace building.

We also know that attitudes and values often follow behavior. When students are encouraged to engage in peaceful actions such as acting as mediators, participating in community service projects, and writing letters to the editor, the values that support those actions are strengthened.

Beliefs about Ability and Outcome

People aren't likely to do peace work unless they believe their actions will either achieve desired outcomes or at least make progress toward them, as research shows.[5,6] Such beliefs develop from personal experience and from observing experiences of others. If positive expectations are essential for developing peaceful people, peace education should provide abundant examples of successful nonviolent actions,[7] diplomatic initiatives, and other peaceful endeavors where individuals and citizen groups have had a significant impact on government policy and social problems. Curricula should also provide opportunities for students to successfully engage in peacemaking and peace-building activities.

A school environment that rewards competition doesn't encourage development of positive outcome expectations for cooperative behavior, but cooperative learning techniques do.[8]

Varieties of Peace Education

Ian Harris outlined five types of peace education.[9] "Global peace education" includes international studies, holocaust studies, and teaching about weapons of mass destruction. "Conflict resolution programs" teach about mediation, negotiation, and communication skills. "Violence prevention programs" emphasize domestic violence, drug abuse, anger management, and teaching tolerance. "Development education" includes human rights education, environmental studies, and an emphasis on power and resource inequities and structural violence. "Nonviolence education" is based on the ideas of Gandhi, King, and other great peacemakers.

For "conflict resolution education," Tricia Jones differentiated between peace education, violence prevention, social and emotional learning, and anti-bias education. Clearly, there's much overlap between these categories, and there's no consensus about which category is most inclusive. But if our goal is developing peaceful people, we can use "peace education" as the most general category. All the programs mentioned here have potential for contributing to developing peaceful people. While programs for violence prevention, social and emotional learning, and conflict resolution education tend to focus rather exclusively on interpersonal conflict, instruction should explicitly make appropriate generalizations of basic principles across levels from interpersonal to international. Global peace education is often in Social Studies or History, but "peace education" more generally can be incorporated into most subjects.

Promoting Peace Education

Although the concept *peace education* may be useful in our thinking and strategizing as peace workers, it's not necessarily the best vocabulary to use to promote peace education in schools. To many conservatives, the concept is associated with political movements and liberal ideologies that oppose military spending, maintenance of a strong national defense, and military actions. If conservatives see our efforts as part of a grand strategy for promoting a particular political agenda different from their own, they'll vigorously oppose us. School systems won't adopt the programs in those circumstances. Therefore, we'll be more effective if we use a more politically neutral vocabulary — *violence prevention, social and emotional learning, conflict resolution education,* and *global security programs.*

There are four primary ways to promote peace education. First, encourage teachers to teach about conflict, violence, and peace within existing courses; and provide them with resources for doing so. Second, encourage school administrators and school board members to adopt programs, providing them with information about programs and how to select and implement them. Third, promote legislation in your state to mandate programs in public schools. Fourth, support peace education organizations.

The distinction between encouraging and helping teachers vs. persuading schools to adopt programs is important. The possibility of institutionalizing peace education by implementing programs implies a more permanent type of change that may affect most students within the system. When new programs are designed to be comprehensive, age appropriate instruction occurs across grade levels, so basic concepts are repeated and elaborated in increasingly complex ways as children progress through the grades. Just as important, the adoption by school officials legitimizes peace education activities. Without an approved program, teachers are likely to see peace education activities as taking valuable time from teaching required subjects. Because students are evaluated by standardized tests on required subjects and teachers may be rewarded according to students' performance, the system motivates teachers to use the available time on required subjects. Still, both strategies — whole systems and individual teachers — can contribute to developing peaceful people, so both should be pursued.

Influencing Teachers to be Peace Educators

Resources for preschool through high school

Even without changes in the basic curriculum, teachers may use information, concepts, and activities with peace and conflict issues to learn required objectives — say, in reading, writing, and critical thinking. "Infusing" concepts into existing courses may be the easiest way to promote peace education; Ian Harris and Mary Lee Morrison offer examples of how.[10] You could encourage teachers you know personally to use such opportunities and provide them with information about teaching manuals and websites that describe activities and lesson plans. While a professor in a teacher-training program would be in an excellent position to do this, any citizen can make an appointment with a teacher or a professor in a teacher-training program to talk about peace education resources.

Educators for Social Responsibility (ESR) is one of the best sources for peace education manuals and has suggestions, lessons, and activities. The ESR Store on the group's website at www.esrnational.org describes and sells many teaching resources organized by grade levels. The website includes an Online Teacher Center with free teaching resources on issues of international security, conflict resolution, peacemaking, violence prevention, and social responsibility. Resources are organized in levels from early childhood to high school. A free E-Newsletter is available. Other websites also offer free teaching materials:

The Ohio Commission on Dispute Resolution and Conflict Management: http://www.disputeresolution.ohio.gov/schools/resourcescm.htm#cur

The Southern Poverty Law Center Teaching Tolerance Program: http://www.tolerance.org/teach/activities/index.jsp

The United States Institute of Peace: http://www.usip.org/class/index.html

The Hague Appeal for Peace (Click Learning to Abolish War, Book 2): http://www.haguepeace.org/index.php?action=resources

Heifer International Read to Feed Program: http://www.rcadtofccd.org/for_teachers_leaders_and_parents

Resources for college teachers

College professors have considerably more freedom regarding the content of their courses. They sometimes also can create new courses with open-ended titles like "Special Topics." If you're acquainted with college teachers who might be interested in contributing to the development of peaceful people, you could discuss this with them and call their attention to available resources.

Although some disciplines may be more relevant to peace education than others, every department probably has something important to contribute to the development of peaceful people. As my own discipline is psychology, I'm more knowledgeable about resources in that field and I coauthored an article of suggestions for various psychology courses.[11] While the following resources are slanted toward psychology, many are also relevant to other disciplines.

Professors can investigate whether there are organizations that address issues relevant to their particular discipline or committees that do so within their professional organizations. For example, the Union of Concerned Scientists (www.ucsusa.org) publishes materials useful to physical or biological science courses. The United States Institute of Peace (www.usip.org) publishes materials useful for political science courses. Psychologists for Social Responsibility (www.psysr.org) has materials for psychology courses. Within the American Psychological Association, there's a division called the Society for the Study of Peace, Conflict, and Violence (www.webster.edu/peacepsychology)

with teaching materials on its website. One of its committees, the Peace and Education Working Group, uses a listserv to share information about peace education at all levels with anyone requesting to join the list (contact me at llnelson@calpoly.edu to be added).

CRInfo (www.crinfo.org) is a free, online clearinghouse, indexing more than 25,000 peace- and conflict resolution-related web pages, books, articles, audiovisual materials, etc. It provides easy browsing on 600 peace- and conflict resolution-related topics. For online syllabi on conflict resolution and related topics (over eighty of them), information about textbooks, and other information for instructors developing conflict studies courses, go to www.campus-adr.org. Click on "Classroom Building" or "Faculty Club."

The Office of Teaching Resources in Psychology at www.lemoyne.edu/OTRP/teachingresources.html#diversity has "Psychology of Mass Violence: Instructional Resources," "Psychology of Mass Violence: War, Ethnopolitical Conflict, Terrorism, and Peace: Informational Resources," and "Psychology of Mass Violence: Genocide, Torture, and Human Rights: Informational Resources." Social Psychology Network includes a good collection of website links on peace psychology at www.socialpsychology.org/peace.htm and a comprehensive list of links on violence, conflict, negotiation, and peace at www.socialpsychology.org/social.htm#violence. The INCORE Guide to Internet Sources on Psychology and Conflict, www.incore.ulst.ac.uk/cds/themes/psyc.html, has online articles and much more.

There are textbooks for teaching about conflict resolution[12,13] peace studies [14], and peace psychology.[15,16] These journals are particularly useful: *Bulletin of the Atomic Scientists*, *Conflict Resolution Quarterly*, *Journal of Conflict Resolution*, *Peace and Conflict: Journal of Peace Psychology*, *Political Psychology*, and the *Journal of Peace Education* (first published in March 2004).

Influencing School Systems to Adopt Peace Education Programs

One of the most effective actions to promote peace education is to talk to members of your local school board or administrators in your school district. You might ask whether your schools have programs for conflict resolution education, violence prevention, or social and emotional learning. This could lead to discussing the benefits of such programs and possibilities for implementing or improving them in your schools. It might be particularly effective to approach school officials as a small group of like-minded citizens who've prepared themselves to discuss this or perhaps as representatives of a parent-teacher association. Ideally, follow up after a few weeks to inquire about any actions the school official has taken or might be willing to consider.

The peace education committees of Psychologists for Social Responsibility and the Society for the Study of Peace, Conflict, and Violence have collaborated in developing a brochure to inform school officials about the benefits of conflict resolution education, violence prevention, and social and emotional learning programs. The "Every Child, Every Day" brochure lists demonstrated benefits, with relevant research studies, and provides websites that describe programs shown to be effective. "Every Child, Every Day" brochures may be ordered from Psychologists for Social Responsibility by email (psysr@psysr.org) or by phone (202-543-5347). The websites are useful for selecting a program appropriate to a school's particular needs, with links to information about implementation and training. These sites are:

Blueprints for Violence Prevention:
   http://www.colorado.edu/cspv/blueprints
Collaborative for Academic, Social, and Emotional Learning:
   http://www.casel.org/about_sel/SELprograms.php
Virginia Best Practices in School-based Violence Prevention:
   http://www.pubinfo.vcu.edu/vabp

In a recent review of research, Tricia Jones reported that conflict resolution education programs increase academic achievement, positive attitudes toward school, cooperation, communication skills, constructive conflict behaviors, healthy interpersonal and intergroup relations, and self-control. They decrease aggressiveness, dropout rates, and discipline referrals and suspensions. Jones concluded, ". . . the research clearly demonstrates that CRE [Conflict Resolution Education] approaches yield impressive results.... Evidence for the efficacy of basic SEL [Social and Emotional Learning] programs and general conflict resolution programs is clear."[17]

School officials are likely to be particularly interested in evidence showing that CRE and SEL programs create conditions that promote academic learning. This evidence is described in a recent book, *Building Academic Success on Social and Emotional Learning: What Does the Research Show.*[18] In the first chapter, the editors state "there is a growing body of scientifically based research supporting the strong impact that enhanced social and emotional behaviors can have on success in school and ultimately in life." This chapter is available online at www.casel.org. Many books inspire interest and give general information.[19,20,21]

Promoting Legislation for Peace Education Programs

Some states, including Ohio, Oregon, New Mexico, and Indiana, have made significant progress in implementing statewide programs for conflict resolution education. The Ohio Commission on Dispute Resolution and Conflict Management (www.disputeresolution.ohio.gov) was established by the General Assembly in 1989 to provide conflict management resources to Ohio schools, colleges, universities, courts, communities, and state and local government. The commission has promoted programs through grants, training, and resource development with the goal of institutionalizing conflict resolution education into the daily operations of the schools. Programs are linked to state curriculum standards and the Ohio Graduation Tests.

Illinois provides a good example of legislation for social and emotional learning programs. In 2003 the Illinois legislature passed the *Children's Mental Health Act.* Section 15(b) states, "Every Illinois school district shall develop a policy for incorporating social and emotional development into the district's educational program." Also, the Illinois State Board of Education was directed to incorporate social and emotional development standards as part of the Illinois Learning Standards for assessing academic success. The connection between "social emotional learning" and peace education is clear in the standards: identify and manage one's emotions and behavior, recognize feelings and perspectives of others, recognize individual and group similarities and differences, use communication and social skills to interact effectively with others, and demonstrate an ability to prevent, manage, and resolve interpersonal conflicts constructively. The full description is at www.isbe.net/il/social_emotional/standards.htm.

Information about legislation in each state is at www.disputeresolution.ohio.gov/legislationscm.htm. For information about legislation throughout the world, go to: www.disputeresolution. ohio.gov/crecountry.htm.

To effectively promote new legislation, you'll need to work closely with legislators who support your objectives and you may need to form a coalition with other groups interested in improving the quality of educational programs in your state. You may also need the help of organizations that have experience working for peace education legislation such as the Collaborative for Academic, Social, and Emotional Learning (www.casel.org) and the Ohio Commission on Dispute Resolution and Conflict Management (www.disputeresolution.ohio.gov).

Supporting Peace Education Organizations

One way to promote peace education is to join and support peace education organizations, for example:

- Association for Conflict Resolution (www.acresolution. org)
- Educators for Social Responsibility (www.esrnational. org)
- Heifer International Read to Feed Program (www. readtofeed.org/for_teachers_leaders_and_parents)
- Psychologists for Social Responsibility (www.psysr.org)
- Southern Poverty Law Center Teaching Tolerance Program (www.tolerance.org)

Conclusion

If we wish to live in a peaceful world, we must concern ourselves with developing peaceful people. Peace education refers to all efforts to facilitate development of peaceful people. There are at least four ways to promote it: encouraging teachers to teach about conflict, violence, and peace; encouraging school administrators and school board members to adopt peace education programs; promoting legislation to mandate peace education programs in public schools; and supporting peace education organizations.

References

1. Nelson, L. L., Van Slyck, M. R., & Cardella, L. A. (1999). Peace and conflict curricula for adolescents. In L. Forcey & I. Harris (Eds.), *Peacebuilding for adolescents: Strategies for educators and community leaders* (pp. 91–117). New York: Peter Lang.

2. Nelson, L. L., & Milburn, T. W. (1999). Relationships between problem-solving competencies and militaristic attitudes: Implications for peace education. *Peace and Conflict: Journal of Peace Psychology, 5*, 149–168.

3. Braithwaite, V. (1994). Beyond Rokeach's Equality-Freedom Model: Two-dimensional values in a one-dimensional world. *Journal of Social Issues, 50*, 67–94.

4. Astin, A. W. (1992). *What matters in college? Four critical years revisited.* San Francisco: Jossey-Bass.

5. Fiske, S. (1992). People's reactions to nuclear war: Implications for psychologists. In S. Staub & P. Green (Eds.), *Psychology and social responsibility: Facing Global Challenges* (pp. 305–326). New York: University Press.

6. McKenzie-Mohr, D. (1992). Understanding the psychology of global activism. In S. Staub & P. Green (Eds.), *Psychology and social responsibility: facing global challenges* (pp. 327–342). New York: University Press.

7. MacNair, R. M. (2004). *History shows: Winning with nonviolent action.* Philadelphia: Xlibris.

8. Stevahn, L., Johnson, D. W., Johnson, R. T., & Real, D. (1996). The impact of a cooperative or individualistic context on the effectiveness of conflict resolution training. *American Educational Research Journal, 33*, 801–823.

9. Harris, I. M. (1999). Types of peace education. In A. Raviv, L. Oppenheimer, & D. Bar-Tal (Eds.), *How children understand war and peace: A call for international peace education* (pp. 299–317). San Francisco: Jossey-Bass.

10. Harris, I. M., & Morrison, M. L. (2003). *Peace education* (2nd ed.). Jefferson, NC: McFarland & Company. pp. 106-109.

11. Nelson, L. L., & Christie, D. J. (1995). Peace in the psychology curriculum: Moving from assimilation to accommodation. *Peace and Conflict: Journal of Peace Psychology, 1*, 161–178.

12. Folger, J. P., Poole, M. S., & Stutman, R. K. (2005). *Working through conflict: Strategies for relationships, groups, and organizations* (5th ed.). Boston: Pearson Education.

13. Pruitt, D. G., & Kim, S. H. (2004). *Social conflict: Escalation, stalemate, and settlement* (3rd ed.). Boston: McGraw-Hill.

14. Barash, D. P., & Webel, C. P. (2002). *Peace and conflict studies.* Thousand Oaks, CA: SAGE Publications.

15. Christie, D. J., Wagner, R. V., & Winter, D. D. (Eds.). (2001). *Peace, conflict, and violence: Peace psychology for the 21st Century.* Upper Saddle River, NJ: Prentice-Hall.

16. MacNair, R. M. (2003). *The psychology of peace: An introduction.* Westport, CT: Praeger.

17. Jones, T. S. (2004). Conflict resolution education: The field, the findings, and

the future. *Conflict Resolution Quarterly,* 22(1–2), 233–267. p. 257.
18. Zins, J., Weissberg, R., Wang, M., & Walberg, H. J. (Eds.). (2004). *Building academic success on social and emotional learning: What does the research say?* New York: Teachers College Press. p. 19.
19. Bodine, R. J., & Crawford, D. K. (1998). *The handbook of conflict resolution education: A guide to building quality programs in schools.* San Francisco: Jossey-Bass.
20. Jones, T. S., & Compton, R. (Eds.). (2003). *Kids working it out: Stories and strategies for making peace in our schools.* San Francisco: Jossey-Bass.
21. Lantieri, L., & Patti, J. (1996). *Waging peace in our schools.* Boston: Beacon Press.

PARENTING FOR PEACE

Rita Sommers-Flanagan and John Sommers-Flanagan

Decades ago, Graham Nash wrote, in the lyrics to the song, "Teach your Children," that all of us traveling on the road of life need "a code that you can live by."[1] If you're reading this book, we assume that the "code" you live by and the code you want your children to live by involves peace activism.

Glancing back through history and given the current wars and violence, it's highly likely peacekeeping will remain an essential activity for a long time to come. Therefore, we not only have the challenging task of working for peace now, but also an obligation to raise our children with the foundation necessary for peacemaking and -keeping in the future. This doesn't mean parents have permission to force children into their own image — and besides, many children eventually rebel against overly controlling parents anyway. But to be honest, it's normal and natural for parents to try to pass their values on to the next generation.

In this chapter, we draw on our experience as parent educators, psychologists, and the humbling, challenging, and gratifying experience of being parents ourselves. Our goal is to help you imagine how you might, in a gentle and positive manner, raise children who'll grow to love peace and continue your social justice and peace activism work.

[Editor's note: This chapter covers parenting as a specialized form of outreach, with children as a specialized audience. Chapter 7 covers parenting as a part of a peaceful home.]

Creating Peaceful and Healthy Parent-Child Relationships

Peace has everything to do with establishing and maintaining healthy egalitarian relationships. Consequently, we begin with a brief review of a model for developing positive parent-child relationships.

Carl Rogers is the eminent psychologist who believed emotional healing and human learning occurs best in a "certain type of relationship." Rogers stated:[2]

If I can provide a certain type of relationship, the other person will discover within himself [or herself] the capacity to use that relationship for growth, and change and personal development will occur.

Presently, overwhelming evidence supports Rogers's claim that relationships ease emotional healing and learning.[3] On specific attitudes that get the best healing and learning, he stated:[4]

. . . the relationship which I have found helpful is characterized by a sort of transparency on my part, in which my real feelings are evident; by an acceptance of this other person as a separate person with value in his [her] own right; and by a deep empathic understanding which enables me to see his [her] private world through his [her] eyes.

Formally, Rogers's three crucial attitudes are referred to as:

- Congruence
- Unconditional Positive Regard
- Accurate Empathy

Below, we describe these, add a fourth component crucial to parenting, and provide a parenting self-statement to help you enact these attitudes.

Congruence

Children need to see and experience their parents' genuine feelings and values. They need parents who can express love and affection as well as disappointment and even anger. In addition, as a parent you should try to live congruent, authentic lives, in and out of the home. You can't hit or harm or neglect your children and preach nonviolence and respect on the street. You can't lie to your children while promoting honesty.

As with each of these parental attitudes, it's impossible to experience and express congruence perfectly. It's also possible to overuse congruence in an attempt to give children ongoing feedback. Your parental goal should be for your child to regularly, but not constantly, experience and understand your feelings and reactions toward them. After all, you probably want your child to glimpse how his/her behavior affects you, but not for him/her to constantly be focusing on how you feel and what you want or need. We'll expand on this point later.

Unconditional Positive Regard

Rogers was very clear that children learn and grow best when their parents like them, accept them as they are, and warmly respect them as a person of unconditional worth. Unfortunately, as parents and realists, we know children don't always behave in ways that evoke warm and positive feelings from their parents. Instead, those independent little rascals often *will not* follow your guidance, absorb your values, and become peace activist clones. They need to find their own way, say outlandish things, and try on different points of view — many of which may be at odds with your values and expectations.

Maintaining unconditional positive regard for children is a huge challenge. You'll undoubtedly fail occasionally. The key is to keep trying to express acceptance and respect for your child's unique thoughts and feelings. If you love music and hate sports and your child loves sports and hates music, you may struggle with accepting his or her preference. Similarly, if you're a proud academic and your child does poorly in school, it will be hard to express unconditional positive regard. The point is for you to treasure your child as a separate individual more than you value your personal preferences and values. You should also strive to value your child more than you value his or her performance or achievements.

We should emphasize that although your goal is to accept your child's thoughts and feelings, it's not healthy to accept all of his or her behaviors. In a recent interview with Natalie Rogers (Carl's daughter, who's now approaching eighty years old and is a renowned therapist herself), she articulated an important distinction between feelings and behaviors:[5]

> . . . in terms of Carl's theories about education, I remember hearing him talk and audiences asking about permissiveness and freedom, but I think the permissiveness often has been misunderstood. He

said that any thoughts and feelings are okay, but not all behavior is acceptable. Unless that is really made clear, both in the theory and in the practice, it can be disastrous.

Accurate Empathy

For children to develop their full potential as human beings, they need to be understood. Even as tiny babies, children need parents who tune into their emotions and mirror them back accurately. Helping children handle their anger and disappointment is essential for the development of peacekeeping adults. Having a parent respond empathically rather than judgmentally is the bedrock of beginning to develop internal acceptance and self-control.

Tuning in to your children's feelings is relatively easy when you and your children agree. But if your child's angry with you or in the midst of a wild tantrum, the difficulty of accurate empathy multiplies. The key is to remember you can simultaneously express empathy by making an accurate emotional reflection ("You sound mad") while at the same time setting limits on behavior.

The Fourth Parental Foundation: Limit Setting

Parents are well advised to maintain their position of authority. Extensive research shows that children develop ideally when their parents are not too permissive (the jellyfish parent) or too authoritarian (the brick wall parent).[6] Instead, the best approach is for you to set firm limits and deliver reasonable consequences when your child misbehaves. Parenting experts agree that children are not ready-made adults; they need guidance and limits. In particular, when you set reasonable limits with fair and consistent consequences, you're helping your child internalize self-discipline, a sense of right and wrong, tolerance, compassion, and generosity.

After learning about Rogers's three idyllic attitudes, parents often complain it's impossible to be congruent, have unconditional positive regard, and have accurate empathy all the time. They rightly complain parents shouldn't be too permissive. In fact, research shows children raised without adults who set behavioral limits turn out to be impulsive, have lower self-esteem, and are emotionally unhealthy adults.[7]

The key to having a home environment conducive to learning and emotional growth is to remember to practice all things in moderation, including Rogers's core conditions. You shouldn't be a perfect parent — there are theories of child development emphasizing that children actually grow up more psychologically healthy if they have fallible parents who make mistakes (and correct themselves) from time to time.[8] Realistically, the following self-statements serve as a good guide for peace activist parents:

- I will be emotionally honest without burdening my children.
- I will respect my children's right to have their own opinions, thoughts, and feelings.
- I will do my best to tune in to my children's emotions as often as is realistic.
- I will set limits on my children's behavior, realizing that respect for their feelings and thoughts is much different than permissiveness for their behaviors.

Teaching Family Values

Experts agree that parents are their children's first and most influential teachers. As a parent, you teach your children directly and indirectly. Many parents begin teaching their children lessons about nonviolence even before age one. If, in response to your child's natural aggressive behaviors (biting, hitting, or kicking), you say something like, "No! I know you're mad, but you need to stop hitting. In our family we don't hit or hurt others," you're directly setting a limit, showing empathy, and teaching your child to contain his or her aggressive impulses. Similarly, if you demonstrate values of peace and respect by living your daily life without violence, without hitting, and by modeling respectful communication with others, you're showing your child how to act peacefully and respectfully.

Sometimes parents teach their children lessons about life in deliberate and intentional ways. Other times the teaching is accidental or completely outside your awareness. In fact, the lessons that last the longest are often the ones you may have been unaware of teaching. Remember how much more interesting it was to overhear something adults were saying than to sit in the middle of their conversations? Children learn by instruction, modeling, example, and a kind of kid radar that picks up, scrutinizes, and either absorbs or rejects their parents' values — the deliberately expressed values as well as those expressed accidentally. The decision about whether to absorb or reject parental values is related to the quality of the relationship between parent and child.

A Pinch of Moral Philosophy

Ethics and morality go far beyond rules and "being good" in that finger-shaking, shame-inducing "Now, you behave yourself" sort of way. Humans have been considering the best ways to live and to live in community for thousands of years. Early texts, such as the Hebrew *Torah* or the Hindu *Rig Gita*, used stories, customs, and laws to guide human relationships with each other, nature, and the sacred. Stories and traditional customs are time-tested strategies for instilling a sense of community and morality in the next generation.

Our sound bite culture has allowed political discourse to shrink the concept of morality into a tiny box. The simple truth is: It doesn't fit. Morality is complex as we attempt to live moral, peaceful lives ourselves and help our children do the same.

There are many ways to think of morality or the good life. One is virtue or character ethics. Aristotle wrote, "The moral virtues, then, are produced in us neither by nature nor against nature. Nature, indeed, prepares in us the ground for their reception, but their complete formation is the product of habit."[9] Aristotle believed becoming virtuous was part of the human blueprint. He wrote that the virtues were attributes that lie in the middle of human extremes — a concept he called the *golden mean*. Therefore, helping our children find a balance between timidity and foolhardiness will yield courageous children. Helping our children find the balance between giving away nothing and giving away too much will yield generous children. Helping our children (and ourselves) find the middle road between violence and weakness will hopefully yield peacemakers.

Another ethical orientation is duty ethics. Eighteenth-century German philosopher Immanuel Kant believed anyone capable of rational thought was accountable for doing his/her duty. He believed we could figure out our duty by following this guide: Would I be willing to have my action become the way everyone acted, at all times and in all places? Second, Kant sternly admonished that our moral duty was to never, ever treat other people as a means to an end but rather as ends in themselves. Parents especially need to remember this second duty. Our children are not a means to an end, in any sense. Practicing these duties and teaching children to live lives with a sense of global, universal duty is a tall parenting order!

Yet another perspective deals with consequences. John Stuart Mill, noted English economist and social theorist of the early nineteenth century, believed the moral way is the one that yields the greatest good for the greatest number. Mill believed the potential for an orientation toward pro-social goodness was inborn, a propensity that can be learned as readily as speech. However, it isn't always learned. This is obviously where parents come in! In contrast to a sense of absolute duty, consequentialists would help children assess how their actions might bring about as much good in the world as possible. Everyone is equal and deserves to be taken into account in any social policy or law.

We offer this brief overview for two reasons. First, it debunks the idea that morality is simple, judgmental, and/or unidimensional. The complexities involved in being moral should be wrestled with from childhood on. Second, those parenting adolescents might find an opening to talk about these and other ethical orientations with their argumentative teen — developmentally, adolescents are beginning to grapple with deep and central abstractions.[10]

Parenting Pointers for Peace

As you think about these strategies for raising peace activist children, try to identify the moral virtues and duties you would like most to instill and contemplate whether the values you want to teach will yield the greatest good.

Notice and Cultivate Your Children's Positive Values

There's an old truism in psychology: Whatever you pay attention to, will grow. It's very important for you, as a parent, to keep an eye out for when your child engages in virtuous, dutiful, or positive moral behavior and to and verbally or nonverbally acknowledge it. For example, if your child is generous and shares a toy with another child, simply state, "I noticed you shared your favorite toy with Melissa." When noticing these positive behaviors, avoid always giving praise or a judgment. Although it's fine to use praise sparingly, too much praise will cause your child to look to you for approval and he/she may not learn to discern his/her own positive and negative behaviors.

Give Character Feedback

As parents, often we naturally focus on our children's negative behaviors. For example, when you notice your child being aggressive, you might say something like, "You need to learn to keep your hands to yourself" or "You're always so mean to Juan when he comes over." Unfortunately, if your child is listening to you, it won't be long before he or she begins to believe the message, "I have trouble keeping my hands to myself" or "I'm the kind of person who is mean to my friends." In other words, over time, your child will begin to think of himself or herself as having a particular negative personal trait.

The trick is for parents to do three things: (a) pay more attention to positive behaviors, (b) specify behaviors (and not traits) when talking about negative behaviors (e.g., you hit Juan and even though you were mad, that's not okay), and (c) identify positive traits your child is beginning to display. For example, even if your child is somewhat aggressive, wait until he or she is gentle and then say, "I noticed you're the kind of boy (girl) who can play nicely and gently with your friends."

Use Passionate Rewards and Boring Consequences

All too often, parents become animated and passionate when giving out consequences. If your teen misses curfew and comes home late, you can either yell and lecture or calmly and boringly give out a negative consequence ("Oops, I guess because you got home late you'll have to stay in tomorrow night and scoop the poop in the back yard"). Interestingly, many teenagers tell us they actually feel powerful and fulfilled when their parents yell; they like to see their parents' veins bulge and pulsate. The point is that when you pay intense attention to your child in response to a negative behavior, you're actually rewarding the negative behavior. Therefore, it's crucial to concentrate on becoming animated when your children behave in appropriate ways and boring when they misbehave or break a family agreement.

Get Curious, Not Furious

Inevitably your child will behave in ways that push your buttons. One way to stop yourself from popping your cork is to practice the mantra, "Get curious, not furious." Generally speaking, when children misbehave, they do so because of physical reasons or psychological purposes.[11] The physical reasons include being hungry, tired, or having physical discomfort or pain. Therefore, if your child is behaving poorly, first consider whether these physical causes can be addressed. The psychological purposes of misbehavior include attention seeking, power and control seeking, revenge seeking, or a display of inadequacy. Again, if your child misbehaves it's more productive to become curious about the causes and address them directly than to immediately react with anger.

Problem Solve with Your Child

Children are natural problem solvers and you can help them improve on these important skills by simply asking them problem-solving or solution-oriented questions.[11] These questions include things like: "How did you manage to stay calm when the teacher gave you that detention?", "What strategy did you use to get that puzzle together so quickly?", "What were you thinking the other day when you got yourself out of your bad mood and into a good one?" As you can see, these questions help children focus on how they successfully accomplished something — as opposed to the more negative and typical parental response of "What in the *#@ were you thinking when you carved your initials on the school bus seat?"

Conclusion

Our overall message is that it's possible to teach your children well — to teach them the attitudes and skills needed to become moral people, whether that takes the form of peace activism or some other productive contribution to society. This teaching comes about best if you do three things:

1. Focus on developing a positive relationship with your child.
2. Become conscious of the moral values you want to teach your child and practice them yourselves.
3. Use positive strategies to nurture and cultivate your child's naturally evolving moral behaviors.

You may have noticed that the approaches we recommend are positive and noncoercive. As peace activist parents, it's important to plant the seeds of nonviolence in our children while avoiding negative or coercive parenting practices. We wish you all the best in your efforts to be an excellent parent.

References

1. Nash, G. (1994) *Teach your children* [Recorded by Crosby, Stills, Nash and Young]. Deja vu: Atlantic: WEA.
2. Rogers, C. R. (1961). *On becoming a person*. Boston: Houghton Mifflin. p. 33.
3. See: Norcross, J. C. (Ed.). (2002). *Psychotherapy relationships that work*. New York: Oxford University Press; Hubble, M. A., Duncan, B. L., & Miller, S. D. (Eds.). (1999). *The heart and soul of change*. Washington, D.C.: American Psychological Association; and Duncan, B. L., & Miller, S. D. (2000). *The heroic client: Doing client-centered, outcome-informed therapy*. San Francisco: Jossey-Bass.
4. Rogers, *op. cit.*, p. 34.
5. Sommers-Flanagan, J. (In press). The development and evolution of person-centered expressive art therapy: A conversation with Natalie Rogers. *Journal of Counseling & Development*.
6. Gershoff, E. T. (2002). Corporal punishment by parents and associated child behaviors and experiences: A meta-analytic and theoretical review. *Psychological Bulletin, 128*(4), 539–579.
7. See: Gershoff [note 5]; and Baumrind, D. (1971). Current patterns of parental authority. *Developmental Psychology Monographs, 4*, 1–103.
8. Kohut, H. H. (1971). *The analysis of self*. New York: International Universities Press.
9. Irwin, T. (1985). *Aristotle: Nicomachean ethics*. Indianapolis, IN: Hackett. p. 34.
10. For more information on the ethical orientations, see the extensive website from Laurence Hinman at the University of San Diego: http://ethics.acusd.edu/LMH/editor.html
11. Dreikurs, R. (1948). *The challenge of parenthood*. New York: Hawthorne.
12. Bertolino, B. (1999). *Therapy with troubled teenagers: Rewriting young lives in progress*. New York: John Wiley & Sons.

REGRETS, REALIZATIONS, AND RESOLUTIONS OF AN ONLINE ACTIVIST

Scot Evans

Hello, my name is Scot and I have a confession to make. I feel guilty about calling myself a social activist when lately there's rarely any *social* in my activism. Yeah, sure, I've attended a few anti-war rallies and marches, and I've marched in support of state-funded health care for the poor, but lately most of my activism is done through the click of mouse, from the safety of my desk chair, alone in a dark room deep beneath the surface of the earth. Ok, that last part is not true, but you get the point: most of my activism is solitary action done through email or the web. I rarely leave my seat to make my voice heard. Even today, as a large group of individuals who are slated to be removed from our state health care rolls are in day twenty-four of their sit-in in the governor's office, I'm in my seat in front of my computer. And I'm worried.

I'm worried about three things. First, I'm not sure if I'm making any difference. Second, is this the best way to make a difference? Last, how can I make optimal use of the available online resources for action and meaningful social change and avoid activism fatigue?

Just this morning, there are twenty-seven messages in my in-box asking me to: "Get the media to demand answers"; "Urge Your Senators to Support Renewable Energy"; "Boycott . . ." "Tell senators to vote no"; "Help toll the bell for thousands being cut from our state health care program"; "Join the No Spray Coalition"; "Come to Washington in September for a major weekend of protests"; and many more requests. And these are just from today! You should see yesterday's. Quite possibly, you're experiencing the same thing. Lately, this overload has created for me a feeling of "dissent dullness." Regardless, I'm poised for action . . . or at least poised to click.

Does It Make a Difference?

We know from the past that the Internet and electronic communications can be powerful tools for change. One example is the 1994 rebellion waged by Zapatista communities in Chiapas, Mexico.[1] The Zapatistas were able to get their messages out rapidly through local supporters who sent them out over the Internet to potentially receptive audiences around the world. As a result, they gained supporters in over forty countries. Communications analysts described it as an "electronic fabric of struggle." With electronic communication, they were effective in pulling together a grassroots movement against the current political and economic order in Mexico.

Another example of successful grassroots organizing through the web is efforts to block the Organization for Economic Cooperation and Development's (OCED) attempt to pass a Multilateral Agreement in Investment (MAI) without the knowledge of or input from many of the world's peoples. The temporary defeat of this agreement has been credited partly to groups who circulated information about the MAI and critiques of the content and undemocratic process.[2] The use of the Net by grassroots organizations to rally people against international organizations has stunned many groups like OCED, the World Bank, and the International Monetary Fund. Several multinational institutions have now developed strategies to either attempt to counter Internet activism or to use it to their advantage.

Other events around the world have demonstrated how the Internet can play a role in mobilizing people for action. In Beijing, 10,000 members of Falun Gong suddenly showed up for a protest outside the government leadership headquarters — due to virtual organizing. In Indonesia, student pro-democracy leaders who were linked by the web mounted mass protests that eroded then President Suharto's authority and sped his ouster.[3] In the United States, online activism plays a role in elections: in 2004, eleven percent of U.S. Internet users, or more than thirteen million people, went online for donating money, volunteering, or learning about political events to attend.[4] There were innovative strategies to connect local people through the house parties phenomenon, swing state phone banks and neighborhood walks were organized online, and volunteers received direction from campaigns without lifting their fingers from their keyboards. There are numerous examples from around the world that illustrate the power of the Internet in helping organize for action.

There have been a few instances where I felt my contributions to change by the Internet were moderately successful. I've participated in many online action campaigns spearheaded by the U.S. group MoveOn.org. They've been very effective in relating successes back to the people who participate in actions. Taking part in their online campaigns has contributed to stopping a House proposal to take away overtime pay from six million Americans and helped restore some of the budget cuts made to National Public Radio (NPR) and the Public Broadcasting System (PBS). During the NPR and PBS campaign, MoveOn.org reports that members sent in more than one million online generated comments.

The "ONE Campaign to Make Poverty History," driven by a large partnership of international nongovernmental aid organizations, has marched dramatically onto the global activism scene. It has recruited support from big-name celebrities such as Bono, Elton John, Cameron Diaz, Brad Pitt, and a crowd of other good-looking people. It has influenced leaders of the Group of Eight (G8) meeting at the G8 Summit to get real financial commitment in fighting the crisis of extreme poverty and global AIDS. I and 1.4 million other Americans joined the campaign, and ONE suggests these efforts helped result in pledges by G8 leaders to provide an additional $25 billion in development assistance for the emergency in Africa as part of an additional $50 billion globally by 2010. Hey, if it's good enough for Brad Pitt, it's good enough for me.

There is also an encouraging trend lately in the field of psychology. Groups within the American Psychological Association (APA) and affiliated with psychology are using the Internet to make calls for action. Some is directed at APA itself. Consider a call by the Society for the Study of Peace, Conflict, and Violence: Peace Psychology (Division 48 of the APA) reacting to APA's soft stance on the role of psychologists in interrogations and torture at U.S. prisons in Guantanamo Bay, Cuba. It called on psychologists to demand that APA issue a clear statement against the direct or indirect involvement of psychologists in using inhumane, degrading, or coercive interrogations and the use of torture either physical or mental in interrogation of prisoners.

Psychologists for Social Responsibility (PsySR) has long maintained a presence on the Internet and has served as a resource destination for psychologists who want to get involved in social and political issues. It also maintains several email lists for a variety of action committees. In 2003, in an informal partnership with PsySR, we started Psychologists Acting with Conscience Together (PsyACT) to further facilitate action on social issues that affect the well-being of individuals and communities. Although the experiment has only achieved moderate success, dialogs at psychology-related conferences demonstrate that PsyACT can be a valuable resource for action. The site (www.psyact.org) has a page on "Everyday Activism" to share ideas on how to live our values by being an activist through our everyday actions (through purchase choices, conserving energy, choice of career, etc.).

Online activism is potentially effective by bringing large numbers of imaginative people into a collective endeavor where their joint efforts can challenge power. Lately, email and web pages have been cited by protagonists on all sides of the political spectrum as playing key roles. Mostly, they play the role of finding otherwise hard-to-obtain information and circulating it widely. Through sharing information that the mainstream media mostly ignore or refuse to seek, groups organize resistance against abuses of power. These email lists and web pages constitute a kind of alternative, oppositional community of dialog and debate outside of and operating much more democratically than traditional policymaking institutions — institutions that for the most part are in business to maintain the status quo. While some might question the effectiveness of online activism in achieving outcomes, at a minimum, it's successful as a democratic process. At its core, online activism is democracy in action.

Is This the Best Way?

Most things that activists can do on the Internet, their opposition can also do, and with more money and force. It seems logical to recognize that no matter how useful the Internet — and for that matter all media — are to activists and advocates of social change, they are, and will always be, more useful to the defenders of current power structures.[5]

Cyberspace is a site of struggle, rather than a straightforward tool of liberation or domination.[6]

Obviously, online activism may not be the best way or only way to promote social change. For instance, while email protest and letter writing campaigns may clog the inboxes of decision makers, how are we to know these letters are really getting into the hands of those in power? What if there is an equal number of messages from groups on the other side of the issue? More than once I've felt a mild sense of futility when clicking through an organization's website to send a letter to my representatives. This is especially true in the current U.S. political climate, where ideology reigns over honest debate and deliberation. Thus the paradox: If we stop our email protests and letter writing, will the voice of the "other side" appear as shared public opinion?

Online activism faces many challenges. Among them, and perhaps most important, the very people who would most benefit from the information sharing and networking the Internet provides — the poor and dispossessed of developing nations — are largely excluded from its use. While many of us have minute-by-minute access to computers and networks, most who need to be participating or leading the charge on many issues have no regular access. This potentially creates another disempowering strategy for liberation that requires those with more power to advocate and act for those with less. Additionally, the technology is rooted in Western traditional values, and for those not familiar with these, they can marginalize and make people feel even more invisible.

Second, the ease of online activism for advocates risks turning activists into "click monkeys." This is how I've been feeling lately as I semi-blindly respond to email action requests by clicking through without really paying much attention to the substance of the issue. If it's from a group that I generally respect, I trust the issue is important enough to demand my "action." This uncritical response is devoid of the necessary deliberation and learning that's a part of the democratic process. Whereas the benefit of online activism is in its ability to inform debate and spur action, the risk of using this technology in activism lies in streamlining the process to such a point that it subdues outrage and passionate connection to the issues.

Last, online activism risks taking people away from physically working in communities in solidarity with others to effect change. This is a fast-paced world. We take on too much work and face a plethora of distractions in the form of material goods, media, and managing our stuff. Social action takes time, and anything that helps save us some time is welcomed and appreciated. So we move to electronic forms of action and stop attending rallies, community forums, group actions, and demonstrations. Our connection to the human and social components of social action is lost, and only the illusion of collective action is preserved. Imagine if the courageous African-American students who organized sit-ins at segregated lunch counters during the civil rights movement had resorted only to email campaigns or blogging. Maybe they would have avoided being arrested or beaten, but the dramatic demonstration of the injustice of the system would have been minimized.

How Can I Maximize the Web for Action?

How can we avoid the perils and maximize the web for social change? I'll highlight four important factors to help maximize:

1. Be selective.

If you're like me, you probably find it easy to sign up for numerous email action lists for progressive causes. As I've turned into a click monkey, I've decided to slim down my involvement and limit myself to those groups and issues I feel most passionate about. When we're talking about change, we're most likely to be engaged and effective when our heart is in it or when we have a personal stake. Find those groups that represent your deep convictions and get involved deeply. Focus on taking action on those issues where you feel outrage, where you know something must be done — by you.

2. Act on- and offline.

As mentioned earlier, one risk is the potential for the Internet to become our only means of taking action. We need to continue to get our hands dirty. We need to connect with others in the human struggle for justice, and not just through message-boards. The Internet can be a great way to organize for action only if you also respond to those local notices about meet-ups, actions, and other forms of physical protest. I've felt the most connected to my community and to the people in it during those moments when I was physically engaged with others in the democratic process. We need to think of our online communication and activism activities as a complement to our in-the-world civic participation. And that in-the-world action mostly happens locally.

3. Think globally, act everywhere.

One of the beauties of online activism is that you can join in social justice fights anywhere in the world. It's important that we join in solidarity with others around the globe to help make a difference. Building a worldwide collective voice against oppressive forces can be a powerful tool for change. Online movements against the Iraq war and efforts to raise awareness about the genocide in Darfur built international coalitions for change.

At the same time, we can be effective in many ways locally. PsyACT has realized the need to connect people locally and has encouraged people to set up local action teams. In many ways, this sums up the goal of online activism — connect people globally and mobilize them locally.

4. Help those directly affected.

Find ways to help those most affected by the issues you care about. Work with those disenfranchised individuals and groups to help them get their message out. As we work to increase access to and application of technology in activism, we challenge power dynamics. Make sure we make the community central to that process. Online activism can be a mysterious, foreign process, seen as something white, Western, and money dominated. We need to invite people into the process, not impose it upon them. Our most effective approach may be to find ways to work alongside disenfranchised individuals and groups to help them learn to use electronic means to take action for their own liberation.

Maybe there is a fifth, which is to use the Internet as a means of connecting with people who you also see in person. Email and websites are good ways of storing information and allowing everyone easy access to it, even if they're all members of a group you meet with regularly. You can also have a website that you direct people you meet (in person) to. It's fun and unifying to have a website as a group, even if it's largely in-house.

Conclusion

I'm simply one individual, like you, who realizes I need many tools to help others and to be an engaged citizen. The Internet is just one. The ability of the Internet to unite people around the world for a common cause is clear. It helps distribute information and knowledge, helps critically evaluate that information, and aids in organizing and mobilizing for action. If used wisely and alongside nonvirtual means, it can help develop our understanding of where power does reside. This understanding can be leveraged into support and resources for struggles wherever they may be. Now, to take my own advice and shed my monkey suit, I'm off to join the sit-in at the state capitol.

References

1. Harry Cleaver describes this in "The Chiapas Uprising and the Future of Class Struggle in the New World Order." This and other essays can be found on the web at: http://www.eco.utexas.edu/faculty/Cleaver/hmchtmlpapers.html
2. How the Net Killed the MAI. *Globe & Mail*, 29 April 1998; and Network Guerrillas. *Financial Times*, No. 109, Fall 1998.
3. Engardio, P. et al. Activists without Borders. *Business Week*, 10 April 1999, 14.
4. Pew Internet & American Life Project and the Pew Research Center for The People & The Press.
5. Meisner, M. (2000). e-Activism. (2000, Fall). *Alternatives Journal*, 26(4), 34.
6. Froehling, O. (1997, April). The Cyberspace: 'War of Ink and Internet' in Chiapas, Mexico. *Geographical Review*, 87(2), 291.

Suggested Readings
(Resources for Action)

MoveOn.org. http://MoveOn.org
NetAction. http://www.netaction.org/
ONE: The Campaign to Make Poverty History. http://www.one.org
Progressive Portal. http://www.progressiveportal.org/
Psychologists Acting with Conscience Together (PsyACT). http://www.psyact.org
Psychologists for Social Responsibility (PsySR). http://www.psysr.org
Society for Community Research and Action (Division 27, APA). http://www.scra27.org
Society for the Study of Peace, Conflict, and Violence: Peace Psychology (Division 48, APA). http://www.webster.edu/peacepsychology/

PART V
PEACEFUL PERSUASION
CHANGING ATTITUDES

They will beat their swords into plowshares and their spears into pruning hooks. Nation will not take up sword against nation, nor will they train for war anymore.

— Isaiah 2:4 and Micah 4:3

CREATING A PEACEFUL CLIMATE FOR PEACE WORK

Jo Young Switzer

During speeches or sermons on peace, many of us who are sympathetic to the peace position find ourselves thinking, "I sure wish the president (or my conservative friend Rick) could hear that!" Although we are quick to agree that communication problems are at the heart of many misunderstandings, most of us also focus on areas in which the *other* person needs to change.

Consider the persons with whom we are most likely to witness disagreements about peace issues:

- a church friend who thinks peace advocates are well meaning but much too idealistic to be taken seriously
- an articulate U.S. senator who contends that peace advocates, while they have a right to speak, do not have access to pertinent, classified information that would cause them to change their views
- a television evangelist who preaches acceptance of war because the Bible says there will always be wars
- a hard-working neighbor who thinks that peace advocates should "stop harping about peace and get jobs!"

When we discuss peace with these people, we can easily see their communication faults. This chapter won't tell how to change them. Instead it will discuss how we can improve ourselves. We cannot directly change the behaviors of others, but we can change our own.

Each of us needs to improve our own communication habits when we talk about any controversial or emotional issues, including peace. Effective communication is often defined as "shared meaning," a situation in which both parties have similar ideas of the message that has been spoken. When a State Department official clearly understands a reporter's question, we say they have communicated effectively, because they have shared meaning. Whether they agree with one another is not important in this definition because effective communication means they understand one another's message clearly.

The suggestions in this chapter are based on the assumption that we genuinely want to achieve more shared meaning, more effective communication. Those who adopt this "shared meaning" definition will work hard to ensure that their messages about peace issues are clear. Moreover, we need to listen to others' messages carefully in order to share meaning with them, even when we do not agree with them. In other words, we must work to change our own communication.

First, although the general tone of all interpersonal exchanges is affected by everyone involved, just one person in the dialog can make the communication climate more open. If a discussion about Israeli-Palestinian relations has become a shouting match, the climate can improve if even one of the parties begins to listen with an open mind.

Jack Gibb, a well-known researcher who studied small group communication, noted that most groups have primarily either "defensive" or "supportive" communication climates.[1] Defensive climates are those in which people feel threatened. Humans nearly always respond to perceived threat with self-protection, and whether the threat is real (a car pulling out unexpectedly in front of the moving car) or imagined (shadows in the bushes, which are spookier after we've seen an Alfred Hitchcock movie), we will work to protect ourselves. This self-protection makes sense when the perceived threats are physical, and it is less obvious when the threats are verbal.

What happens to communication when people feel defensive? A person who perceives a threat and puts up defenses against the threat is less likely to listen well, especially on controversial topics. As is often experienced in arguments with spouses or children, one may feel so heavily attacked verbally as to develop a verbal "battle plan" even while the other is talking. At the first pause for breath, the already well-rehearsed verbal attack is launched! This practice hurts communication effectiveness because time that could be spent on listening and comprehending is instead spent mentally developing one's own arguments. Poor listening and low comprehension will not help anyone speak openly with others about peaceful alternatives to violence.

What then can be done to improve dialog so that the communication can be as effective as possible? What can we do to create a "supportive" climate and make shared meaning possible?

Certain behaviors lead to openness, while others lead to defensiveness. We all need to develop skills for making the climate more trusting and more supportive.

Use Descriptive Words: Avoid Judging

One behavior that leads to more trust is using descriptive words and phrases rather than those that *evaluate* or *judge* another person. People like to hear their ideas and work responded to descriptively, and they feel threatened when people judge them.

A college student recently said to her mother, "I know you're sincere, but you are so gullible and naive to believe everything the president says." The mother naturally became defensive. What could the daughter have said to keep communication channels open? A better statement might have been: "I've read in several places that the president just reads a one page summary of the news each day. I think citizens should learn about issues more thoroughly than that and not assume that the president is always right." This statement leaves room for the mother to disagree and does not pass judgment on her for taking a "naive" position. No one likes to be called "gullible" or "naive."

One long-time advocate for peace publicly described a government leader as a "total idiot." While the professor clearly believes that his evaluation is accurate, the remark will make any person sympathetic toward the official feel more defensive. When such judgment occurs, the communication effectiveness decreases. Although most of us do not think we are judgmental toward others, we would do well to become more aware of our own comments to make sure we are not making judgmental remarks that might hurt communication if, indeed our goal is to communicate more effectively.

Be Open-Minded: Avoid Rigidity

Communication also improves when the parties are open minded, open to each others' views. An open-minded person is not wishy-washy but rather is willing to hear opposing arguments, even while staying strongly committed to a particular position. Being open minded is difficult for many peace movement people, especially those who are well read but who limit their reading to such peace position sources as *Sojourners* and *The Progressive*. Ironically, we want our opposition to follow sources other than *Fox News* or *U.S. News & World Report*. We will all benefit from reading a variety of sources, those with which we disagree as well as those with which we agree.

Reading only those sources with which one agrees tends to foster certainty, a rigid "I know what is right, don't confuse me with the facts," attitude. It is easier to identify this rigidity in those with whom we disagree than in ourselves. When faced with such rigidity, other people's defensiveness increases. When people state their opinions in a spirit of open-mindedness, full discussion is much likelier to occur — in part because people sense that their ideas will be heard, even by their opponents.

In a class at a college with an active peace studies program, a business major presented a well-researched, well-reasoned speech on the necessity of "balance of power" for worldwide nuclear stability. He used historical analogies and supported his views with good research. Two peace activists nearly hooted him from the room. Their criticisms of the speech were not based on what he had presented but on a knee-jerk response about peace and the craziness of balance of power arguments. These critics were rigid in their own views and did not give serious consideration to his. It was apparent that the speaker, a man who was moderate in his political positions, was defensive — so defensive, in fact, that I suspect he moved further away from the peace position because of the demeaning ridicule from its supporters.

Persons with a strong peace commitment need to be open to opposing views. If their ideas about peace are sound, alternative views will not threaten them. Moreover, we can grow by welcoming those views. We may decide to subscribe to journals that present an alternative view; we may read columnists who consistently support military build-up; we may occasionally find ideas within these and other "enemy" sources with which we can agree! Such openness will enable those with whom we talk to speak freely, knowing that they will be heard with an open mind.

Display Equality: Avoid Appearing Arrogant

People who treat others as equals produce trust in those with whom they communicate. Perhaps because the issue of peace is so vital to many, some who are long associated with the peace movement feel morally superior to the rest of "misguided" humanity. If other people detect that superior attitude, as they usually will, they may be put off by the arrogance. A sense of superiority may be expressed in different ways: sometimes it is a "know-it-all" attitude in discussions about the U.S. government and its involvement around the world; sometimes it is in-group jokes that exclude the nonpeace people present; sometimes it is use of a jargon that excludes others. The inverse of the golden rule seems good advice here: if you do not like people acting morally superior and arrogant toward you, you would do well not to act that way toward them.

Use Sensitive Language: Avoid "Hidden Antagonizers"

Language has considerable impact on communication effectiveness. All peace advocates who have been called "unpatriotic" know that certain words can hurt. Often, however, words operate with more subtlety; one writer refers to these words as "hidden antagonizers."[2] These are words or phrases that are not intended to hurt or exclude anyone but that, nevertheless, have that effect. The speaker means no harm, but the listener takes offense and becomes less open to the message. For example, many peace workers find themselves labeled "idealistic." While that label is not necessarily negative and the person using it may not intend to be critical, the phrase may still be a hidden antagonizer. Why? Because being called idealistic might suggest that the person is naive or uninformed, and thus easily disregarded. Peace workers also use words that hurt clear communication, words that can function as hidden antagonizers like "flag waver."

Emotional statements like "you wouldn't kill your own children, would you?" breed powerful defensiveness because of the implied judgment about the listener. While the speaker may intend to make a point rather than provoke anger, the overall effect still harms the quality of communication. What can you do to be more sensitive in using language?

- Avoid unnecessary use of abbreviations. Provide full names of agencies and weapons, assuming that not everyone is knowledgeable of the abbreviations.
- Avoid overly technical words; talk directly and clearly about the issues. If the aim is good communication then we need to adapt to our listeners.
- When you have a choice, use short words rather than long ones.
- Do all you can as speakers to keep the doors of communication open by careful language choice.

If the goal is to share ideas about peace with others, and not just to win the argument, then we must work hard to create a communication climate that allows good discussion. To do that, we need to reduce (or eliminate) judgment, rigidity, attitudes of superiority, and use of antagonizing language; and we need to increase our descriptiveness, open-mindedness, equality, and sensitive language (see the exercise below to practice this).

By making these skills more a part of our daily communication, we can work toward peace in our interpersonal relations. Then, messages about alternatives to violence can move into wider circles.

The Andy Murray song that says, "What can one person do is a very good question if you don't do nothing at all," lets us know that each step toward peace, whether in Afghanistan, Iraq, Sudan, or over our backyard fences, will help.

A Communication Exercise

In small groups, label the following statements as exhibiting judgment, rigidity, superiority, or hidden antagonizers. After doing that, rephrase them to be more descriptive, open minded, equal, or sensitive in language.

(a) "The Republican plan for moving tanks through the desert will never work."
(b) "Those Homeland Security planners are absolutely crazy if they think we can evacuate New York City to Syracuse!"

(c) "Joe's reasons for joining the Army are bizarre."

(d) (on the phone): "All right, Ms. Winter, I'll get the registration material in the mail today. Good-bye, honey."

(e) "You may think you understand the complexities of the terrorist problem, but I know when something is over your head."

(f) "Oh, Susan. You're so funny for thinking you can believe what the State Department says. Well, I guess that's a woman for you."

References

1. Gibb, J. (1961). Defensive communication. *Journal of Communication, 11,* 141–148.

2. Brooks, W. D., & Emmert, P. (1980). *Interpersonal communication* (2nd ed.). Dubuque, IA: Wm. C. Brown. (out of print)

Suggested Readings

Adler, R., Rosenfeld, L. B., & Proctor, R. (2004). *Interplay: The process of interpersonal communication* (9th ed.). New York: Holt, Rinehart, and Winston.

   This introductory interpersonal communication textbook devotes an entire chapter to communication climate, providing clear explanations and earthy personal examples of its application.

Stewart, J. (Ed.). (2001). *Bridges not walls* (8th ed.). Reading, MA: Addison-Wesley.

   This collection of readings adopts a humanistic viewpoint to interpersonal communication, and includes Gibb's original article (cited in the References above) as well as related articles and exercises.

PRINCIPLES OF OPINION CHANGE

Neil Wollman and John P. Keating

Get at the Reasons for Your Listeners' Beliefs

People hold beliefs for particular reasons, and you'll need to take this into account when you try to change those beliefs. Let's say you're talking to someone who feels the United States must be very aggressive in its dealings with any enemy. She might not state this directly, but it would emerge in her arguments concerning policies the United States should pursue, weapons it should produce, or tactics it should take. In this case, rather than initially discussing specifics of foreign policy, it would be better first to explore the underlying reason for those specific beliefs. Ask *why* the United States must be aggressive; after she gives her response ask, "Why?" again. Gently probe deeper into the person's attitudes. She'll be more open to talking about such matters if at the same time you reveal the underlying reasons for your own beliefs.

Assuming the circumstances allow you to probe your listener, figure out the apparent reason for her aggressive beliefs. Is it a desire to appear "strong?" Is it a well-reasoned view of the global situation? Is it a need to maintain a "good guy vs. bad guy" view of the world? If it's the last, try to satisfy a "good guy vs. bad guy" view with another perspective — for example, that the good guys are those working hard for peace and the bad guys are those pushing for more violence.

Admittedly, it's not always practical or possible to first explore underlying reasons for beliefs and then plan an appropriate and successful argument. However, if you have the time, energy, and desire, doing so could make a difference — especially if you will be talking to someone over a long period of time.

Don't Use Arguments Too Extreme for Your Audience

People judge new information and appeals in terms of how they already feel about a topic. Any argument that differs too much from their current beliefs will likely be rejected. If you know your listener believes every weapons system on the drawing board should be produced, don't push for stopping them all; he'll probably reject your proposal outright, and be even more rigid. Instead a more moderate appeal, perhaps suggesting that the United States not build a *particular* weapon, might be more effective.

It all depends on where your listeners are on the topic to begin with. Remember two things: don't decide on the arguments to use before you find out the person's attitude, and don't expect a major change from that attitude unless you plan on working to change that attitude gradually, over time.

Compare Benefits of Your Policies with Alternatives

Let your listeners know what they and our country will gain by adopting your policies rather than the alternatives. For instance, you might note that if we stopped building more weapons, each citizen would have more money, more could be spent on health care and other benefits, and we would be looked upon favorably by the world for our peacemaking efforts.

Arouse Fear under Certain Conditions

Arousing fear in an audience — perhaps regarding continuing nuclear threats or the possibility of a military draft — can be a very effective means of changing an attitude. Researchers have noted, however, that the danger must seem real and that audience members — even when fearful — won't adopt the proposed new attitude or behavior unless they feel doing so will counteract the feared outcome. If you use scare tactics, be sure also to present specific concrete actions your audience can do to help prevent the feared outcome. Presenting your audience with a list of peace activities they could engage in and discussing past successes of the peace movement can help people feel they can do things to work for peace. Without such options, your audience will remain threatened and will likely discount your message.

Use New Arguments

Good arguments that the audience hasn't heard are tremendous catalysts for persuasion. It's important, then, to remain up to date on peace issues and to introduce new information and arguments (or twists on arguments) within your same basic theme. When surveyed, people have expressed impatience over hearing what they consider to be repetitious arguments on both sides of a subject. Consequently, you should use novel approaches when presenting material and introduce recent findings.

Make Your Conclusions Obvious

Don't just present the facts, but also clearly draw the conclusions to your argument. All too often speakers believe if they clearly state the facts, the audience will draw the desired conclusions and decide on appropriate actions. Research shows this is true only when your audience is *highly* intelligent and the conclusion is *exceedingly* obvious.

Know Whether Peace Issues Are Important to Your Listeners

There's evidence that the more important an issue is to someone, the more she'll be affected by the quality of the arguments (if understood) than by "secondary" factors — those not related to the argument itself, but to aspects of the speaker, the listener, or the situation. Secondary factors (such as the similarity of the speaker or whether the discussion occurs in a pleasant setting) have more influence when the issue is less important to a listener. Also, as you might expect, a change of attitude brought on by arguments (rather than secondary factors) will last longer and influence behavior more.

These findings point out the value of knowing how important a topic is to your listeners before speaking to them. When you address a politically sophisticated audience, be aware that secondary factors like flashy language, good jokes, and neat appearance won't be particularly effective unless your political arguments are sound, and weak arguments can really damage your case. On the other hand, when you address people who are not highly motivated politically (a majority of our citizens), concern yourself more with those secondary factors. Research has even shown that for those who have little concern about a topic, the number of arguments presented may affect persuasion more than the strength of the arguments.

Create Good Moods, Bad Moods, and Word Associations

Research has shown that a person who happens to be in a good mood while listening to an argument will be more receptive to the message. You might employ this principle, for example, by serving food at some peace-oriented activity or by presenting peace literature at a county fair booth.

You can also apply this principle by linking your position or argument together with political or other ideas that listeners would likely feel good about. For example, associate your suggested policies with a popular past president, or say your position is "patriotic" or "morally right." Or you might use a political bumper sticker along with a heart warming, nonpolitical one ("Hugs are better than drugs").

Likewise, use ideas that associate bad feelings with a position you oppose. Link government policies with those leading to the Vietnam War, or refer to a government as a "bandit" when it "steals" money that could go to help needy people and uses it to make more weapons.

Similarly, use terms together regularly in various communications so that listeners will begin to think of one word when they hear the other. Words help shape the way we see the world and form opinions. Use them to your advantage.

Inconsistencies

Point out inconsistent government policies that your pro-military listener(s) may support. This will result in tension because the listener is made aware of holding beliefs that are not consistent. The more inconsistencies you can point out, the greater the discomfort (see also chapter 37).

Here is a wide-ranging list of inconsistent U.S. policies that you can use in your arguments: providing weapons to both sides of military conflicts (such as the Middle East), condemning human rights violations in some nations but excusing them in our allies, condemning a relatively few welfare cheaters while allowing weapons manufacturers to make millions in cost overruns, not allowing citizens to withhold that portion of their taxes going for military purposes while allowing many large profit-making companies to legally pay little or no tax at all. The inconsistencies go on and on; it's not hard to make a collection of them — they emerge with surprising regularity.

Take care in using this approach because it has the potential of making listeners feel stupid. Be gentle and make your statements in a way that your listeners know you're trying to inform them rather than show them up.

Once inconsistencies are clear, you should present specific new beliefs your listener could adopt to no longer support and believe in inconsistent policies. Accepting these new beliefs would relieve the tension.

It's important to present specific and sensible alternative beliefs about policies. Otherwise, your listeners may reduce the tension by rejecting or distorting the new information you've presented to them. They may do this anyway — to maintain their attitudes. The more deeply ingrained the attitudes, the less likely they'll accept new information.

If your listeners are to make a basic attitude change, they'll need to feel psychologically secure with the new beliefs you propose. If, say, you suggest the United States reduce its conventional or nuclear forces, be sure to present an alternative policy with which your listeners can feel safe (you might need to explore this during the course of the conversation). People will feel more secure if they don't see their attitude (or behavior) change as an abandoning of relatives and friends who share their political outlook. Try to convince your listeners that their relatives and friends, who are similarly concerned about world tensions, would likely find your arguments sensible as well.

Get Your Listeners to Do Something Small for Peace

Sometimes individuals don't form their opinions until they become fully aware of their own behavior. Someone may realize she's in love with another person only after becoming aware that she always gets excited around that person, spends a lot of time around the other, and often gets presents for the person. But why do we form opinions this way? Because we need to explain our behavior to ourselves. If we start taking certain actions, we feel it tells us something about what kind of person we are or what we believe in.

You can apply this principle by getting people to voluntarily make any statements or take any actions favorable to your cause.

After they do so and then become aware of their small support for peace, they'll begin to feel more favorable to the cause.

Try (in a noncoercive way) to get others involved in small activities favorable to peace: signing a petition, giving a small donation, reciting back to you some of your arguments, becoming involved in any activities at a peace group meeting, or publicly making or endorsing any statements favorable to promoting peace.

For example, at a presentation you might ask for a show of hands from people who believe that "peace is the first order of business for all countries." Or during a presentation to a pro-military audience, lead listeners through an exercise in which they imagine and describe the steps needed to peacefully resolve or lessen a particular world conflict. Ask members of the audience to consider on their own what specific actions are required to peacefully resolve or lessen the conflict. Then break the audience into small groups (or pairs if small groups are not feasible) to share their ideas.

Note that the above exercise can cause attitude change in two ways: it induces individuals to make statements favorable to peace, and it has those individuals thinking about peaceful solutions. The more a person thinks over an argument without criticizing it, the more favorable he will become toward it. Thus you might ask listeners to think over your argument on their way home that day. They'll be more likely to do so if you tell them you'll do the same if they have ideas they wish to share.

Balance Your Presentations

If your arguments are so one sided that you seem to misunderstand the complexity of an issue or the other side's arguments, your audience will see you as unknowledgeable. You'll be more persuasive if you present both sides, showing you understand those points an adversary might make. After you present both sides, offer clear rebuttals to the main thrusts of opposing arguments. (The exception is you shouldn't present both sides if you're sure your audience is familiar with only your position or is already completely in agreement with it — don't put opposing ideas in their heads.)

Reward Appropriate Statements

Another way to get a listener to start talking more favorably about peace is to reward her whenever she makes *any* statement supporting the cause of peace. Rewards come in many varieties: nodding your head, giving particularly good eye contact, giving (legitimate) compliments, promising (and then doing) a favor. Remember to give rewards only when listeners agree with your statements or make statements favorable to peace interests; don't give them continually. As long as your listeners don't feel they were forced into behaving or saying what they did or they did so only to get a reward, they'll probably see their actions as representing some part of who they are or what they believe in. This should lead to attitude change.

Conclusion

These are basic principles for changing attitudes. Each has something a little different to offer. Explore how you can use them together in your work. If you're creative in using and combining these attitude change approaches, you'll give yourself the best chance of changing people's opinions on peace issues.

Suggested Readings

Cialdini, R. B. (1984). *Influence: How and why people agree to do things.* New York: William Morrow.

    Using everyday language and examples, Cialdini creatively examines a number of factors that influence citizens and consumers.

Zimbardo, P. (1972). The tactics and ethics of persuasion. In B. T. King & E. McGinnies (Eds.), *Attitudes, conflict, and social change* (pp. 84–99). New York: Academic Press.

    This is a small chapter in an older, but still relevant book. It focuses on useable peace-oriented suggestions rather than on a presentation of attitude change research.

TECHNIQUES OF BEHAVIOR CHANGE

Christopher S. Grundy and Richard Osbaldiston

Activists' Goal: Change Behavior

The primary goal of activism is to get people to change their behaviors. This may seem obvious, but if not, consider a few quick examples. Peace and social justice activists want people to behave in just and humane ways: avoid products made in sweatshops, support political candidates who advocate for peace, and encourage people to avoid violence in their jobs and lives. Health activists want people to practice healthy behaviors: eat healthy diets, exercise regularly, practice safe sex, and use sunscreen. Environmental activists want people to engage in environmentally friendly activities: conserve energy, recycle, and refrain from using pesticides.

Changing people's behaviors is the cornerstone of activism. This chapter starts with the assumption that you and your activist group are considering embarking on a campaign, project, or activity to get people to perform a desired behavior. You want to reach out to nonactivists and get them to do something. You may even have some specific behaviors in mind now.

Given that behavior change is the ultimate objective of activism, the question becomes, "How do we change behavior?" That is, what techniques are effective for bringing about the desired behaviors? There are many possible answers to this question. Two common ways of changing behavior are making laws and educating the public. Both of these techniques are capable of changing behavior, but they don't give us much insight into what individuals can do to influence others' behaviors.

There is no "silver bullet"; that is, there is no one technique that's effective for every person or in every situation. Activists will often have to try different techniques (or combinations of techniques) to determine which ones work best for them. We will also present a method for determining which techniques may be most effective.

Six Techniques for Behavior Change

1. Provide procedural information

Procedural information is "how to" information; it's specific directions that detail how to perform the desired behavior. Sometimes people literally don't know what to do. In these cases, a campaign that informs them how to do the desired behavior is a good starting place. After all, people can't perform the desired behavior if they don't know how to do it.

Because activists are already conscious of what behaviors need to be done, they might overlook the level of specificity and simplicity that needs to be addressed. Remember that the target audience is people who don't know what to do and have never done anything like this. Break the instructions down into very specific, manageable tasks. Presenting the desired behavior as a three-step process is often effective.

The authors occasionally try to get students to write postcards to elected officials on a variety of political topics. To a person who frequently communicates with these officials, the process of sending a postcard, letter, or fax is very simple. But to a person who has never done this before, the process can seem intimidating and overwhelming. At political events on our campus, we set up a postcard writing station that includes blank cards, sample letters of what to say, a list of contact addresses, and even stamps. Even with these clear directions and examples, it's surprising how much assistance is needed to get a postcard written.

2. Link persuasive information to values

Persuasive information is "why to" information; it details the reasons a person should perform the desired behavior. It's difficult to imagine a campaign for a certain behavior that would not include persuasive information. It's common in our culture that anytime people ask other people to do something, they include an explanation or rationale as to why the behavior should be performed.

Persuasive information can be persuasive in two ways. First, the information can change beliefs. Beliefs are statements or ideas that a person thinks are true (they don't necessarily have to be true, but if a person "believes" they are true, they're called beliefs). It's quite possible that someone simply holds incorrect beliefs, and persuasive information is designed to change the beliefs from inaccurate to accurate.

Second, information can be persuasive because it makes a connection between beliefs and deeper values. Values are personal feelings about what's important, including feelings about what's right and wrong. Most people have value systems that help them decide if specific behaviors are worth doing. Ideally, people can identify which behaviors support their values and then engage in those behaviors. However, sometimes there is a disconnection between behaviors and values: people don't realize that certain behaviors are in line with their values. Persuasive information seeks to make this connection.

Consider a person who believes that most children in the United States are adequately provided for by public services like welfare programs, food stamps, and reduced lunch prices at schools. This belief is not an accurate reflection of reality, but the person believes it to be true. One way to persuade this person to do something about the situation would be to show him or her facts that more accurately portray the true state of affairs.

However, presenting information is rarely enough to change behavior. Once this person understands that there are many hungry children, this new belief needs to be linked to his or her values. If this person holds values like, "We should promote the general welfare of the people of the United States" or "It takes a village to raise a child" or "Do to others as you would have them do to you," then these new facts about child hunger can be linked to the values to encourage the person to take action. For example, a persuasive message might state that "It's important that we care for those people who are less fortunate, including children in the United States who don't have enough to eat."

3. Request a commitment and set a goal

Commitment and goals are keys to behavior change. Making a commitment is the process of declaring that a person will take an action; and setting a goal is the process of specifying exactly what the action will be. A common strategy for activists' campaigns is to ask people to make a commitment to do a specific behavior for a length of time. Further, this commitment isn't just a verbal commitment — it's a written, signed pledge or statement. This pledge has a specific psychological effect: once people say they are going to do something, they feel more obliged to do it and therefore are more likely to do it.

There are three features that make commitment work effectively. First, commitment works best when it's combined with an explicit goal. Goals are specific, observable behaviors that people can undertake and should be clear enough that people can determine for themselves if they're meeting or failing to meet them. Second, commitments that can be made public or known to other people are more likely to be effective than commitments that remain private. Third, commitments by individuals are more likely to be effective than commitments that are signed by groups or people who represent groups.

The most common form of making a commitment is asking a person to sign a pledge card. The card specifically states the goal, and it has two places for a signature. When people sign the card, they are given one part for their own personal record to serve as a reminder, and the activists keep the other part in order to publicize the commitment and to follow up on people in the future. Other forms of commitment include petitions and advertised messages bearing signatures, although rarely do these documents lock people into action.

For example, activists may try to start a grassroots campaign by asking concerned citizens to sign a pledge card that says that they will talk to three of their neighbors about a certain issue within the next week. The signed pledge card serves as a commitment; people feel obligated to undertake the behavior if they say they will. And the behavior of talking to three neighbors within the week is a goal. People making the commitment will be able to determine for themselves if they have accomplished this action or not.

4. Use social norms

One of the most interesting findings in psychology is that humans are by nature social creatures, and as such, we are likely to do what people around us do. Various terms can be used to describe this effect — conformity, social influence, obedience, role modeling — but the net effect is that we do what other people around us do. Norms are the unwritten rules that prescribe normal or appropriate behavior. Each individual determines the norms by observing what other people do. Norms serve to govern our behavior in all kinds of social situations — from cocktail parties to church services to basketball games.

When designing campaigns, social norms can be quite useful. Demonstrating what many other people are doing causes the target audience to begin to learn what normal behavior is. People are more likely to engage in behaviors if they perceive that many other people are also doing them. This kind of information is already common in our society. We frequently hear statements like "Polls show sixty percent approval for . . ." or "Most people support . . ." Activists can take advantage of this information, too.

Phrases that imply appropriate behavior can be used judiciously in campaigns to harness the power of social norms. Sentence stems like "There is a growing concern in our community about . . ." or "Many people have been asking about . . ." introduce a topic and imply a public consensus of concern. Further, stems like "Many people are now doing . . ." and "It is becoming more and more common that people are . . ." imply that the norm is an established behavioral routine. These statements encourage people to jump on the bandwagon.

Social norms are most powerful in ambiguous situations, that is, in situations where an individual might not know what the appropriate behaviors are. Imagine going to a religious gathering that is much different from your own, possibly a Buddhist ceremony or a Quaker Meeting. Or imagine being a dinner guest at a party thrown by a host from a different culture. In these situations, you would probably watch what everyone else does and mimic those behaviors. These examples show the power of social norms. When we don't know exactly what to do, we get this information from other people around us. As people join an activist group or participate in activities, they are watching and learning what is appropriate behavior. If your group behaves in a positive manner — respectful, welcoming, informed, focused — newcomers will be likely to pick up those behaviors and carry them forward. Unfortunately, the opposite is also true: negative behaviors will likewise be mimicked.

5. Provide incentives

Some psychologists have argued that many of our behaviors are due to the incentives and rewards that we have received over time. Certainly this point is true at the level of training animals. Seals, dolphins, and most other animals can be taught to do very clever and complex tricks by appropriately rewarding them with treats. Similarly, incentives can motivate and encourage people to behave in certain ways.

The most common incentive in our culture is money; to the extent that there is money in it, people are generally willing to do anything. However, small gifts can sometimes have a greater effect than the money that they actually cost. Thus, in designing a campaign that includes incentives, try to find gifts that have a greater perceived value than actual value.

Incentives can be given either before or after a behavior occurs. Those that are given beforehand serve to entice people to perform the behavior; those that are given afterward serve to reward them. Enticements and rewards have slightly different psychological properties. Enticements show good faith on the part of the campaigners and they're easy to distribute, but they can be abused by people who accept the enticement but don't follow through with the behavior. Rewards show appreciation, but they require a confirmation that the behavior has been performed. Thus, the campaign has to have some method to ensure that rewards are distributed only to those people who have done the behavior.

There are several variables to consider when designing a campaign that includes incentives. First, the incentive should be tied to a specific behavior; there should be no ambiguity as to what behavior was necessary in order to receive the incentive. Second, the incentive should be delivered as soon as the desired behavior has been performed. Third, incentives are of limited use because typically the behavior stops being performed once the incentives are withdrawn. This is an unfortunate side effect of incentives, and it's important to keep it in mind.

6. Provide feedback

Feedback is the process of providing information to people that lets them know how well they've done in performing a certain behavior. One form of feedback is rewards (as mentioned in number 5); the reward is information that the behavior has been satisfactorily completed. Yet the information doesn't have to be of a rewarding nature; rather, it can just inform the person that they have or have not done the behavior. In this way, it also relates to goal setting (number 3) by letting people know whether or not they've achieved their goal.

Feedback is common in our culture, but most people don't perceive it as feedback. For example, an invoice or bill is feedback about how much of a certain behavior was performed. In the case of credit cards, it's information about how much money was spent; and in the case of utility bills, it's also information about how much electricity, water, or natural gas was used.

People seem to have a natural curiosity about "how they're doing" in achieving their goals. Feedback takes advantage of this curiosity. It serves as a motivating force because it lets people evaluate their progress. Feedback that shows a person is falling short of his or her goals can serve as a positive motivational force, indicating that more effort needs to be applied to achieve the goals. However, it can also be a negative motivational force. A person can adopt a mindset of "I'm not doing that well, so I probably ought to abandon this goal." Thus, activists must be careful to use positive language when providing feedback.

The Activist Process

There is no silver bullet for behavior change. Each of these six techniques for behavior change work some of the time; none of them work all of the time. So the question becomes, which strategies are likely to work for you?

When considering this question, consider the level of involvement of the target audience. Your audience may be in one of three possible stages: unaware, unengaged, or unmonitored. If you can identify which stage your audience is in, you have a better shot at pitching your message effectively. Naturally, this three-stage model is a simplification. Rarely is every member of a target population at the same stage, so it's often appropriate to combine techniques.

People who are at the unaware stage need information. They need to be made aware of the situation and what they can do to help. Thus, if the target audience is unaware of the behaviors to perform, then the campaign should focus on providing procedural information and persuasive information.

Once people are aware of why and how to do something, they move to the unengaged stage. These people need a motivating force to help them start to take action. If the target audience is unengaged, the campaign should focus on techniques like using social norms, making commitments, and setting goals. These techniques help people take action on what they know. They provide the basic psychological forces to get people to start doing something.

Once people become engaged, they may perform the desired behavior irregularly or inconsistently, and thus they're at the unmonitored stage. These people need help monitoring their behavior so that they become consistent. Providing incentives and providing feedback help people monitor their behavior so that they perform it whenever it's appropriate.

Once people are performing a behavior regularly, they move back to the unaware stage because they're unaware of what other behaviors they should also be performing. Thus, the stages cycle back on themselves in an ever-expanding mindful exploration of the right way to live. For example, once people understand and take action on issues of injustice and human rights, they expand their vision of justice and rights to include related issues, like poverty, discrimination, or the environment. Hopefully, once people have gone through several cycles, they will understand the need to continually expand their ways of thinking and doing, and they will become activists themselves who then continue to fuel the process.

Suggested Readings

Tools of Change: Proven Methods for Promoting Health, Safety and
  Environmental Citizenship. http://www.toolsofchange.com/English/firstsplit.asp
    Tools of Change has some good information for activists to use.
  Particularly useful is the list of eight techniques under the "Tools of Change"
  button.
Social Norms and Social Marketing. http://www.edc.org/hec/socialnorms/
    Higher Education Center has some great information on how to use social
  norms.
Campus Action: Web Center. http://www.campusaction.net/activist_toolbox/
  activist_toolbox_frontpage.htm
    Campus Action provides a number of general tools for activists, including
  a brief section on how to organize a campaign effectively.
Cialdini, R. B. (2001). *Influence: Science and practice*. Boston, MA: Allyn &
  Bacon.
    This is the classic book on influence and persuasion.

DIALOGS ACROSS DIFFERENCES

Susan E. Hawes

The dialectical process that allows individual self-knowledge and self-acceptance presupposes a radical change in social relations, to a condition where there would be neither oppressors nor oppressed, and this change applies whether we are talking about psychotherapy, or formal schooling, production in a factory, or everyday work in a service institution.

— Ignacio Martín-Baró[1]

The turn to dialog has come about in order to help people, who cannot talk to one another without arguing, dominating, withdrawing into silence, or fighting, begin a process of mutual understanding. Dialog assumes that every one of us is at our best when we can *both* express our core beliefs, values, and needs *and* to be truly heard. Dialog is different from discussion and debate for a number of reasons. It's exciting to see the rich variety of approaches to "doing" dialog that are now available to any who wish to lay the groundwork for peaceful relations, from the interpersonal to the global (you can find a modest list of such resources at the chapter's end). I think it's important, before searching for the best toolkit, to understand what dialog means. Here are seven of the most important characteristics of dialog:

Our Own Contexts

Each of us has distinct contexts that define our ability to understand others and to understand ourselves — interpersonal, historical, cultural, and social. Therefore, we can't be "neutral" or "objective" or ever "get the whole picture" in trying to make sense of our world and each other. This is a very important assumption underlying dialog, because it means: (a) that no one person's truth can be identical to another's and (b) that no one can claim she has exclusive access to or ownership of the "truth" of the matter — because understanding is always incomplete.

This doesn't mean we're all islands that can't ever understand the other person. After all, the one thing we can say that *all* humans share is the effect of context and history! Therefore, in contrast to what distinguishes us from one another, we also have multiple contexts we share in common. Both our commonalities and differences form the conditions for mutual understanding. To be in dialog involves listening for similarities and differences between ourselves, as well as a sense of humility because of the limits of our capacity to know the whole truth.

Imagine having a conversation with someone on something of great importance to you and *not* wanting him to see it the way you do, but hoping to learn from what he says because that resembles your beliefs and is different. Would you understand him better than if his words simply fit neatly into your own ideas? Imagine being listened to without judgment but with curiosity for what is common and what is surprising in what you say. Would you feel understood better by him than had he said, "I agree" or "I don't agree?"

Back and Forth

While each of us may long for one-half of dialog — that is, the experience of being seen, heard, and understood — the side of seeing, hearing, and understanding another is neither automatic nor easy. Yet dialog is an act of cocreating mutual understanding, and understanding is based on a process of dialog; that is, there's a circular back and forth between self and another, a process of "call" and "response," of question and answer.

It's not surprising that we often hear the words *dialog* and *circle* used together. Dialog groups are said to happen in circles, and circle groups often have dialog as a goal. Another characteristic of dialog is that it involves circular movements back and forth, between part and whole, between an individual and her or his group, family, society, and culture. This means that dialog can occur within me as the tensions between my individual needs, experiences, and perceptions and those of everyone else. How am I unique and also a reflection of my world and everyone in it? In what ways do the differences I experience in you have the potential to expand my sense of common humanity?

Understanding Differently

Dialog assumes that to understand is to understand *differently*. Often we think we understand someone when her words seem to reflect views or experiences similar to our own. These are the times when we may find ourselves nodding our heads as someone speaks and having quick associations between what she has said and specific experiences of our own. We might then say, "Yes, I know exactly what you mean!" What we have done is to plug what that person has claimed as hers neatly into our own repertoire, and we come away understanding little more than that someone else has validated our views of the world.

This is a comfortable transaction because it asks nothing of us. Our memories may record little or nothing of the details given by the other person, only that she reinforced what we already knew. That exchange, if we can call it that, is not the same thing as "understanding" because we have not come away with anything "new" or "different." At the minimum when we understand another person, we calibrate our preexisting views to accommodate some of what was not there before. You'll know that you've understood someone when you hear yourself saying, for example, "Oh, I never thought of that, but I see what you mean," or "I never would have thought that was possible."

Leaping into the Unknown and Being Changed

Dialog asks that each participant submit to the other with the intention of discovering the strength of that person's point of view. When you're in dialog, you mindfully seek to make yourself open to what is foreign, unfamiliar, or even incomprehensible. To enter into dialog is a risk, a leap into the unknown. Not only does dialog call for a willingness to risk facing what is unknown, but it also asks us to bear the consequences of being changed or transformed in the process. The leap into the unknown that happens when we truly seek to understand another person through dialog has to result in some change in us, if only that we have understood differently.

Whenever we suspend our usual way of seeing things in order to understand differently, whenever we open ourselves to change, we also make ourselves vulnerable. This feeling of vulnerability comes from several common, naturally occurring fears. For example, it's a common fear that giving in to another's way of seeing means we're giving up our sense of security in being "good" or "right." We might also worry that our partner in dialog might not keep up his or her end of the bargain, might not be open and vulnerable for us.

We naturally seek consistency in our lives, and we're drawn more to what is like us than what is strange. This stance becomes exaggerated when we feel uncertain or defensive; under those conditions, we tend to resist change as if it threatens our very existence. However, even under optimal circumstances, we don't readily embrace even small changes to our perspectives. Nor do we accommodate ourselves to the differences we find in others. Therefore it's very important whenever we enter a dialog that we remind ourselves of two things: (a) we want to leap into the unknown in the other person and (b) it's natural that we experience this process as unsettling.

The Public Conversations Project (PCP) builds into its process a moment for participants to reflect on the ambiguity, uncertainty, or mixed feelings they might have about their own point of view.[2] I understand the purpose of this reflection to provide an opportunity for each participant to create openings for understanding by revealing the weakness of holding an "either-or" position. For example, a PCP facilitator might ask participants to do a go-round speaking to this question: "Do you have uncertainties about any of the views you've held in the past? Can you say something about both the certainties and uncertainties you bring to this conversation?" This question is only introduced after all participants have had several opportunities to express their experiences and values and to listen to those of others. This ambiguity and opening up shouldn't be introduced until participants have experienced these trust-building procedures.

Equality and Safety

Trust building emerges only under certain conditions. A key requirement for dialog is that *all participants must be accorded equal value* in the process. They must have the same chances to speak and be heard, to express ideas, and to express feelings, wishes, and needs without fear of retaliation. Only when the conditions of equality and safety are met can the optimal conditions for dialog such as openness, curiosity, and vulnerability occur.

Most practitioners and facilitators of dialog have come to rely on creating a structure for the dialog process that tries to build in these optimal conditions. It's all too easy for any of us to fall into styles of interaction that end up leaving people out, interrupting, intellectualizing, and debating. For example, there are dialog circles where participants speak in turns and, at least at first, are asked to speak from their experience and are restrained from talking to another person or about what another person has said. Ground rules for participants' safety are either presented by facilitators or elicited from the dialog group at the outset.

An Act of Love That Requires Hope, Humility, and Faith in Humanity

What would make us want to take the risks of opening ourselves to the differences in others? Paulo Freire thought of dialog as an act of love that requires hope, humility, and faith in humanity that becomes an equal relationship that builds mutual trust between the participants.[3] Dialog requires that we care for and want to learn from the other person. Like the Golden Rule, dialog can be described as a core human responsibility. The promise then is that when we participate in dialog fully, we experience joy in recognizing our shared humanity, as it is expressed in all our differences and similarities.

Some forms of dialog practice, such as the Ojai People's Way of Council, make explicit the call for love and compassion as a foundation for dialog.[4] The Way of Council builds into its simple structure four "intentions," two of which are to "speak from the heart" and to "listen from the heart."

The Process of Dialog Is Its Own Outcome

With dialog, the outcome (consensus, conversion, victory) doesn't drive the process. The process *is* the outcome. It needs to be created mutually and over time, with no other purpose than to realize our humanity. With its focus on the here and now, on understanding in the present moment, and on vulnerable authenticity, dialog serves functions that call for making judgments or expect unity at the cost of differences and diversity.

Sometimes dialog gets confused with consensus building or decision making. Dialog practice may lead to consensus or result in a group decision, but those are consequences that are possible because dialog occurred to lay a foundation for collaboration, consensus, action, and so on. Dialog, using just means, builds understanding and mutuality, without which just action cannot be formed.

The Zen Peacemaker Circles often use council practice (from the Way of Council) to begin their meetings because it creates an intimacy and group connection that makes the action and business components of every meeting go smoothly. Dialog can also be introduced when a conflict arises within a group to provide a safe and compassionate framework for members to express their feelings without having to defend them to each other. Dialog can also serve as a way to practice being silent and focused, listening, and mindful. There are surely other uses for us to discover.

Conclusion

Now that you have these seven essential characteristics of dialog and are oriented to the process, you have the foundation for identifying those structures and procedures that best suit your peacemaking goals. In the Suggested Readings below are three different approaches to dialog practice that I have found valuable, along with an encyclopedic resource website — National Coalition for Dialogue and Deliberation. I recommend visiting there first.

References

1. Martín-Baró, I. (1994). *Writings for a liberation psychology*. Cambridge, MA: Harvard University Press, p. 42.
2. Public Conversations Project. PCP Dialogue Toolbox. Retrieved July 9, 2005 from http://www.publicconversations.org/pcp/uploadDocs/toolbox.pdf
3. Freire, P. (2000). *Pedagogy of the oppressed* (30th anniversary ed.). New York: The Continuum International Publishing Group, Inc.
4. Center for Council Training. http://www.counciltraining.org/index2.html

Suggested Readings

Flick, D. (1998). *From debate to dialogue: Using the understanding process to transform our conversations*. Boulder, CO: Orchid Publications.
Zimmerman, J., & Coyle, G. (1996). *The way of council*. North Bergman, NJ: Bramble Books.
Public Conversations Project. PCP Dialogue Toolbox. http://www.publicconversations.org/pcp/uploadDocs/toolbox.pdf
National Coalition for Dialogue and Deliberation: Fostering a World of Conversation, Participation and Action: D & D Models & Techniques. http://thataway.org/resources/understand/models/models.html

USING THE MIND'S DRIVE
FOR CONSISTENCY

Rachel M. MacNair

In examining the arguments by which war is defended, two important considerations should be borne in mind — first, that those who urge them are not simply defending war, they are also defending themselves. If war be wrong, their conduct is wrong; and the desire of self-justification prompts them to give importance to whatever arguments they can advance in its favor. . . . The other consideration is that the defenders of war come to the discussion prepossessed in its favor. They are attached to it by their earliest habits. They do not examine the question as a philosopher would examine it, to whom the subject was new. Their opinions had been already formed. They are discussing a question which they had already determined. And every man who is acquainted with the effects of evidence on the mind knows that under these circumstances, a very slender argument in favor of the previous opinions possesses more influence than many great ones against it.

— Jonathan Dymond, 1824[1]

Mental Gymnastics and Belligerency

People sometimes reason in very strange ways. Have you ever wondered about how this could happen?

Consider: Individuals have predicted some catastrophic event. They quit their jobs and sold their houses to prepare. When the event didn't happen, they didn't conclude their prediction was wrong. They came up with a reason it was right. Then they pushed this especially hard on everyone they could find.

Consider: Government leaders in the United States knew their war in Vietnam was unwinnable Nevertheless, they continued sending soldiers to their deaths.

Back in 1957, Leo Festinger became interested in that first group, the one that predicted catastrophe. He proposed a psychological explanation (called *cognitive dissonance*) that has since been applied in many other situations. People had taken fairly drastic actions by giving everything away. They had put themselves in a position of being in deep trouble if they were wrong. Accordingly, they were highly motivated to convince themselves they weren't wrong. They figured out some idea whereby the prediction was right after all. According to his theory, they should insist on their new ideas all the more than they did before. To convince themselves that the original claim was right and that they were therefore not fools for thinking so, they must also convince others that the claim was right.

In the same way, the war planners had gotten themselves into a fix when so much effort and so many resources had gone into the war — and so many young American soldiers had been killed. If they stopped the war at any point, they would be unable to justify why they had been fighting up to that point. With no victory, a mere pullout would have meant all the effort and previous deaths were wasted. So they kept the war going to justify having kept it going before.

What many studies over the years have shown is that people have such a strong drive for consistency that inconsistency is a form of stress, of tension. It makes people so uptight they'll go to great lengths to relieve it. In many cases, this means they sensibly change their *views* to make them consistent with their behavior or with the facts. In others, they change their *behavior* to make it consistent with their views or newly discovered facts. They'll generally change the thing that's easiest to change. In either case, your job as an activist is easy enough: bring the inconsistencies to their attention and show how what you're proposing is more consistent. Do what comes naturally by way of persuasion.

Other times, holding on to the thing that's harder to change leads to some impressive mental gymnastics. People do this to convince themselves they really are consistent after all. If it's hard to convince other people, and especially if they're not entirely convinced themselves, then they can be quite belligerent.

In 1811 Hannah Moore, in a book called *Religion of the Heart*, noted, "Violence and belligerence are the common resource of those whose knowledge is small, and whose arguments are weak." More recently John Noonan developed this idea for puzzling behavior of slave owners in the early years of the United States. Unemotional political advice was to make allowances here and there. Yet slavery advocates insisted on extremes such as the *Dred Scott* court case that made Northerners watch as escaped slaves were taken off in chains. The slave holders would not allow slavery to be contained within Southern borders. Noonan sees this poetically connected to the ancient Greek mythical beings called the Furies:

> Why did the slave-holders act as if driven by the Furies to their own destruction? . . . Why did they take such risks, why did they persist beyond prudent calculation? The answer must be that in a moral question of this kind, turning on basic concepts of humanity, you cannot be content that your critics are feeble and ineffective, you cannot be content with their practical tolerance of your activities. You want, in a sense you need, actual acceptance, open approval. If you cannot convert your critics by argument, at least by law you can make them recognize that your course is the course of the country.[2]

Once we understand why people see this belligerence as necessary, we have better tools for dealing with them. Sometimes that will mean we're less puzzled over what is otherwise some astounding reasoning. Other times it may help to find a way to get through and be persuasive. Yet when we can't persuade, we can at least understand what's underlying the wave of hostility. This means not merely scoffing at ridiculous posturing but treating people more as people — people like us — we, after all, may find the same dynamic working in our own reasoning.

Persuading Others

Consider the task of explaining that something terrible is happening to people currently unaware of it. Advocates often use the approach of giving statistics to show how truly horrifying the situation is. They think their readers and listeners will share their anger, arise, and take action. When they find that doesn't happen, they get mad at the listeners — not pausing to think that maybe they didn't really use the best approach.

There's an underlying message the advocates may not be catching, but members of their audience are. There are two ideas at once. One idea is there to start with, before the communication: we are a noble and virtuous people. Whoever "we" are, this is a point that many people already have in the back of their minds and feel strongly about. The second idea is that we're allowing terrible things to go on. Those two points can't both be true.

The eager advocates may have given up on that first point long ago, and expect the audience to do the same. But people will more likely give up what's easiest to give up. Maintaining group self-esteem is a lot more important to a lot of people and therefore more difficult to give up than some new piece of information.

Therefore, members of the audience could decide the information can't be true. It's just an exaggeration for propaganda. Or — much worse — they could decide the situation must be ok. If it happens while we're a noble and virtuous people, then it must be something consistent with nobility and virtue. Instead of arousing anger, the writers may have actually increased support! Being ignored is a better alternative.

This makes it wiser to take a different tack. The group self-esteem doesn't require a rosy view of group perfection; most people know better than that. But if behavior is in fact changing for the better, or there are stirrings to change, that can be highlighted. After all, a noble and virtuous people would be expected to make things right. The two ideas no longer contradict. This approach is far more effective in persuading.

Most issues are amenable to this either in the short term or in the long term. Even if, say, war sentiment is cranking up or executions are accelerating in a state, the overall historical trend is that both war and the death penalty are far less accepted than they were a century ago. An upsurge can be presented as an exception that would naturally alarm people when brought to their attention, rather than being presented as a sign that things are going to hell in a handbasket. Simply keeping the group self-esteem in mind when formulating the wording can make a big difference in how well it's accepted.

The Need to Explain

It may seem rather obvious that people like to think well of the group they're in, but there's more to the idea of the drive for consistency. If people know a practice is subsiding (if it is), they'll seek to *explain* the new situation. Rather than using information as an accusation, information that accounts for why the practice is lessening makes people more eager to hear it.

The practical application of this is that in your writing and in your interviews, you might think to start out by explaining, if there's a reasonable and accurate way of doing so, that behavior is indeed changing. Or, if more suitable, slip the point in at an appropriate place along the way.

The exact same information about what's wrong with a policy may be better listened to if people understand first that it's not an oncoming juggernaut but a dwindling difficulty. There is a psychological tendency to want to explain why it's dwindling. You're supplying the reasons.

Leroy Pelton shows another way the drive for consistency works when behavior has in fact already changed.[3] White businessmen in Montgomery, Alabama, had said a lot of vicious racist things before the boycotts there. Because of the boycotts, they changed their behavior, consistent with their business philosophy of making money. Ten years later, the racist remarks were considerably lessened. Yet remarks made out of Black customers' earshot would have no impact on profits.

The explanation? The businessmen noticed their own behavior had changed, so they changed their everyday rhetoric to match their new behavior. Indeed, the new language helped account for the behavior — and to make the change more permanent. The drive for consistency means that it's not always that we persuade people of new views and thereby change their behavior. Sometimes, we change their behavior and thereby change their views.

Calling on Consistency

There are times when you can use the principles people have asserted on one issue to bring up the question of consistency on others. For example U.S. senator Sam Brownback, a conservative Republican reflecting on consistency, told a reporter, "If we're trying to establish a culture of life, it's difficult to have the state sponsor executions."[4] It may seem obvious, but at times it must be brought up that those who, like Brownback, oppose abortion or the hastening of death or physician-assisted suicide will be more effective in persuading others if they're consistent by opposing the death penalty and being much more strict and sincere in opposing wars. A wide variety of worldviews and ethical systems will have aspects of them that would be consistent with violence reduction and peace, and often the task is to find it.

Note here, however, that finding a consistency will have to go both directions. For example, if you want to appeal to someone's patriotism for peace, as many a bumper sticker does, it will only be effective if you share the sense of patriotism. If you think patriotism should be replaced by love for all of humanity (also a common peace movement view) then it would be cynical manipulation to use it. You could expect the other person to have a negative response accordingly. After all, you can't appeal to someone else's consistency by being inconsistent within yourself. Similarly, in the above example, someone who believes in abortion accessibility won't be able to make an appeal to consistency in the same way as someone who agrees with the "culture of life" point being drawn upon. In such cases, the best tack may be to refer listeners on to those who can make the appeals sincerely.

Persuading Ourselves

When you are not feeling particularly friendly but know you ought to be, the best thing you can do, very often, is to put on a friendly manner and behave as if you were a nicer person than you actually are. And in a few minutes, as we have all noticed, you will be really feeling friendlier than you were. Very often the only way to get a quality in reality is to start behaving as if you had it already.

— C. S. Lewis[5]

If other people can make their feelings fit their actions, so can we. Logic or an intellectual desire to be helpful can control the actions. Feelings follow. This makes actions more permanent. Greater harmony and more effective peace action ensue.

References

1. Dymond, J. (1824). An inquiry into the accordancy of war with the principles of Christianity, and an examination of the philosophical reasoning by which it is defended, with observations on some of the causes of war and on some of its effects, pp. 67-68. Available at http//www.qhpress.org/texts/dymond/
2. Noonan, J. T. (1979). *A private choice*. New York: The Free Press, p. 82.
3. Pelton, L. H. (1974). *The psychology of nonviolence*. New York: Pergamon.
4. Borger, G. (2005, April 11). A Time for uncertainty. *U.S. News and World Report*.
5. Lewis, C. S. (1943). *Mere Christianity*. New York: The Macmillan Company, p. 161.

HUMOR FOR PEACE: FINDING LAUGHING MATTERS

— Gary A. Zimmerman

If I didn't have a sense of humor I would long ago have committed suicide.

— Mohandas Gandhi

You can't say civilization don't advance. In every war they kill you in a new way.

— Will Rogers

A government that robs Peter to pay Paul can always depend upon the support of Paul.

— George Bernard Shaw

Military intelligence is a contradiction in terms.

— Groucho Marx

The benefits of humor and laughter have been widely acclaimed:
1. Laughter is healing [1,2], socially contagious [3], improves learning [4,5], and reduces tension.[6,7,8,9]
2. Laughter liberates us from fear, sorrow, and inhibition and can help calm us during uncomfortable, awkward, or terrifying situations.[10]
3. Laughter releases feelings of embarrassment, surprise, and low levels of fear and anger, making it possible to think more clearly.[11,12]

4. Laughing with others helps build rapport and diminishes social distance between people, causing a sense of connectedness.[4]

5. Laughter can create a mood in which other positive and beneficial emotions, such as zestfulness, hopefulness, and cheerfulness can emerge.[1,11,13]

6. Laughter enables group members to release anxiety, stress, and conflict and brightens members' outlooks and spirits.[14]

7. Political or educational messages can be presented effectively through the use of humor. [15,16]

8. Finding humor in a troublesome situation allows us to see the problem from a different perspective.[15] An example is the story of a Palestinian college student about how unfair, harsh, and inconvenient Israeli checkpoints are for Palestinian people, often requiring them to stand in line for hours. But she couldn't contain her laughter as she explained that these checkpoints have become creatively known as "duty-free" areas, where Palestinians buy and sell food, drink, and other items. She called it "sad humor" as she laughed some more. Her laughter was more than just a tension release. She truly saw how Palestinians were making the best of a bad situation, spawning a whole new economic industry.

The Benefits of Humor for Peace Work

Humor (and its accompanying laughter) can be important in a wide variety of ways in active nonviolence and in the peace movement, whether the sayings or jokes you use are related specifically to peace or not. For example, humor can be used:

- To reduce tensions during conflict, such as in a demonstration, a mediation session, or a discussion with others about peace.
- To help people's minds better absorb the information and message you are sharing in a speech or in a letter to the editor.
- To create a positive tone at the beginning of a group meeting.
- To help put you and the other person at ease when you canvass door to door.
- To help alleviate burnout that you or co-workers are beginning to experience.

- To provide a vehicle for deflating all-too-easy pretensions and their resulting arrogance and violent thoughts, on either side of an issue.[17]
- To make peace work more fun.

These are but a few examples of how humor can help in particular situations that arise in peace work. Look over the group of benefits listed earlier; stay attuned to situations in your work in which such effects would be helpful; and use humor when it seems appropriate to the situation.

As with any information or power, humor can be abused. Making fun of others ultimately widens the gap between you. What are your goals? Are you trying to open up lines of communication with people on the other side or who are uncommitted? Or, are you trying to be prophetic, point out power abuses, and rev up your group? Even if the latter is your primary goal, there are many humorous options available and your "thoughtfulness about how, when, and why to employ humor will ensure, in humor consultant Joel Goodman's words, that we 'elevate, not devastate.'"[4] This is particularly hard to do when we're in the low-power position and we want to "get even" or "get heard," but it is possible. Many bumper sticker examples were passed over in choosing the ones that appear later in this chapter.

Some Hints on Improving Your Use of Humor

Some bright boy over at NBC once told me there were only thirty-two basic jokes. Another bright boy reduced it to eleven. Somebody else has it down to two — comparison and exaggeration.

— Fred Allen

Using comparisons or exaggeration are two ways to create humor and make people laugh. Comparisons are made automatically by the mind. If you present an idea that is out of context, unexpected, illogical, unreasonable, exaggerated, or inappropriate, the incongruity between the new idea and a related one already in the listener's mind creates laughter and a release of tension. For example, you can put two ideas together in a new way: "The meek shall inherit the earth — but not the oil rights."[15] Or you can change words in a popular phrase or saying: "The CIA and the KGB are equal opportunity destroyers"; "The Meddle East"; "The Axis of Pretty Bad"; "I wonder who's Kissinger now"; "The business of the U.S. is none of your business"; or "Some songs are anti-folk songs."[18]

Exaggeration can also elicit laughter, again because of the incongruity involved. In the summer of 2005, several teachers were in a seminar studying "The Troubles" in Northern Ireland. During a tour of Catholic and Protestant neighborhoods in Belfast that have had decades of tension, at the third stop the local bus driver announced, "This is the only place on the tour where we ask that you, for your own personal safety, not go someplace when you get off the bus. Please stay off the grass here...it's booby-trapped...the dogs use it as a toilet." This comment not only exaggerated the present situation, but also tapped into our feelings of surprise, embarrassment, and low-level fear — perfect components for helping us lighten up with spontaneous laughter.

What can you do to improve your ability to make people laugh? Work at developing your own humor [5,10,19]; read more about how humor works [4,19,20,21]; study humorous peace sources, including some of the numerous Internet sites; here are a few examples [18,22,23,24,25,26]. Cut out relevant comic strips or editorial cartoons, start a file of them, and use them on your peace group's bulletin board, your refrigerator door, or your office door. Jot down good jokes that you hear and also humorous sayings, songs, and jokes on buttons, T-shirts, or bumper stickers such as: "You can no more win a war than you can win an earthquake"; "Ignore your rights and they will go away"; "The labor movement: the folks who brought you the weekend"; "I love my country...but I think we should start seeing other people"; "Global economy: survival of the richest"; "No justice, no peace — know justice, know peace"; "Support faith-based missile defense systems"; "Watch this patriot act!"; "Actions speak louder than bumper stickers."[16]

Ultimately it's important to act, yet there can be scary moments. Humor can be helpful. Richard Deats recounts a story about Dr. Martin Luther King, Jr.:

> At a rally in Philadelphia, Mississippi, following the brutal killing of (Andrew) Goodman, (James) Chaney, and (Michael) Schwerner, King called on (Reverend Ralph) Abernathy to pray before a crowd of hostile whites that included the local sheriff. Afterwards someone asked King

why he did not lead the prayer. "In that crowd, I wasn't about to close my eyes!" said King, to the guffaws of his friends, who were accustomed to the humorous banter that pervaded the movement.[25]

Some of you may not have laughed yet while reading this chapter. Is that because I'm saving the best jokes for the end or for my own book? No. Your mind and its characteristics are different from mine. I may not have used the best exaggerations, incongruities, or comparisons for you personally. But more importantly, you are probably reading this to yourself, and we tend not to laugh out loud when we're alone.[3,15] Try some of the humor in this chapter on a group of people. Have fun laughing with co-workers, the people you canvass, your Representative, or your neighbor who supports more military spending. If you do, they'll be more relaxed. Having "emptied their attics" of old feelings a bit and also feeling more connected to you, they'll be more likely to appreciate you and consider letting some of your ideas into their heads.

References

1. Cousins, N. (1979). *Anatomy of an illness, as perceived by the patient: Reflections on healing and regeneration.* New York: W.W. Norton.
2. Moody, R. A. (1978). *Laugh after laugh: The healing power of humor.* Staunton, VA: Headwaters.
3. Chapman, A. J., & Foot, H. C. (1976). *Humor and laughter.* London: Wiley.
4. Cornett, C. (2001). *Learning through laughter . . . again.* Bloomington, IN: Phi Delta Kappa Educational Foundation.
5. Berk, R. A. (2003). *Humor as an instructional defibrillator: Evidence-based techniques in teaching and assessment.* Sterling, VA: Stylus.
6. Freud, S. (1905/1960). *Jokes and their relationship to the unconscious.* New York: Norton.
7. Berlyne, D. E. (1971). *Aesthetics and psychology.* New York: Appleton-Century-Crofts.
8. Mendel, W. (1970). *A celebration of laughter.* Los Angeles: Mara.
9. Nichols, M. P., & Zax, M. (1977). *Catharsis in psychotherapy.* New York: Gardiner.
10. Mindess, H. (1971). *Laughter and liberation: Developing your sense of humor, the psychology of laughter.* Los Angeles: Nash.
11. Jackins, H. (1973). *The human situation.* Seattle: Rational Island.
12. Scheff, T. J. (1979). *Catharsis in healing, ritual, and drama.* Berkeley: University of California.
13. Mullen, T. (1989). *Laughing out loud, and other religious experiences.* Richmond, IN: Friends United.

14. Chapman, A. J. (1977). *It's a funny thing, humor.* New York: Pergamon.
15. Peter, L. J., & Dana, B. (1982). *The laughter prescription.* New York: Ballantine.
16. Cramer, S. (Bumper stickers and other materials — Northern Sun, 2916 East Lake Street, Minneapolis, MN 55406).
17. MacNair, R. M. (2003). *The psychology of peace: An introduction.* Westport, CT: Praeger.
18. Lippman, D. (Several CDs, cassettes, and videos of activist humor available from Urgent Records, P.O. Box 781, Chapel Hill, NC 27514).
19. Bailey, J. (1976). *Intent on laughter.* New York: Quadrangle/Times.
20. Eastman, M. (1938). *The enjoyment of laughter.* New York: Simon & Schuster.
21. Gruner, C. R. (1979). *Understanding laughter: The workings of wit and humor.* Chicago: Nelson-Hall.
22. Munnik, L. (1983). *Nothing to laugh about.* New York: The Pilgrim Press.
23. ZNet Toons. http://www.zmag.org/cartoons/
24. Peace Corps Online Humor. http://peacecorpsonline.org/messages/messages/2629/2027665.html
25. Deats, R. (1994). *How to keep laughing even though you've considered all the facts.* Oklahoma City: Fellowship.
26. Langer, V., Thomas, W., & Richardson, B. (1982). The nuclear war fun book. New York: Holt, Rinehart, and Winston.

EPILOGUE

Anne Anderson, LICSW

How delightful: I do not know many of the authors of this book! For the longest time, back in the 1980s, in my first years as Psychologists for Social Responsibility's (PsySR) Coordinator, I think I actually had met or communicated with most of the folks in the social sciences/mental health professions who were working for peace. Now the numbers of people using their skills and talents for peace has grown to the point where one person can't keep track of us all. The range of contributors and multiplicity of topics covered here are a hopeful sign for our future.

When PsySR was founded in 1982, its focus was on the increasing tensions between the US and the USSR and the dangers of nuclear holocaust, should these tensions lead to an outbreak of violent confrontation. Psychologists realized they had much to say on the making of exaggerated enemy images, on psychological responses to overwhelming issues like nuclear winter, and on techniques to manage and reduce tensions among groups. Within ten years, the Berlin Wall had fallen, but the much desired "peace dividend" did not materialize and more wars broke out. PsySR expanded its mission to contribute to building a culture of peace with social justice. We understood that the roots of violent conflict often lie in the less visible social injustices that plague every society on this planet.

Now our mission reads: PsySR "applies the research, knowledge and practices of psychology to promote durable peace at the community, national and international levels. To accomplish this mission, our members mobilize and train psychologists, social scientists and mental health professionals to apply their knowledge in ways that foster peace, social justice and sustainable development. We support each other's projects and join in coalitions for effective action. We supply critical information from psychology for use in local, national and international public policy making."

At the turn of the 21st Century PsySR launched a new set of stand-alone conferences focused on building more community among us, and sharing skills, ideas and resources to work more effectively for social change. PsyACT (see chapter 28) came out of one of them, and this book has come out of our 2005 Conference in Portland, OR, "Beyond Talk: Tools and Training for Advocacy and Action" Our co-sponsoring organization, Counselors for Social Justice, is continuing the series in 2006 with a conference at George Mason University in Virginia. True to our mission, we are reaching out across disciplinary boundaries, building coalitions, finding ways to work together, as a glance at the authors list for this book confirms.

I remember once sitting at dinner with some folks deeply involved in the endeavor of social change and community development. Someone expressed their frustration this way: "If it weren't for having to deal with people, we could get so much done!" This is exactly our point — policy is developed by people, carried out by people, and affects people, and other living things. Where there are people, there is psychology. Psychology can be used cynically and manipulatively to influence individuals and groups to attain misguided goals (e.g. using exaggerated enemy images to go to war, or advertising poor nutrition to children). Doris Miller, one of PsySR's founders, cogently pointed out back in the 80's, that many commentators from other professions feel free to discuss the psychology of current events — political scientists, historians, journalists — so it is incumbent on those of us in the profession to do so, responsibly and with full commitment to the ethics of our professions. Our understanding of human psychological processes must also be used to promote the most effective policies to nurture and sustain our home planet and all of its inhabitants.

But what to do? How to choose which problem to take on? My answer is two-fold: Which problem do you care about, and which one do you see a way to address? I opened my neighborhood listserve this morning and read about a young mother who was horrified to find broken glass under a jungle gym at a neighborhood playground. She described how everyone on the playground helped pick up the glass and now she's alerting the rest of us. She is contributing to the local peace. On a larger playing field, but no more important, I remember consulting with the International Tribunal for Yugoslavia and Rwanda back in the 1990s. Our international group of mental health professionals and human rights activists were stumped as to why women witnesses to rape as a war crime were refusing to use the counseling services provided by the Tribunal for the support of those who were testifying. Someone finally asked, out of curiosity, how many counselors there were, and through her question it became clear that with so few counselors, they were serving both the witnesses for the prosecution and the defense in the same trial, a clear break in the basic rules of confidentiality. No wonder women were refusing! Fortunately, we were in a position to put in an immediate request to the European Union for more funds to hire more counselors and solve this problem. But, we didn't know that we were going to be able to do anything when we started.

One of my basic tenets throughout these twenty-some years has been that everyone can do something, and that all of these small acts contribute to building a culture of peace. Barry Childers' list (chapter 1) is an excellent example of the many ways that people can contribute. My PsySR computer is decorated with M. K. Gandhi's comment: *"Almost anything you do will seem insignificant, but it is very important that you do it,"* a most heartening reminder on many days. We know from research on durable peace that it is multi-layered, held together by interlaced social norms (chapters 26, 27, 13), nurtured by non-violent communication (chapter 19), and that individual actions, while small, can contribute to social change. Do something about what you feel passionate about. Then, tell us about it! (psysr@psysr.org) Maybe you'll prevent someone else from reinventing the wheel. Don't allow yourself to get overwhelmed by the enormity of our difficulties. After all, last time I looked I — and you — were only one person. Using the tools in this book we become more capable of working together effectively for the well being of all of us traveling on this space ship, Earth.

So, it is with urgency that we have gathered these chapters together for you. This book, *Working for Peace*, provides you with critical information to apply to the issues that are closest to your heart. And, we need you and your friends and colleagues working at many levels to make the changes this world needs to survive and thrive. We need you working together, laughing together, healthy, energized, thinking strategically, using every psychological tool to promote the many varieties of cultures of peace around the world.

About the Authors

Robert E. Alberti, Ph.D., is a licensed psychologist and fellow of the American Psychological Association. Now semiretired, his academic career included a tenured professorship at California Polytechnic State University. He is author of several books of popular psychology and editor of more than 100 books of popular and professional psychology. His special interest is in facilitating self-expression.

Anne Anderson, LICSW, has been Psychologists for Social Responsibility's Coordinator since 1984, and is the recipient of their 2005 Distinguished Contribution Award. She has a clinical social work practice with the Washington Therapy Guild in Washington, DC. She has served with Christian Children's Fund's International Technical Assistance Group, which included authoring *Remembering September 11, 2001: A Manual for Caregivers.*

Charles T. Brown, Ph.D. (1912–2003), a long-time researcher and teacher in the field of interpersonal communication, introduced the study of conflict into the curriculum of Western Michigan University. His chapter also appeared in the 1985 edition.

Pat Bullen, B.Sc., B.A. (Hons.), is a doctoral candidate in psychology at the University of Auckland, New Zealand. For several years she was an active volunteer for an organization promoting well-child health. Her current interests include positive youth development and youth-driven health initiatives and programs.

Shawn Meghan Burn, Ph.D., is Professor of Psychology and Child Development at California Polytechnic State University, San Luis Obispo. She has written books and research articles on group dynamics, the social psychology of gender, international women's studies, and social psychology and the environment. (Email: sburn@calpoly.edu).

Barry Childers, Ph.D., is a clinical psychologist by trade (now retired), and a peace activist by choice. Barry and his wife live in Geneva, Switzerland, where he works with the International Peace Bureau and she works for the World Council of Churches.

Jane Connor, Ph.D., is director and associate professor in the Division of Human Development at Binghamton University. She is also coauthor of Connecting across Differences: A Guide to Compassionate, Nonviolent Communication.

Larissa G. Duncan, M.S., is a doctoral candidate in human development and family studies at Penn State University. She is developing and testing mindfulness-based interventions for parents and youth as part of her Ph.D. work. She has worked for peace in a variety of ways for ten years and attributes her motivation toward alleviating suffering in the world to her parents.

Scot D. Evans, Ph.D., is an assistant professor of community psychology at Wilfrid Laurier University in Waterloo, Ontario, Canada. He is the cofounder of Psychologists Acting with Conscience Together (PsyACT) and researches and writes about the role of nonprofit human service organizations in social action and social change. (Email: sevans@wlu.ca).

Donelson R. Forsyth, Ph.D., holds the Colonel Leo K. and Gaylee Thorsness Endowed Chair in Ethical Leadership in the Jepson School of Leadership Studies of the University of Richmond (Richmond, VA 23173). He studies leadership, ethical decision making, and identity processes in groups and interpersonal settings.

Miriam L. Freeman, Ph.D., LISW, is a professor in the College of Social Work at the University of South Carolina where she teaches social work practice with families, social work practice with groups, and the Satir Growth Model. (Email: miriam.freeman@sc.edu).

Carolyn Gellermann, M.A., has twenty-five years of consulting experience and is currently on the adjunct faculty in the University of Washington College of Education. In addition to degrees, including her M.A. in Organizational Development from Antioch University, Carolyn completed the MIT/Harvard Public Disputes Program and has partnered with Bill Ury, author of *Getting to Yes*, in the Global Negotiation Project. (Email: carolyng@peoplepc.com).

Mary E. Gomes, Ph.D., is a professor of psychology at Sonoma State University and coauthor, with Theodore Roszak and Allen D. Kanner, of *Ecopsychology: Restoring the Earth, Healing the Mind* (1995, Sierra Club Books). She is codirector of Altars of Extinction, which creates memorials to species that have gone extinct at human hands. (Email: Mary.Gomes@sonoma.edu).

Christopher S. Grundy received his B.A. in psychology from Southwestern University, Georgetown, Texas. His research interests are in social psychology, particularly as it pertains to addressing social and environmental problems.

Niki Harré, Ph.D., is a senior lecturer in social and community psychology at the University of Auckland, New Zealand. She has a particular interest in developing methods to understand and encourage social activism in young people. She belongs to a number of local and international action groups. (Email: n.harre@auckland.ac.nz).

Susan Hawes, Ph.D., is associate professor of clinical psychology at Antioch New England Graduate School in Keene, New Hampshire, where she teaches a workshop on dialog across differences, as well as courses on qualitative research, and a critical social history of psychology. She is also a member of Zen Peacemaker Circles USA, part of a worldwide community working for peace through the integration of Zen practice and social action. (Email: shawes@antiochne.edu).

JW P. Heuchert, Ph.D., is an associate professor of psychology at Allegheny College. He is the editor of *Peace Psychology*, the newsletter of the Society for the Study of Peace, Conflict and Violence: Peace Psychology Division of the American Psychological Association. He teaches classes mostly in the clinical psychology area and does related research as well as research on aspects of personality and peace. He obtained his qualifications in South Africa and at Boston University. (Department of Psychology; Allegheny College; 520 North Main Street, Meadville, PA 16335; Telephone: (814) 332-2397; Email: jw.heuchert@allegheny.edu).

John P. Keating, Ph.D., is a social psychologist and Chancellor of the University of Wisconsin, Parkside.

Matt Keener is a filmmaker who lives and works in Hollywood (both the town and the industry). A former corporate media consultant and documentary filmmaker, he remains active in media communications as a volunteer founding fellow at Media Action Project. (www.MediaActionProject.org).

Paul W. Keller, Ph.D. (1913–2003), was a teacher of speech communication and offered courses in conflict resolution starting in 1962. He taught at Manchester College, and is now deceased. His chapter was in the 1985 edition of *Working for Peace*.

Susan M. Koger, Ph.D., is professor of psychology at Willamette University in Salem, Oregon. She coauthored *The Psychology of Environmental Problems* with Deborah Winter (2004, Lawrence Erlbaum Associates). As a physiological psychologist, Sue is particularly interested in the effects of environmental toxins on brain development and function. (Department of Psychology, Willamette University, 900 State St., Salem, OR 97301; Email: skoger@willamette.edu).

John W. Kraybill-Greggo, Ph.D., L.S.W., A.C.S.W., is coordinator of the Social Work Program and also coordinator of the University-wide Service-Learning Initiative Committee at East Stroudsburg University of Pennsylvania. Previously, he was co-director of the Social Justice Education Project at the University of Scranton. (Email: jkgreggo@po-box.esu.edu).

Marcella J. Kraybill-Greggo, M.S.W., L.S.W., is supervisor of the Mentoring, Training and Internship Programs at Valley Youth House, Allentown, Pennsylvania. She is also a trained spiritual director and serves as a clinical director and adjunct professor in the Pastoral Counseling Program at Moravian Seminary, Bethlehem, Pennsylvania. (Email: marcellak2@aol.com).

George Lakey, M.A. (Sociology), has led over 1,000 social change workshops on five continents while writing seven books and leading activist projects. His first time in jail was for a civil rights sit-in. He has taught peace studies at Haverford and Swarthmore Colleges and the University of Pennsylvania. He is founder/director of Training for Change in Philadelphia, Pennsylvania: www.TrainingforChange.org. He updated his chapter from the 1985 edition of the book.

Rachel MacNair, Ph.D., majored in Peace and Conflict Studies at Earlham College, a Quaker school, and is a Quaker. She's the author of the college textbook *The Psychology of Peace: An Introduction*, along with other books (www.rachelmacnair.com/books). She's the director of the Institute for Integrated Social Analysis, research arm of Consistent Life. (811 East 47th Street, Kansas City, MO 64110; Telephone: 816-753-2057; Email: drmacnair@hotmail.com).

Roxanne Manning, Ph.D., is a clinical psychologist in Raleigh, North Carolina. She is interested in bringing Nonviolent Communication to ethnically diverse populations and to those working in social change. (Email: connect@rationalminds.com).

Helen Margulies Mehr, Ph.D. (1916–1992), was a clinical psychologist in private practice and Chair of the Committee on Social Issues of the California State Psychological Association, and she served on the National Steering Committee of Psychologists for Social Responsibility. She is now deceased. Her chapter appeared in the 1985 edition under the title "Peace Work and Your Mental Health," and for updating, it has been lightly edited and shortened.

Christina Maslach, Ph.D., is a professor of psychology at the University of California, Berkeley, and is the author of several books about burnout, as well as of the research measure, the Maslach Burnout Inventory (MBI). (Email: maslach@berkeley.edu).

Carol Merrick is a graduate of the Evergreen State College in Olympia, Washington. She trained as a medical laboratory technician and a biological laboratory research technician. She has been a community organizer, activist, and speaker for twelve years. She is one of the founding members of Northwest VEG and is currently the secretary. (Email: nwveg@juno.com).

Christina Michaelson, Ph.D., is a clinical psychologist who teaches psychology at Le Moyne College in Syracuse, New York. Her teaching and research interests include Eastern psychology, meditation, and inner peace. (Department of Psychology, Le Moyne College, 1419 Salt Springs Road, Syracuse, New York 13214; Email: michaec@lemoyne.edu).

Linden L. Nelson, Ph.D., is a professor emeritus in the Department of Psychology and Child Development at California Polytechnic State University. He has served as president of Psychologists for Social Responsibility (PsySR) and is currently chair of PsySR's Peace Education Action Committee. (Email: llnelson@calpoly.edu).

Kurt O'Brien, M.A., is an organization development consultant, trainer, and coach with an M.A. in organization development from the University of San Francisco. He works as an internal consultant at the University of Washington Medical Center and has his own independent consulting business. He lives in Poulsbo, Washington with his wife and two children. (Email: obrien.consulting@comcast.net).

Brad Olson, Ph.D., is an applied social and community psychologist who is involved in and studies the psychology of community action. He presently has various roles with the Society of Community Research and Action (SCRA) as chair of the Community Action Interest Group, and as the representative to Divisions of Social Justice (DSJ) within the American Psychological Association. He is also closely involved with Psychologists Acting with Conscience Together (PsyACT) and Psychologists for Social Responsibility (PsySR).

Richard Osbaldiston, M.S., M.A., is an assistant professor in the Department of Psychology at Southwestern University, Georgetown, Texas. His research interests (and his political activism) focus on issues of social justice and environmental problems. (Department of Psychology, Southwestern University, 1001 E. University Ave., Georgetown, TX 78626; Email: osbaldir@southwestern.edu).

Gerald D. Oster, Ph.D., is a psychologist in private practice in Maryland, where he specializes in individual and family therapy. A past Clinical Associate Professor of Psychiatry at the University of Maryland Medical School, he provides consultations and assessments for Montgomery General Hospital and the Expressive Therapy Center.

Robert Pettit, Ph.D., is a sociologist with widespread interests ranging from religion, sexuality, and pop culture to the promotion of social justice. (Department of Sociology, Manchester College, North Manchester, IN 46962).

Susan M. Sisk, M.S., is the cofounder of Tekoa, Inc., a group of psychological treatment facilities and alternative schools in Virginia that were designed, in part, to bring peace to the lives of emotionally disturbed adolescents and their families. She has thirty years of experience as a counselor, nondenominational minister, and mother to three children and two stepchildren and has recently become a grandmother.

John Sommers-Flanagan, Ph.D., is a clinical psychologist, clinical consultant at Trapper Creek Job Corps, and counselor educator at the University of Montana. John provides continuing education workshops nationally and internationally. He's an aspiring farmer and devoted advocate for peace.

Rita Sommers-Flanagan, Ph.D., is a clinical psychologist, farmer, peace activist, and counselor educator at the University of Montana. She and her husband, John, have raised two intense, radical, and globally concerned daughters.

Together, John and Rita are the authors of many articles and books, including *Tough Kids, Cool Counseling; Problem Child or Quirky Kid; Clinical Interviewing; Counseling and Psychotherapy Theories in Context and Practice: Skills, Strategies, and Techniques;* and, with their older daughter Chelsea Elander Flanagan Bodnar, *Don't Divorce Us!: Kids' Advice to Divorcing Parents.*

Jo Young Switzer, Ph.D., serves as president of Manchester College in Indiana. She updated her chapter from the 1985 edition of *Working for Peace.*

Deborah Du Nann Winter, Ph.D., taught psychology at Whitman College for thirty years before retiring in 2006 to the Big Island of Hawaii where she performs community service. She served as president of Psychologists for Social Responsibility and has written or edited books on the psychology of environmental problems and peace psychology.

Neil Wollman, Ph.D., is senior fellow of the Peace Studies Institute and Professor of Psychology, Manchester College (North Manchester, IN 46962). He is an activist and psychologist who believes the time has come for people to pool their knowledge and resources to work for a better world. Neil was the editor of the 1985 edition of Working for Peace and his chapters and introduction are updates of those that appeared in that volume. (Email: njwollman@manchester.edu).

Gary A. Zimmerman, Ph.D., is chair of the Psychology Department and for over twenty years has taught both conflict resolution and mediation courses in the Peace Studies program at Manchester College. He continues to learn from young people, especially his grandchildren, about peacemaking and finding laughing matters. He updated his chapter from the 1985 edition of *Working for Peace*. (Psychology Department, Manchester College, North Manchester, IN 46962; Email: gazimmerman@manchester.edu).

RESOURCES FOR PEACE WORK

1. Programs that offer workshops based on sound psychology

- *Enemy Images: A Resource Manual on Reducing Enmity* (2004), by Stephen Fabick, 80 pgs

This manual examines the psychological processes involved in making people into enemies. Its focus is the new East/West conflict of Western imperialism vs. Islamic terrorism. Enemy imaging is described as the psychological fuel for war. Such images are typically distorted representations of one's adversary. Often enemies are depicted as thoroughly diabolical, aggressive, and untrustworthy. Exaggerated representations of adversaries are generated at the preconscious level in all of us through selective attention and memory, double standards, self-fulfilling prophecies, and ignorance. The manual cites historical, media, and research examples of these mechanisms. A sample lecture is included as well as a variety of exercises that behavioral scientists can use to moderate such unconscious and regressive thinking. It can be used in a classroom or workshop setting and can be downloaded at http://www.psysr.org.

- *US & THEM: Moderating group conflict presenter's manual* (2004), by Stephen Fabick, 159 pgs

The manual focuses on conflict in our post 9/11 world. The US & THEM program highlights the dynamics common to prejudice and conflict along many dimensions — race, class, culture, nationality, religion, and ethnicity. Education about these common dynamics relies upon a balance of teaching basic concepts, experiential learning, dialog, and action. Brief sample talks are accompanied by overhead materials, followed by related experiential exercises. A second phase entails dialog groups, and the third phase involves a joint project developed and implemented by participants from the diverse groups. Selected as one of the top intergroup dialog programs in the country by the Center for Living Democracy, the manual can be downloaded from http://www.psysr.org.

- The Help Increase the Peace Program (HIPP)

This is an interactive conflict transformation program with experiential training that empowers youth to reduce violence and become active agents for social change. Through activities that build community, break down stereotypes, and teach communication skills, HIPP teaches children habits of nonviolence. More information is at http://www.afsc.org/hipp.htm.

- Alternatives to Violence Project (AVP)

Founded in and developed from the real life experiences of prisoners and others and building on a spiritual base, AVP encourages all to use their innate power to positively transform themselves and the world. AVP/USA is an association of community-based groups and prison-based groups offering experiential workshops in personal growth and creative conflict management. More information is at http://www.avpusa.org.

2. Peace psychology organizations

- Psychologists for Social Responsibility

  Website: http://www.psysr.org
  Email: psysr@psysr.org
  208 "I" Street, NE
  Washington, D.C. 20002-4340
  Telephone: (202) 543-5347
  Fax: (202) 543-5348

- American Psychological Association — Division 48

  Society for the Study of Peace, Conflict, and Violence: Peace Psychology Division

  Website: http://www.webster.edu/peacepsychology

- American Psychological Association — Division 9

  Society for the Psychological Study of Social Issues

  Website: http://www.spssi.org/
  Email: spssi@spssi.org
  208 "I" Street NE
  Washington, D.C. 20002-4340
  Telephone: (202) 675-6956
  Fax: (202) 675-6902

INDEX

298

More Books With *IMPACT*

We think you will find these Impact Publishers titles of interest:

You Can Beat Depression
A Guide to Prevention and Recovery (Fourth Edition)
John Preston, Psy.D.
Softcover: $15.95   176 pages
The most readable book on depression, with proven strategies for self-help — and how to get good professional help when needed. Information on latest drug therapies and other methods of treatment.

The Stress Owner's Manual: *Meaning, Balance and Health in Your Life* (Second Edition)
Ed Boenisch, Ph.D. and C. Michele Haney, Ph.D.
Softcover: $15.95   224 pages.

Up-to-date edition of the popular practical guide to stress management with self-assessment charts covering people, money, work, leisure stress areas. Life-changing strategies to enhance relaxation and serenity.

Calming the Family Storm
Anger Management for Moms, Dads, and All the Kids
Gary D. McKay, Ph.D. and Steven A. Maybell, Ph.D.
Softcover: $16.95   320 pages
Practical manual teaches families how to deal effectively with anger. Provides effective techniques for anger expression to create a happier, more harmonious family life.

Master Your Panic and Take Back Your Life!
Twelve Treatment Sessions to Conquer Panic, Anxiety & Agoraphobia (Fourth Edition)
Denise F. Beckfield, Ph.D.
Softcover: $16.95   304 pages

Includes the latest information and research findings on exposure therapy, medication, and other treatments. Proven, research-based methods presented in easy-to-follow instructions.

Impact Publishers®
POST OFFICE BOX 6016
ATASCADERO, CALIFORNIA 93423-6016

Please see the following page for more books.

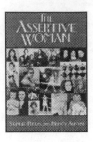